IVAN GOGIN, ALEXAN!

FIGHTING SHIPS OF WORLD WAR TWO 1937 - 1945

Volume V

FRANCE

NAVYPEDIA LLC
Gatchina
2021

FIGHTING SHIPS OF WORLD WAR TWO 1937 - 1945

SERIES

1. UNITED KINGDOM AND COMMONWEALTH
2. UNITED STATES OF AMERICA
3. JAPAN
4. GERMANY
5. FRANCE
6. ITALY
7. SOVIET UNION
8. EUROPE
9. ASIA, AFRICA, LATIN AMERICA

Dear reader!

We immediately admit: English is not the native language of the authors. Therefore, we are not trying to write books containing large literary texts. We offer you references. We provide you primarily with information - digits, dates, graphics. These texts were written by us in Russian and translated into English.

We hope that some roughness of the text will not prevent you from using our references. English literature has given the world many geniuses. If the reader wants to feel all the depth and beauty of the English language, then Shakespeare, Byron, Dreiser, and other titans will satisfy any, the most delicate taste. Alas, we do not hope to get into this row. Please, dear reader, forgive us for this.

But we vouch for the accuracy of the information and the quality of the drawings. First of all, we want to offer you information.

Navypedia.org team

Contents

Foreword	4
1937	5
Abbreviations	6
Organization of the French Navy during the World War Two	8
Order of battle of the French Navy on September 3st, 1939	10
Battleships	13
Aircraft carriers and seaplane tenders	21
Cruisers	23
Destroyers and torpedo boats	36
Submarines	47
Escort and patrol ships	57
Riverine and coastal forces	71
Mine warfare ships	78
Miscellaneous vessels, intended for combat support	83
Ship-based aircraft	84
Naval weapons	88

Foreword

Dear reader!

We are pleased to present you the fifth volume of «Fighting ships of World War Two», dedicated to Marine Nationale. Volume I «United Kingdom and Commonwealth» and volume II «United States of America» were published in February 2021, volume III «Japan» followed in March. Volume IV «Germany» was published in May.

Below is the standard text on the structure of the presentation of information in the books of the series. It exactly repeats similar texts in the previous volumes.

The reference contains the maximum possible number of side views, reduced in terms of common sense and volume limitation, in two scales: the main one: 1:1000 and 1:500 for units less than 40m long. The format of the publication, proposing also printed edition, is forced to limit us in the information on merchant and fishing vessels with less than 500grt capacity, used for patrol, minesweeping and other combat duties, and purpose built craft if the total displacement of class was less than 100ts (that were, in the vast majority of cases, experimental boats). Data for these units is provided briefly. Also articles dedicated to small amphibious craft are short.

Ships' data blocks include name of the ship (Builder, laid down, launched, completed or commissioned -the reason and date of deletion from fleet list) Technical data blocks include standard/full load displacement in tons (generally long tons) or displacement surfaced/submerged for submarines, length overall (oa) (if the length between perpendiculars is indicated, pp is witten, if tthe length by waterline - wl) x breadth x mean draught in meters (or maximal draught (max)), composition of machinery (if necessary, number of shafts in brackets), maximal power of main engines in horse powers, maximal speed in knots, maximal fuel stowage in tons, maximal endurance in nautical miles at cruising speed in knots (in brackets), complement, maximal operational depth for submarines in meters. Armour protection is described briefly, detailed description of protection arrangement the reader can find in the text. Armament is described according to the following system: Artillery - number of mounts x number of guns in the mount - caliber of guns in millimeters/barrel length in calibers and mark or common name of the gun. NB: In all cases where we can, we indicate a bore length under British/US system, without length of the breech. If the ship had gunmounts with different gun number, these mounts are marked with «+» sign. As example, (2 x 4 + 1 x 2) — 356/45 BL Mk I means that ship was armed with two quadruple and one twin mount with 356/45 Mk I breech loaded guns. Machine guns with caliber less than 20mm are marked without barrel length and gun mark. Torpedoes - number of mounts x number of tubes in the mount - torpedo caliber for turnable mounts or number of tubes - torpedo caliber for fixed tubes (for example, on submarines, MTBs or old ships). Digits in brackets after number of DCTs and DCRs mean total number of carried depth charges.

Data of aircraft should be read as follows:

Hellcat Mk II: 13.08x10.17x4.11m, 31.0m^2, 4155/6400kg, 1 Pratt & Whitney R-2800-10W, 2200hp, 611km/h, 2600(270)km, 15.1m/s, 11500m, 1p; 6 x 12.7 MG or (2 x 20 guns + 4 x 12.7 MG), 6 x 127mm rockets or 908kg bombs (2 x 454kg).

Means: Data of Hellcat Mk II model: wing span 13.08m, length 10.17m, hight 4.11m, wing area 31.0m^2, empty mass 4155kg / maximum take-off mass 6400kg, 1 Pratt & Whitney R-2800-10W engine with 2200hp power, maximal speed 611 km/h, flying range 2600km at 270km/h speed, maximal rate of climb 15.1m/s, service ceiling 11500m, 1 seat; armament consisted of 6 12.7mm MGs or 2 20mm guns and 4 12.7mm MGs, 6 127mm rockets or 908 kg bombs.

Hellcat Mk II (fighter-bomber, 854 transferred spring 1944- 1945 (including FR Mk II and PR Mk II), serv. spring 1944-8.1946, USN F6F-5, Pratt & Whitney R-2800-10W (2200hp), strengthened armour, 6 x 12.7 MG or 2 x 20 guns and 4 x 12.7 MG, 6 x 127mm rockets or 908 kg bombs (2 x 454-kg));

Means: modification Hellcat Mk II, purpose fighter-bomber, 865 were served in the RN, received by Navy spring 1944-1945 and served spring 1944 - August 1946, further differences from previous modification are briefly described.

Navypedia.org team

1937

Dear reader! In this place we have to repeat the text of previous volumeы. If you've read it in previous volumes, ignore it. But if volume V is the first book in the series that you are familiar with, then we must explain to you: why did we start from 1937?

Our opinion is expounded below.

The first echoes of the thunder of a thunderstorm, which would later engulf the whole world and remain in the memory of mankind as the most destructive and murderous war, rang out on October 25, 1936, when Germany and Japan signed an Agreement against the Communist International, which provided for the destruction of communism in general and the Soviet Union in particular. 6.11.1937 Italy joined the pact. The Axe was formed and set as its goal the creation of a new order. The order in which the German Nazis, Japanese militarists and Italian fascists were to receive the right to decide which of the peoples inhabiting the planet would live.

The Axis nations did not initially face serious resistance to aggression. In 1935-1936, Italy invades Ethiopia. In 1936, German troops occupied the Rhine Demilitarized Zone. In March 1938 Germany annexed Austria, in October - the Sudetenland, and in March 1939 occupied Czechoslovakia. But war broke out at the other end of Eurasia.

Back in 1931-1932, Japanese troops captured Chinese Manchuria, establishing a puppet state on its territory. The League of Nations did not react in any way to the aggression. The creeping aggression associated with constant armed clashes and the seizure of new territories continued for another five years, but in 1937 Japan switched to full-scale military operations. Multimillion armies clashed in a huge theater of military operations that covered all of eastern China. On July 7, 1937, World War II began.

Precisely on the basis that in July 1937 the first large-scale conflict began, which undoubtedly was part of the Second World War and lasted until September 1945, we propose to consider the incident on the Marco Polo Bridge on July 7, 1937 as its actual beginning. And so, our series is an overview of all the world warships for the period from July 1937 to September 1945.

Abbreviations

AA - anti-aircraft
AEW - airborne early warning
AP - armour-piercing
ap - air propeller
ASW - anti-submarine warfare
ASWRL — anti-submarine war-fare rocket launcher
aw - above water
b — boiler
BDE - British destroyer escort
bhp - brake horsepower
BL — breech-loading
brt - British registered tons
BU — broken up
CIC - combat information centre
CMB - coastal motor boat
Compl. — complement
CT — conning tower
CTL - constructive total loss
cwt - hundredweight
cyl - cylinder
d — Diesel engine
DC — depth charge
DCR — depth charge rack
DCT — depth charge thrower
DE - destroyer escort
DP - dual-purpose
DYd — dockyard
ECM — electronic countermea-sures
em - electric motor
FNFL - Forces Navales Françaises Libres (Free French Naval Forces)
FY - Fiscal Year
GM - metacentric height
grt - gross registered tons
gsgt - geared steam-gas turbine unit
gst — geared steam turbine unit
HA - high angle
HDML - harbour defence motor launch
HMS - His/Her Majesty's Ship
h.p. — horse power(s)
HP - high pressure
HQ - headquarters
ihp - indicated horsepower

kts — knots
LA - low angle
lb - pound(s)
LCA - Landing Craft, Assault
LCF - Landing Craft, Flak
LCG - Landing Craft, Gun
LCG(L) - Landing Craft, Gun (Large)
LCG(M) - Landing Craft, Gun (Medium)
LCI(G) - Landing Craft, Infantry (Gun)
LCI(L) - Landing Craft, Infantry (Large)
LCI(S) - Landing Craft, Infantry (Small)
LCM - Landing Craft, Mechanical
LCP - Landing Craft, Personnel
LCP(R) - Landing Craft, Personnel (Rocket)
LCS - Landing Craft, Support
LCS(L) - Landing Craft, Support (Large)
LCS(M) - Landing Craft, Support (Medium)
LCS(S) - Landing Craft, Support (Small)
LCT - Landing Craft, Tank
LCT(R) - Landing Craft, Tank (Rocket)
LCV - Landing Craft, Vehicle
LCV(P) - Landing Craft, Vehicle (Personnel)
LP - low pressure
LSC - Landing Ship, Carrier
LSD - Landing Ship, Dock
LSF - Landing Ship, Fighter Direction
LSG - Landing Ship, Gantry
LSH(L) - Landing Ship, Headquarters (Large)
LSI - Landing Ship, Infantry
LSI(H) - Landing Ship, Infantry (Hand)
LSI(L) - Landing Ship, Infantry (Large)
LSI(M) - Landing Ship, Infantry (Medium)
LSI(S) - Landing Ship, Infantry (Small)
LSS - Landing Ship, Stern Chute
LST - Landing Ship, Tank
MA/SB - Motor anti-submarine boat
max - maximum
MG — machine gun
MGB - motor gunboat
Mk - Mark
ML - motor launch
MMS - motor minesweeper
Mod - model

MTB - motor torpedo boat
nm — nautical mile(s)
No(s) - number(s)
NYd - Navy Yard
oa - overall
pdr - pounder(s)
pe — petrol engine
pp - between perpendiculars
QF — quick-firing
RAN - Royal Australian Navy
RCMP - Royal Canadian Mounted Police
RCN - Royal Canadian Navy
RIM - Royal Indian Marine
RIN - Royal Indian Navy
RL - rocket launcher
RN - Royal Navy
RNVR - Royal Naval Volunteer Reserve
RNZN - Royal New Zealand Navy
RSAN - Royal South African Navy
SAN - South African Navy
SAP - semi-armour piercing

SB - Shipbuilding
SE - single-ended
sd - semi-Diesel engine
shp - shaft horsepower
st — steam turbine unit
std - standard
sub - submerged
t — ton(s)
TC — torpedo cradle
TNT - trinitrotoluene
TS - training ship
TT — torpedo tube(s)
US - United States
USCG - United States Coast Guard
USN - United States Navy
VC - steam engine, vertical compound steam engine
VQE - steam engine, vertical, quadruple expansion
VQuiE - steam engine, vertical, quintuple expansion
VTE — steam engine, vertical, triple expansion
Wks - Works

Organization of the French Navy during the World War Two

After the First World War, despite the interwar economic upheavals and the pacifism that gripped the country, energetic measures were taken to create a powerful modern navy.

In France (as in other countries), the threat from aviation and submarines was underestimated, although the French were in the lead in the development of radar technology for a long time. However, the lack of submarine detecting measures and full-fledged naval aviation (by the beginning of the war, the navy had only 159 ship-based and 194 land-based aircraft) sharply limited the abilities of the navy. The terms of the 1922 Washington Treaty had a huge impact on the development of the French Navy. Having established the parity of the French and Italian navies, politicians predetermined the transformation of Italy into the main rival, and the Mediterranean Sea into the main theater of the future naval war. In the strategic "division of roles" in the British-French tandem, which took shape by the end of the 1930s, the French Navy was "responsible" for the Mediterranean.

But the "German threat" was not ignored either. *Dunkerque* class battleships were specially designed as a counterweight to the German "pocket battleships".

With hostile Germany and neutral Italy, the French Navy had to control the English Channel, the Bay of Biscay and the western Mediterranean.

Many colonies and overseas territories left their mark on the development and deployment of the navy - in the pre-

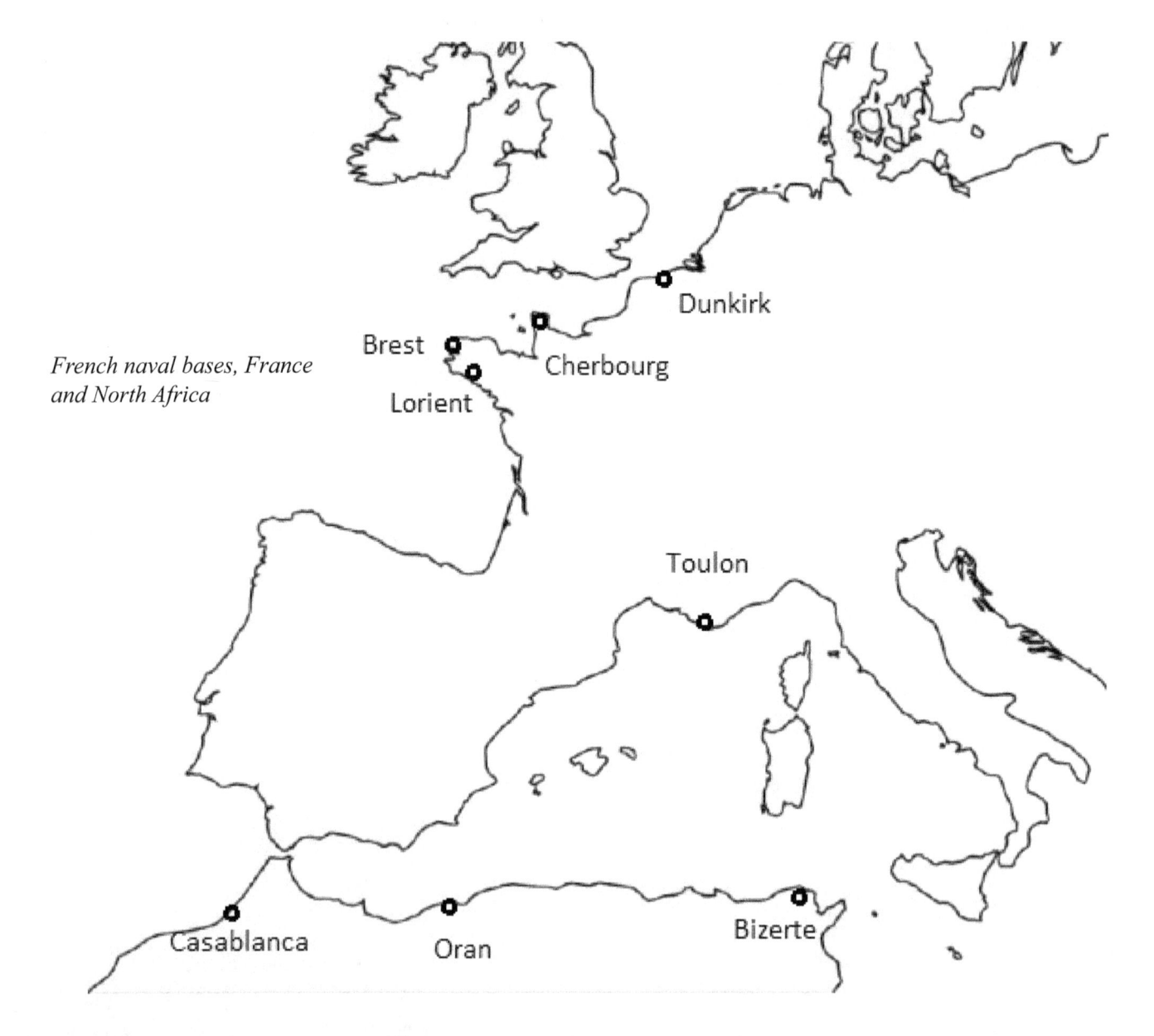

French naval bases, France and North Africa

French naval bases, overseas

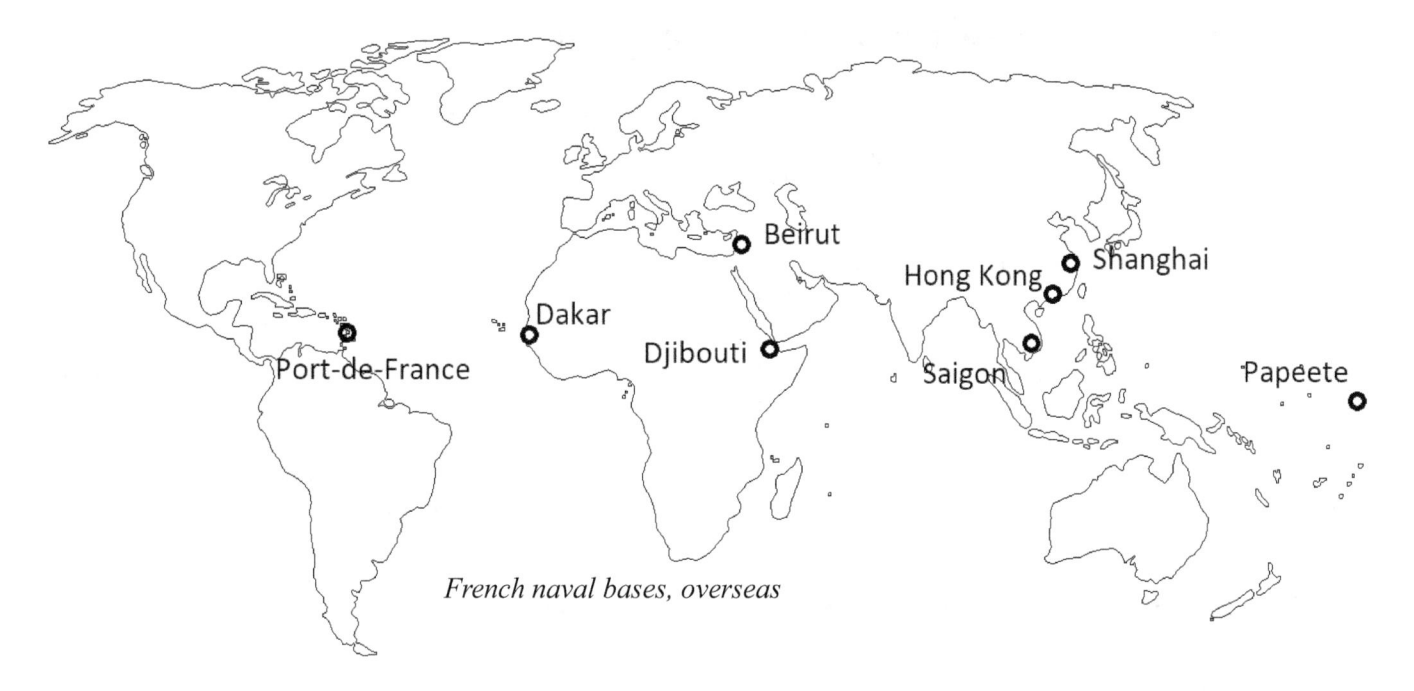

war period, many colonial avisos were built, and many ships before the war were based in the Far East, Oceania, Africa, and Latin America.

On May 10, 1940, Germany started an offensive in the Netherlands and Belgium. On June 22, France capitulated. According to the terms of capitulation, all ships of the French Navy were to be assembled in bases with reduced crews. In fact, all the ships that were in French waters at the time of the defeat came under German control - nothing could, with an appropriate decision, keep the Germans from raising their flags on them.

However, many ships were in British ports - two battleships, two leaders, 8 destroyers and many other ships. On the night of July 2 to 3, they were all captured by the British. After the capture, some of them, which could be manned by crews, became part of the forces of the French Navy, fighting on the side of Britain against Germany. On July 3, British Force H, consisting of a battlecruiser, two battleships, an aircraft carrier, two cruisers and 9 destroyers, approached Mers-el-Kebir, where there were 4 battleships, 6 leaders and a seaplane tender, and transmitted an ultimatum containing a choice of 4 proposals - to leave for Britain and continue to fight against Germany, leave for a British port and repatriate the crews, disarm their ships, or sink their ships. The commander of the French force chose the fifth decision - to fight against the British. Operation Catapult entered a hot stage. After two days, the French force ceased to exist, the remaining ships passed to Toulon, thereby announcing their subordination to the Vichy collaborationist government. Later, some of them fought against the Royal Navy in the waters of West Africa. There were also ships previously based at Oran and Algiers. The squadron stationed at Alexandria declared its neutral status.

The French managed to fight against everyone: against Germany in 1939-1940, against Britain in 1940-1942, against Italy in 1940, against the USA in 1942, against Thailand in 1941. This war against everyone ended tragically: November 11, 1942 German troops crossed the demarcation line and entered the territory they had previously assigned to the Vichy government. On November 27, a French Navy committed suicide in the harbor of Toulon. All ships were blown up or sunk to avoid capture by the German army. The Germans were able to capture only 11 small ships. In March 1945, to avoid capture by Japan, French ships were sunk in the Far East.

The French Navy, fighting against Germany, rose from the dead August 7, 1940, when Charles De Gaulle and Sir Winston Churchill signed an agreement "Establishing the Free French Forces (FFL)". However, the ships of the Free French Navy (FNFL) fought as part of the Royal Navy and did not have independent operational control. France received again a full-fledged navy only after the end of the war.

Order of battle of the French Navy on September 3rd, 1939

High Sea Force (Oran, Algeria)
   2nd Flotilla (Oran, Algeria) – battleship Provence (F)(FF)
      2nd Battle Division (Oran, Algeria) – battleships Lorraine (2 Lore 130) (F), Bretagne
      1st Light Destroyer Squadron (Oran, Algeria)
         1st Light Destroyer Division (Oran, Algeria) – destroyers La Palme (F)(SF), Le Mars, Tempete
         2nd Light Destroyer Division (Oran, Algeria) – destroyers Le Fortune (F), La Railleuse, Simoun
         7th Light Destroyer Division (Oran, Algeria) – destroyers Tramontane (F), Typhon, Tornade
   3rd Flotilla (Toulon)
      1st Cruiser Squadron (Toulon)
         1st Cruiser Division (Toulon) – heavy cruisers Algerie (2 Loire 130) (F)(SF)(FF), Foch (2 Loire 130), Dupleix (2 Loire 130)
         2nd Cruiser Division (Toulon) – heavy cruisers Duquesne (1 Loire 130) (F), Colbert (2 Loire 130), Tourville (1 Loire 130)
      3rd Light Squadron (Toulon)
         5th Destroyer Division (Toulon) – destroyers Tartu (F), Chevalier Paul, Vauquelin
         7th Destroyer Division (Toulon) – destroyers Vautour (F), Gerfaut, Albatros
         9th Destroyer Division (Toulon) – destroyers Maille Breze (F)(SF), Cassard, Kersaint
Raiding Force (Brest)
   1st Flotilla (Brest)
      1st Battle Division (Brest) – battlecruisers Dunkerque (2 Loire 130, 1 L.N.210) (F) (FF), Strasbourg (2 Loire 130, 1 L.N.210)
      Aircraft carrier Bearn (1 PL.7)
      4th Cruiser Division (Brest) – light cruisers Georges Leygues (2 Loire 130) (F), Gloire (2 Loire 130), Montcalm (2 Loire 130)
      2nd Light Squadron (Brest)
         6th Destroyer Squadron (Brest) – destroyers Mogador (F) (SF), Volta
         8th Destroyer Division (Brest) – destroyers L'Indomptable (F), Le Malin, Le Triomphant
         10th Destroyer Division (Brest) – destroyers L'Fantasque (F), L'Audacieux, Le Terrible
Admiral North (Dunkirk)
   1st Maritime Region (Cherbourg)
      11th Destroyer Division (Cherbourg) – destroyers La Cordeliere (F), L'Incomprise, Branlebas
      16th Submarine Division (Cherbourg) – submarines Orphee (F), Amazone, La Sybille, Antiope
      1st Sloop Squadron (Cherbourg) – Arras, Quentin Roosevelt, Amiral Mouchez, Gaston Rivier, Epinal, Amiens
      Sloops Belfort, Diligente, minelayer Pollux
      AC1 (Calais, 9 D.376)
      T2 (Cherbourg, 10 Late 298)
      1S1 (Cherbourg, 3 CAMS.55, 3 Loire 130)
      1S2 (Cherbourg, 3 Lae 290, 3 CAMS.37/11)
      E2 (Cherbourg, 5 Br.521)
Admiral West (Brest)
   2nd Maritime Region (Brest)
      3rd Battle Division (Brest) – battleships Paris (F), Courbet
      2nd Destroyer Division (Brest) – destroyers Jaguar (F), Leopard, Chacal, Panthere
      2nd Light Destroyer Squadron (Brest)
         2nd Light Destroyer Division (Brest) – destroyers Fougueux (F), Frondeur, L'Adroit
         4th Light Destroyer Division (Brest) – destroyers Bourrasque (F), Ouragan, Orage
         5th Light Destroyer Division (Brest) – destroyers Brestois (F), Foudroyant, Boulonnais
      6th Light Destroyer Squadron (Brest) – destroyers Cyclone (F) (SF), Sirocco, Mistral
      4th Submarine Squadron (Brest)
         Submarine Surcouf (1 MB.411)
         2nd Submarine Division (Brest) – submarines Casabianca (F), Sfax, Achille, Pasteur
         4th Submarine Division
         6th Submarine Division (Brest) – submarines Persee (F), Poncelet, Ajax, Archimede
         8th Submarine Division (Brest) – submarines Agosta (F), Ouessant, Beveziers, Sidi Ferruch
      2nd Sloop Squadron (Brest) – sloops Elan, Commandant Riviere, Commandant Duboc, Epinal, Vauquois, Coucy, Somme, Suippe
      AB1 (Brest, 9 PL.7)

FRANCE

AB2 (Brest, 9 PL.101)
2S1 (Brest, 6 CAMS.55, 3 GL.812)
E6 (Brest, 3 Late 523)
E8 (Brest, 1 Br.730, 1 Late 611, 1 Po-CAMS.141)

5th Maritime Region (Lorient)
14th Light Destroyer Squadron (Lorient) – destroyers Bouclier (F), La Melpomene, La Flore
5th Sloop Squadron (Lorient) – sloops Ailette, Commandant Bory, Chamois, Le Chevreuil, Dubordieu, Luronne
2S2 (Rochefort, 3 CAMS.55, 3 GL.812)
2S4 (Lorient, 3 CAMS.37/11, 3 GL.812)

Admiral South (Toulon)
3rd Maritime Region (Toulon)
4th Destroyer Division (Toulon) – destroyers Tigre (F), Lynx
13th Light Destroyer Division (Toulon) – destroyers Baliste (F), La Bayonnaise, La Poursivante
1st Submarine Flotilla (Toulon)
3rd Submarine Squadron (Toulon)
1st Submarine Division (Toulon) – submarines Le Heros (F), Le Glorieux, Tonnant, Le Conquerant
3rd Submarine Division (Toulon) – submarines Protee (F), Acteon, Fresnel, Acheron
5th Submarine Division (Brest) – submarines L'Espoir, Pegase, Monge
5th Submarine Squadron (Toulon)
13th Submarine Division (Toulon) – submarines Doris (F), Thetis, Calypso, Circe
15th Submarine Division (Toulon) – submarines Iris (F), Venus, Pallas, Ceres
Toulon Submarine Base (Toulon)
7th Submarine Division (Toulon) – submarines Redoutable, Vengeur
19th Submarine Division (Toulon) – submarines Galatee (F), Naiade, Sirene, Argonaute
21st Submarine Division (Toulon) – submarines Le Diamant, La Perle
3rd Sloop Squadron (Toulon) – sloops Amiens, Lassigny, Les Eparges, Dedaigneuse
F1B (Berre, 1 LeO H.257bis)
B2 (Berre, 6 LeO H.257bis)
B3 (Berre, 6 LeO H.257bis)
AC2 (Hyeres, 9 D.376)
HC1 (St. Mandriet, 9 L.210)
T1 (Berre, 10 Late 298)
E5 (Berre, 5 Br.521)
3S1 (Hyeres, 6 GL.812)
3S2 (Cuers, 6 LeO C.30)
3S3 (Berre, 6 GL.812)
3S4 (Berre, 4 NC.470, 2 Br. Calcutta)
3S5 (Hyeres, 6 Po.25)
3S6 (Aspretto, Corsica, 4 PL.15, 2 GL.812)

4th Maritime Region (Bizerte, Tunisia)
4th Light Squadron (Bizerte, Tunisia)
3rd Cruiser Division (Bizerte, Tunisia) – light cruisers Marseillaise (2 Loire 130) (F) (FS), Jean de Vienne (2 Loire 130), La Galissoniere (2 Loire 130)
Bizerte Destroyers (Bizerte, Tunisia) – cruiser-minelayer Emile Bertin (2 GL.832)
1st Destroyer Division (Bizerte, Tunisia) – destroyers Vauban (F), Lion, Epervier
3rd Destroyer Division (Bizerte, Tunisia) – destroyers Guepard (F), Valmy, Verdun
11th Destroyer Division (Bizerte, Tunisia) – destroyers Milan, Bison
6th Light Squadron (Oran, Algeria) – submarine tender Jules Verne (F)
8th Light Destroyer Division (Oran, Algeria) – destroyers Bordelais (F), L'Alcyon, Trombe
2nd Submarine Squadron (Oran, Algeria)
12th Submarine Division (Oran, Algeria) – submarines Minerve (F), Junon, Orion, Ondine
14th Submarine Division (Oran, Algeria) – submarines Diane (F), Ariane, Eurydice, Danae
18th Submarine Division (Oran, Algeria) – submarines La Psyche (F), Driade, Meduse, Amphitrite
Seaplane tender Commandant Teste (1 L.130, HB1 – 6 LeO H.257bis, HS1- 6 L.130)
Bizerte Submarine Base (Bizerte, Tunisia) – destroyer Aigle (F), submarine tender Castor
6th Submarine Squadron (Bizerte, Tunisia)
9th Submarine Division (Bizerte, Tunisia) – submarines Caiman (F), Morse, Souffleur
10th Submarine Division

(Bizerte, Tunisia) – submarines Phoque (F), Espadon, Dauphin

11th Submarine Division 17th Submarine Division (Bizerte, Tunisia) – submarines La Vestale (F), La Sultane, Atalante, Arethuse

20th Submarine Division (Bizerte, Tunisia) – submarines Turquoise (F), Saphir, Nautilus, Rubis

Morocco Naval Forces (Casablanca, Morocco)

9th Light Destroyer Division (Casablanca, Morocco) – destroyers Basque, Forbin 4th Submarine Division (Casablanca, Morocco) – submarines Le Centaure, Argo, Pascal, Henri Poincare

Sloop D'Entrecasteaux (1 Po.452)

B1 (Port Lyautey, Morocco, 6 LeO H.257bis)

E1 (Port Lyautey, Morocco, 6 Br.521)

12th Light Destroyer Division (Bizerte, Tunisia) – destroyers La Pomone (F), Le Bombarde, L'Iphigene

4th Sloop Squadron (Bizerte, Tunisia) – sloops Ypres, Tapaguese, Engageante

E3 (Karouba, Tunisia, 5 Br.521)
E7 (Karouba, Tunisia, 6 L.70)
4S1 (Karouba, Tunisia, 6 CAMS.55)
4S2 (Karouba, Tunisia, 6 CAMS.55)

Far East naval Forces (Saigon, French Indochina)

5th Cruiser Division (Saigon, French Indochina) – heavy cruiser Suffren (2 Loire 130), light cruiser Lamotte-Picquett (1 Po.452) (F)

Yangtse Gunboats (Shanghai, China) – river gunboats Francis Garnier, Doudart de Lagree, Balny

West River Gunboats (Hong Kong, China) – river gunboat Argus

Indochina Gunboats (Saigon, French Indochina) – gunboats Vigilante (F), Commandant Bourdais, Avalanche, Mytho, Tourane

Submarine L'Espoir, sloops Amiral Charner (1 Po.452), Rigault de Genouilly (1 Gl.832), Savorgnian de Brazza (1 Gl.832), Tahure, Marne, Laperouse

Antilles Naval Station (Fort de France, Martinique)

SS Antilles (Port de France, Martinique, 4 GL.812)

Levent Naval Station (Beirut, Lebanon)

11th Submarine Division (Beirut, Lebanon) – submarines Marsouin (F), Requin, Narval

Sloop D'Iberville (1 GL.832)

West Africa Naval Forces (Dakar, Senegal)

5th Light Squadron (Dakar, Senegal)

6th Cruiser Division (Dakar, Senegal) – light cruisers Duguay Trouin (1 GL.832) (F) (FS), Primauguet (1 GL.832)

7th Cruiser Division (Dakar, Senegal) – light cruisers Jeanne d'Arc (2 Loire 130), La Tour d'Auvergne

E3 (Dakar, Senegal, 4 Late 301/302)

Djibouti Naval Station (Djibouti, French Somaliland)

Sloop Bougainville (1 Po.452)

Tahiti Naval Station (Papeete, Tahiti)

Sloop Dumont d'Urville (1 GL.832)

SS Tahiti (Fate Ute, Tahiti, 2 CAMS.55, 1 CAMS.37/11)

FRANCE

Battleships

COURBET class battleships

Courbet (Arsenal de Brest, 1.9.1910/23.9.1911/19.11.1913 - FNFL 7.1940, scuttled 9.6.1944)
Océan (ex-Jean Bart) (Arsenal de Brest, 15.11.1910/22.9.1911/5.6.1913 – TS, training hulk late 1937)
Paris (F C de la Méditerranée, La Seyne, 10.11.1911/28.9.1912/1.8.1914 - FNFL 7.1940, accommodation ship 7.1940)

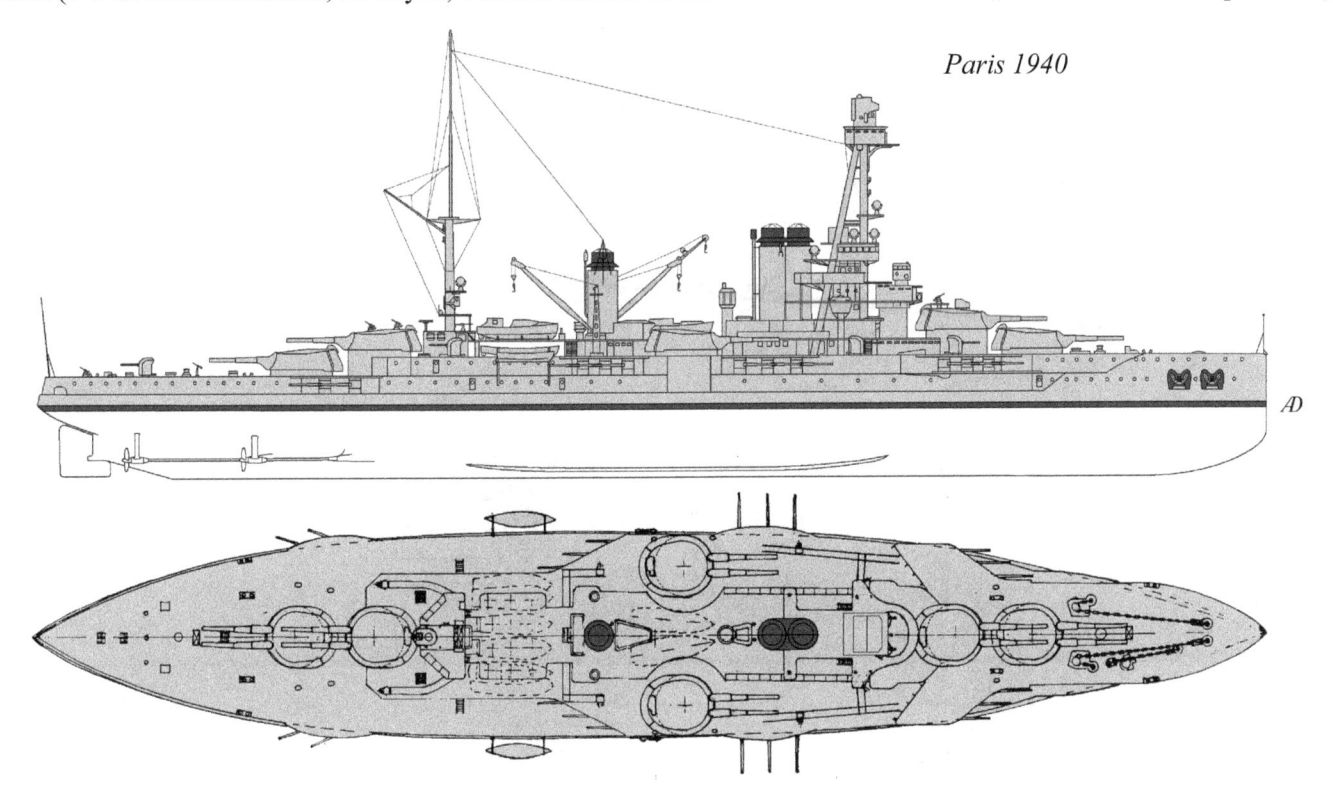

Paris 1940

22189/25000-26000t, 168.0x27.9x9.0m, 4st/26b(*Océan, Paris*) or 4gst/26b(*Courbet*), 28000hp, 20kts, 2500t oil, 4200(10)nm, 1085-1108p; belt 270-180, deck 70+50, turrets 290, CT 300; 6 x 2 – 305/45 M1906-10, 22 x 1 – 139/55 M1910, 4 (*Océan, Courbet*) or 7 (*Paris*) x 1 – 75/50 M1922, 4 x 1 – 47/50 M1902, 4 – 450 TT (beam, sub) (*Océan, Courbet*)

Authorized under the 1910 (*Courbet and Jean Bart*) and 1911 (remainder) Programmes, these were the Marine Nationale's first dreadnoughts. Designed by M Lyasse. Although the armor thickness was increased in comparison with the *Dantons,* it was much thinner than in the US and even the Royal Navy.

Complete main belt had 4.75m height (2.35m above water), its thickness was 270mm at 99m length amidships and 180mm aft. Upper 180mm belt covered the part between the bow and aft casemate. Forecastle casemate had also 180mm protection. Main deck had 40mm thickness at flat part and was connected to lower edge of main belt with 70mm slopes. Flat 45mm upper deck laid on the top of the main belt. There was 40mm forecastle deck. Main turrets had 290mm faces, 250mm sides and 100mm crowns. Barbettes were protected with 270mm armor. CT had 300mm sides and 270mm roof.

9.1938, *Courbet*: - 4 - 450 TT; + 2 x 1 - 75/50 M1922.
1939, *Paris, Courbet*: + (6 x 2 + 2 x 1) - 13.2 MG.

Jean Bart late 1937 was disarmed and converted to training hulk, 1.1.1937 she was renamed *Océan*. 27.11.1942 she was scuttled at Toulon but later salvaged

Courbet after 1924 modernization

by Germans and used as a target. 7.3.1944 ship was damaged by Allied aircraft, 15.3.1944 sank during German explosive trials, salvaged after war and sold for scrap 14.12.1945.

Courbet and *Paris* served since 1931 as training ships. Before the war *Courbet* served as gunnery TS and *Paris* as signal TS. Maximal speed of both ships did not exceed 16kts. 3.7.1940 both ships were captured by British. *Courbet* 11.7.1940 was transferred to FNFL, used as AA and radar TS and in April 1941 disarmed and converted to target for FAA pilots. 9.6.1944 during Normandy landing she was scuttled at Arromanche as breakwater. *Paris* was transferred to FNFL also 11.7.1940 and served as barrack ship for Polish Flotilla. Ship staffing by Polish crew was supposed. After war she was returned to France.

BRETAGNE class battleships

Bretagne (Arsenal de Brest, 1.7.1912/21.4.1913/9.1915 - sunk 3.7.1940)
Lorraine (A C de la Loire et Penhoët, St-Nazaire, 1.8.1912/30.9.1913/7.1916 - FNFL 12.1942, TS 6.1945, accommodation ship 2.1947)
Provence (Arsenal de Lorient, 1.5.1912/20.4.1913/6.1915 - scuttled 27.11.1942)

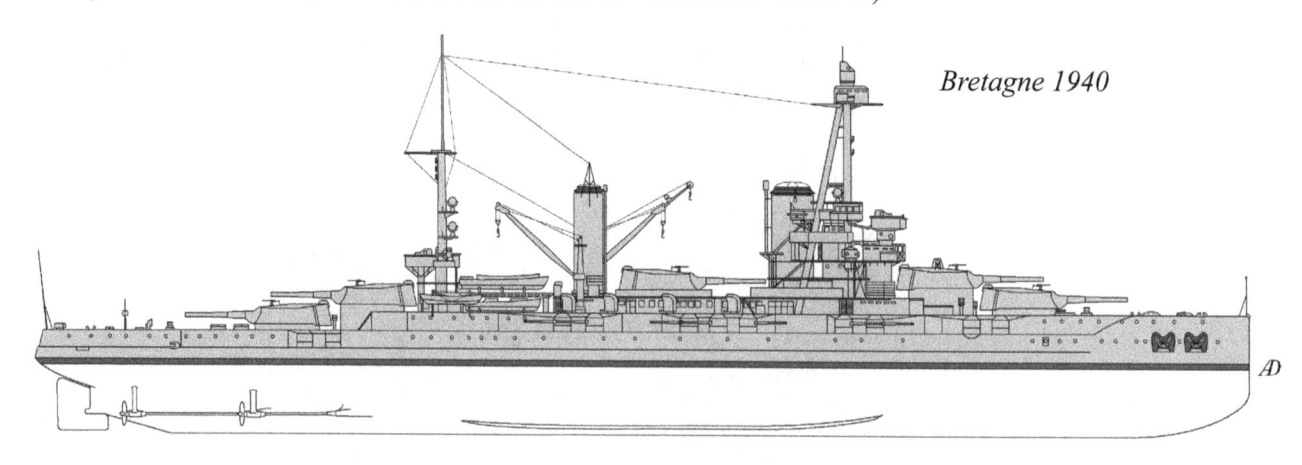

Bretagne 1940

23230/25000t,. 166.0x26.9x9.8m, 4gst/6b, 43000hp, 21.4kts, 2680t coal + 300t oil or 2600t oil(*Lorraine*), 4700(10)nm, 1124-1133p; belt 250-160, decks 45+40, turrets 400-250, CT 300; 5 (*Bretagne, Provence*) or 4 (*Lorraine*) x 2 – 340/45 M1912, 14 x 1 – 139/55 M1910, 4 (*Lorraine*) or 2 (*Provence*) x 2 – 100/45 M1930, 8 (*Bretagne*) or 4 (*Provence*) x 1 – 75/50 M1922, 4 x 1 – 47/50 M1902, 4 (*Bretagne, Provence*) or 8 (*Lorraine*) x 1 – 37/50 M1925, 2 x 4 – 13.2 MG, 1 catapult (*Lorraine*), 4 seaplanes (2 Loire 130) (*Lorraine*).

Built under the 1912 Programme, first and unique French superdreadnoughts. The basic changes from *Courbet* design were brought to introduction of new main guns, and protection even was a little weakened, and armor thickness mismatched artillery caliber. Ships received very thin longitudinal anti-torpedo bulkhead.

Complete main belt was 4.05m-high (2.35m above water), its thickness was 250mm at 99m length amidships (tapering to 220mm at upper and to 100mm at lower edges) and 160mm at ship ends (tapering respectively to 140 and 80mm), 10m-long fore part of waterline became unprotected after modernization in 1920s. Upper 160mm belt covered the part between turret No1 and aft casemate. 60m long forecastle casemate had also 160mm protection. Main deck had 45mm thickness at flat part and was connected to lower edge of main belt with 70mm slopes. Flat 40mm upper deck laid on the top of main belt. There was 40mm forecastle deck. Main turrets had 152mm sides

Bretagne 1920s

FRANCE

and 72mm crowns, turrets No1 and No5 had 340mm faces, turrets No2 and 4 had 250mm and turret No3 400mm. Barbettes of turrets No1 and 5 had 248mm protection and No 2, 3 and 4 270mm. Longitudinal torpedo bulkhead had only 8mm thickness. CT had 300mm sides and 2709mm roof.

1939, *Provence*: - 2 x 2 - 100/45; + 4 x 1 - 75/50 M1922.
1940, *Provence*: + 1 x 4 - 13.2 MG. 4.1940, *Lorraine*: - 4 x 2 - 100/45; + 8 x 1 - 75/50 M1922, 2 x 4 - 13.2 MG.
5.1944, *Lorraine*: - 4 x 4 - 13.2 MG, seaplanes with hangar and catapult; + 14 x 1 - 40/56 Bofors, 25 x 1 - 20/70 Oerlikon, presumably SA, SF radars.

Bretagne 3.7.1940 at Mers-el-Kebir was sunk by British Force "H" (battleship *Resolution*) during operation "Catapult", *Provence* was damaged by two hits and ran aground. The same year she was salvaged and passed to Toulon where in November 1940 disarmed. She was

Provence

scuttled together with remaining French ships but salvaged by Italians 11.7.1943. In August 1944 *Provence* was scuttled by Germans, salvaged again in 1949 and scrapped.

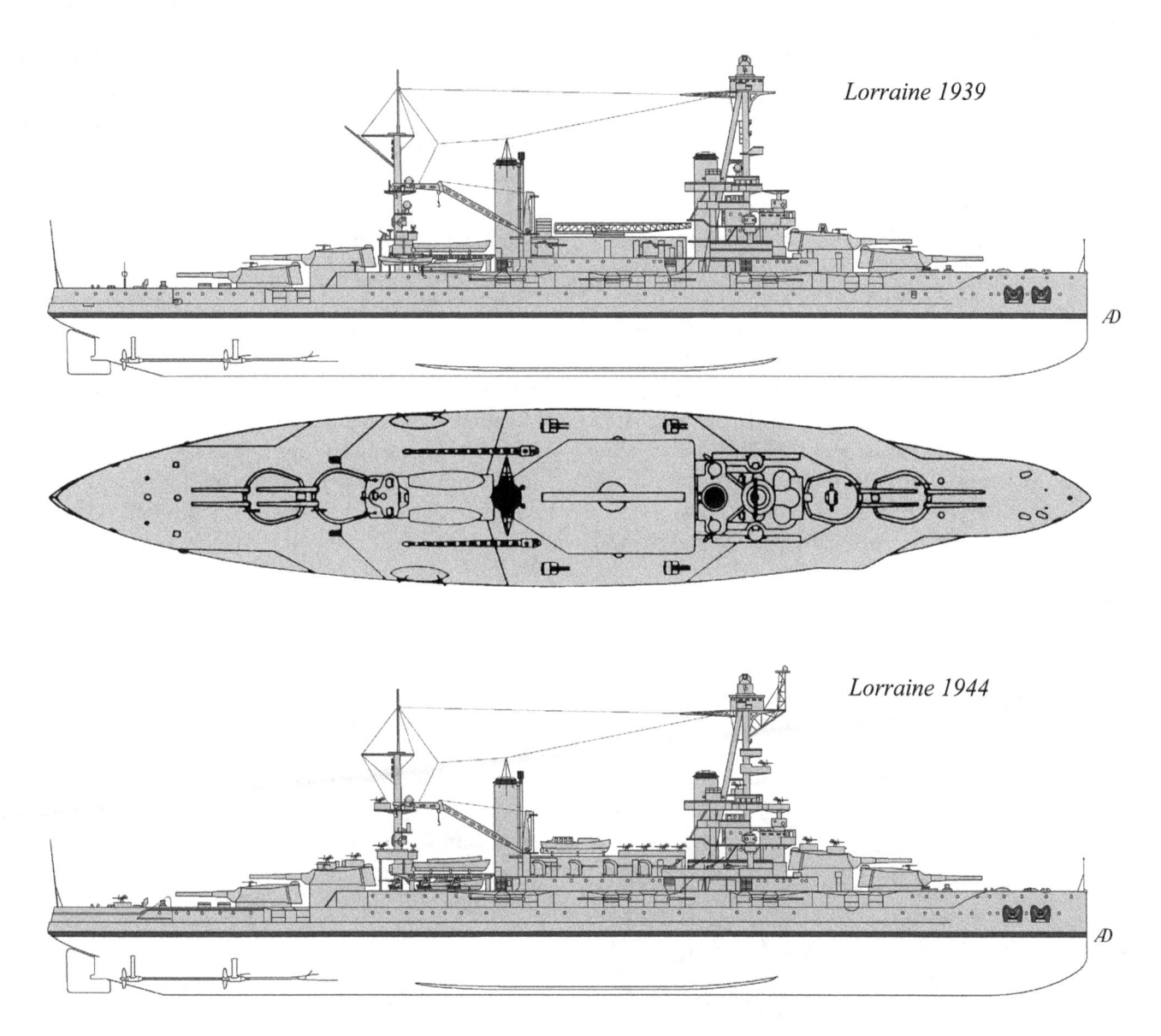

Lorraine 1939

Lorraine 1944

Lorraine in June 1940 participated in operations in Mediterranean. In July as a part of Force "X" she was disarmed at Alexandria but remained under the French control. She joined FNFL in December 1942 and 30.5.1943 *Lorraine* came to the side of the Algerian Government. In 1944-1945 as a part of Allied squadron she served at the Mediterranean coast of France. *Lorraine* served as training gunnery hulk since June 1945 and was converted to accommodation ship in February 1947.

DUNKERQUE class battleships

Dunkerque (Arsenal de Brest, 24.12.1932/2.10.1935/1.5.1937 - scuttled 27.11.1942)
Strasbourg (A C de la Loire et Penhoët, St-Nazaire, 25.11.1934/12.12.1936/6.4.1939 - scuttled 27.11.1942)

26500/34884(*Dunkerque*)-27300/36380(*Strasbourg*) t, 215.1(*Dunkerque*)-215.5(*Strasbourg*) x31.1x9.6(*Dunkerque*)-9.8(*Strasbourg*)m, 4gst/6b, 110960(*Dunkerque*)-112000(*Strasbourg*)hp, 29.5kts, 5664(*Dunkerque*)-5948(*Strasbourg*)t oil, 16400(17)nm, 1431p; belt 225(*Dunkerque*)-283(*Strasbourg*), decks 130+40, turrets 330(*Dunkerque*)-360(*Strasbourg*), CT 270; 2 x 4 – 330/52 M1931, (3 x 4 + 2 x 2) – 130/45 M1932, 4 x 2 – 37/50 M1933, 5 x 4 – 13.2 MG (*Strasbourg*), 1 catapult, 3 seaplanes (2 Loire 130, 1 Loire 210).

First French capital ships designed after WWI and the first-ever fast battleships. Built under 1931 and 1934 Programmes. They were intended for operations against German diesel-powered "Panzerschiffen" ("pocket battleships"). Characteristics of battleships were below limits supposed by Washington and London Treaties. French authorities considered that it should induce other countries to similar steps. For the first time capital ships received dual-purpose guns, and already at the design stage the aviation armament was provided. Often (and quite well-grounded), in view of rather light protection and high speed, they were rated as battlecruisers.

The scheme of main gun turrets arrangement and belt plates declination obviously borrowed from British battleships of *Nelson* class. At the same time French design was distinguished by using of quadruple main gun turrets. Their concentration in a bow allowed to shrink a length of an armored citadel and, as consequence, economy of displacement, increased horizontal fire angles (the dead angles for 1st and 2nd main gun turrets astern were only 37° and 30° aboard respectively), simplified fire control, the stern was exempted for aviation armament. Turrets were divided by the bulkhead on twin "semi-turrets", capable to operate independently. Ships had strong for their time DP and AA batteries though quadruple DP turrets had too low turning and elevation rates, and to the beginning of war firing rate of 130mm guns was already insufficient for air defense. Splinter protection was insufficient, some doubts were called by absence of counterflooding system. On *Strasbourg* protection was a little strengthened and fuel stowage was increased. Besides, she was differed by presence of one more bridge level.

11°inclined internal 225mm (283mm on *Strasbourg*) thick main belt covered 126x5.75m area, tapering to 125mm at lower edge. Its upper edge was connected to outside plating. Many small compartments between plating and belt were filled with special water-resistant material. Main belt was closed with 210mm fwd and 180mm aft bulkheads. Flat main deck laid on upper edge of main belt and had 125mm thickness over magazines and 115mm over machinery. Lower 40mm splinter deck was connected to lower edge of main belt with 50mm slopes. Part of hull aft of citadel was protected with 100mm lower deck with 100mm slopes, being closed with 100mm aft bulkhead of steering gear compartment. Main turrets had 330mm (340mm on *Strasbourg*) faces, 250mm sides, 345mm rears (for balancing) and 150mm (160mm on *Strasbourg*) crowns. Barbettes had 310mm (340mm on *Strasbourg*) armor on 30mm plating, but between armored decks its thickness was decreased to 50mm. Quadruple secondary turrets had 135mm faces, 90mm sides, 80mm rears, 90mm crowns; barbettes had 120mm armor. Twin secondary turrets had only 20mm protection. 7m-deep underwater protection was ended by 30mm torpedo bulkhead, its thickness was increased to 40-50mm at ship ends, it should protect against explosion of 300kg TNT. CT had 270mm sides.

10.1937, *Dunkerque*: + 6 x 4 - 13.2 MG.

Dunkerque

FRANCE

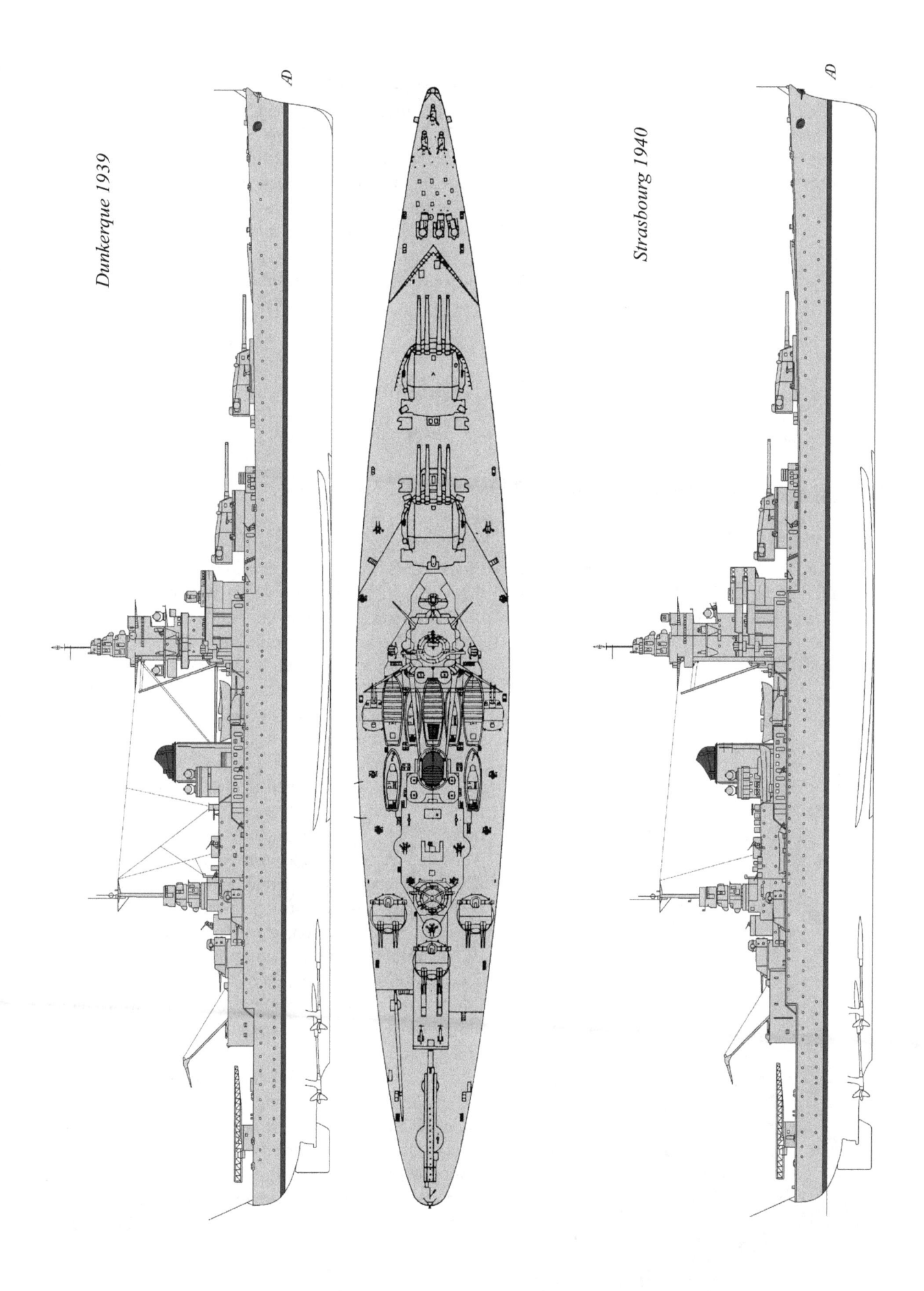

17

Dunkerque 1939

Strasbourg 1940

5.1938, *Dunkerque*: - 4 x 2 - 37/50; + 2 x 4 - 13.2 MG.
2.1939, *Dunkerque*: + 4 x 2 - 37/50 M1933.
Summer 1939, *Dunkerque*: + 1 x 2 - 37/50 M1933.
8.1939, *Strasbourg*: + 1 x 4 - 13.2 MG.
4.1942, *Strasbourg*: + 3 x 1 - 13.2 MG, Sadir M.E.140 / M.E.126 radar.

At the time of armistice with Germany *Dunkerque* and *Strasbourg* were at Mers-el-Kebir. 3.7.1940 during "neutralisation" of French squadron by British force "H" *Dunkerque* was hard damaged (4 hits of 15" shells) and ran aground. On July 6th she received additional damages after explosion of DCs onboard patrol *Terre-Neuve*, torpedoed being moored aside. *Strasbourg* could break from the Mers-el-Kebir and on July 4th arrived at Toulon.

During capture of Toulon by Germans both ships were destroyed by crews, thus *Dunkerque* was scuttled in dock. Italians salvaged *Strasbourg* 17.7.1943, but 18.8.1944 she was sunk by US bombers.

RICHELIEU class battleships

Richelieu (Arsenal de Brest, 22.10.1935/17.1.1939/15.7.1940 - FNFL 12.1942, TS 1.1956, accommodation hulk 5.1956)
Jean Bart (A C de la Loire et Penhoët, St-Nazaire, 12.12.1936/6.3.1940/16.1.1949, really 1.5.1955 - gunnery training hulk 1.1961)
Clemenceau (Arsenal de Brest, 17.1.1939/6.1943/ - scuttled incomplete 27.8.1944)

Richelieu as completed: 35000/47548t, 247.9x33.0x9.6m, 4gst/6b, 150000hp, 30kts, 6796t oil, 10000(12)nm, 1550p; belt 330, decks 150 + 40, turrets 430, CT 340; 2 x 4 – 380/45 M1935, 3 x 3 – 152/55 M1936, 6 x 2 – 100/45 M1930, 4 x 1 – 90/50 M1936, 4 x 2 – 37/50 M1933, (4 x 4 + 2 x 2) – 13.2 MG, 2 catapults, 3 seaplanes (Loire 130).

Jean Bart as completed: 42806/49850t, 247.9x35.4x9.2m, 4gst/6b, 162000hp, 32kts, 6476t oil, 5850(18)nm, 2134p; belt 330, decks 150 + 40, turrets 430, CT 340; 2 x 4 – 380/45 M1935, 3 x 3 – 152/55 M1936, 12 x 2 – 100/55 M1945, 14 x 2 – 57/60 M1951, 20 x 1 – 20/70 Oerlikon; ABM, DRBV-10, DRBV-20, DRBV-30 radars.

Richelieu and *Jean Bart* were built under the 1935 Programme, third ship of class, *Clemenceau*, under the 1938 Programme. They became development of *Dunkerque* and were the last and, probably, most perfect "Washington" battleships. Despite the most severe measures on weight economy to be entered into "Treaty" 35000t, in the design it was possible to reach good equation of general performances. Many progressive constructive decisions included in it were tested on *Dunkerque*. *Richelieu* was distinguished with main artillery, concentrated in two turrets, strong dual-purpose battery and 30kts speed. Though they could not make 152mm guns rather dual-purpose.

A complex pooling a superstructure, mast, and funnel, added originality to external appearance. The design was outlined also by strong underwater protection: at the time of construction, it was "deepest" in the world, up to 7m amidships. It in general repeated the system accepted on *Dunkerque* (alternating of empty and liquid filled compartments). Adding of 1.27m-wide bulges during modernization additionally improved underwater protection.

15°-inclined internal 330mm thick main belt covered 131.5x 5.96m area, tapering to 170mm at lower edge. Inclination ensured the resistibility equivalent of 478mm of vertical belt. Its upper edge was connected to outside plating. Many small compartments between plating and belt were filled with special water-resistant material, "Ebonite Mousse". Main belt was closed with 355-233mm fore and 233mm aft bulkheads. Flat main deck laid on upper edge of main belt and had 170mm thickness over magazines and 150mm over machinery. Lower 40mm splinter deck

Richelieu 1943

Richelieu 1941

Richelieu 1943

connected to lower edge of main belt with 50mm slopes. Part of ship aft of citadel was protected with 100mm lower deck with 100mm slopes, closed with 150mm aft bulkhead of steering gear compartment, thickness of this deck over steering gear increased to 150mm. Main turrets had 430mm faces, 300mm sides and 195-170mm crowns. Barbettes had 405mm armor, but between armored decks its thickness decreased to 80mm. Secondary turrets had 130mm faces, 70mm sides, rears, and crowns; barbettes were 100mm. 7m-deep underwater protection was ended with 30mm torpedo bulkhead, its thickness increased to 40-50mm at ship ends. *Jean Bart* had tear-shaped torpedo bulges and depth of her underwater protection was 8.5m. CT had 340mm sides.

11.1940, *Richelieu*: + 2 x 2 - 37/50 M1933.

2.1941, *Richelieu*: + (1 x 4 + 1 x 1) - 13.2 MG, Sadir M.E.140 / M.E.126 radar. 6.1941, *Richelieu*: + 2 x 1 - 13.2 MG. 7.1941, *Richelieu*: + 2 x 2 - 37/50 M1933.

1.1943, *Richelieu*: - 8 x 2 - 37/50, (5 x 4 + 2 x 2 + 3 x 1) - 13.2 MG, 3 seaplanes, 2 catapults, hangar: + 14 x 4 - 40/56 Bofors, 50 x 1 - 20/70 Oerlikon, SA-2, SF radars. Late 1943, *Richelieu*: + type 284 radar.

Late 1944, *Richelieu*: + type 281B, type 285, SG-1 radars.

8.1945, *Richelieu*: - 9 x 1 - 20/70; + 11 x 1 - 40/56 Bofors, full displacement became 48500 t.

Incomplete *Richelieu* 19-23.6.1940 passed to Dakar, 8.7.1940 she was damaged by torpedo bombers from British carrier *Hermes*. Artillery of this ship played the important role in failure of British-French (Gaullist) attempt of capture of Dakar 23-25.9.1940. Thus, two main guns failed for technical reasons. *Richelieu* joined FNFL in December 1942. After entering of French forces to the Allies *Richelieu* 30.1.1943 departed to the USA for repair and modernization. Works proceeded till August and 20.11.1943 *Richelieu* become a part of British Home Fleet. In March 1944 *Richelieu* arrived in the Far East and as a part of British squadron operated at coast of Indochina, returned to Toulon 11.2.1946.

Incomplete *Jean Bart* 19-22.6.1940 passed to Casablanca. There she was partially fetched to efficient condition. 1st main turret was prepared. By autumn of 1942 search radar was installed. By November 1942, except bow main gun turret, ship had 5 twin 90mm/50 guns, 2 twin and 1 single 37mm MGs, 4 twin and 14 single 13.2mm MGs and 1 light MG. 8-10.11.1942 she resisted the landing of Allies at Casablanca. During battle she was hard damaged by aircraft and gunfire of USN battleship *Massachusetts* (hits of three bombs and five or seven shells) and ran aground by the stern. She was completed after war and became last completed battleship in the world. Hull of *Clemenceau*, laid under a little changed design, in 1943 was taken out by Germans from construction dock and 27.8.1944 sunk by US aircraft at Brest. After war, the hull was salvaged and broken up.

GASCOGNE battleship

35000/48000t, 247.9x33.0x9.6m, 4gst/6b, 150000hp, 30kts, 6796t oil, 10000(12)nm, 1550p; belt 320, decks 150 + 40, turrets 430, CT 340; 2 x 4 – 380/45 M1935, 3 x 3 – 152/55 M1936, 8 x 2 – 100/45 M1937, (4 x 4 + 2 x 2) – 37/50 M1937, 5 x 4 – 13.2 MG, 1 catapult, 2 seaplanes (Loire 130).

Gascogne was ordered to A C de la Loire et Penhoët, St-Nazaire in 1940 but never laid down. She was a further development of *Richelieu* with changed armament arrangement. Main gun turrets should be installed fore and aft, 152mm turrets on the centerline (two superfiring fore and one aft), aviation armament was concentrated amidships between mast-funnels.

15°-inclined internal 330mm thick main belt covered area 131.5x 5.96m, tapering to 170mm at lower edge. Inclination ensured the resistibility equivalent of 478mm of vertical belt. Its upper edge was connected to outside plating. Many small compartments between plating and belt were filled with special water-resistant material, "Ebonite Mousse". Main belt was closed with 355-233mm fore and 233mm aft bulkheads. Flat main deck laid on upper edge of main belt and had 170mm thickness over magazines and 150mm over machinery. Lower 40mm splinter deck was connected to lower edge of main belt with 50mm slopes. Part of ship aft of citadel was protected with 100mm lower deck with 100mm slopes, being closed with 150mm aft bulkhead of steering gear compartment, thickness of this deck over steering gear increased to 150mm. Main gun turrets had 430mm faces, 300mm sides and 195-170mm crowns. Barbettes had 405mm armor, but between armored decks its thickness decreased to 80mm. Secondary turrets had 130mm faces, 70mm sides, rears, and crowns; barbettes were 100mm. 7m-deep underwater protection was ended with 30mm torpedo bulkhead, its thickness was increased to 40-50mm at ship ends. CT had 340mm sides.

Aircraft carriers and seaplane tenders

BÉARN aircraft carrier

Béarn (F C de la Méditerranée, La Seyne, 10.1.1914/15.4.1920/6.1927 - FNFL 6.1943, aircraft transport 3.1945, submarine depot ship early 1950s)

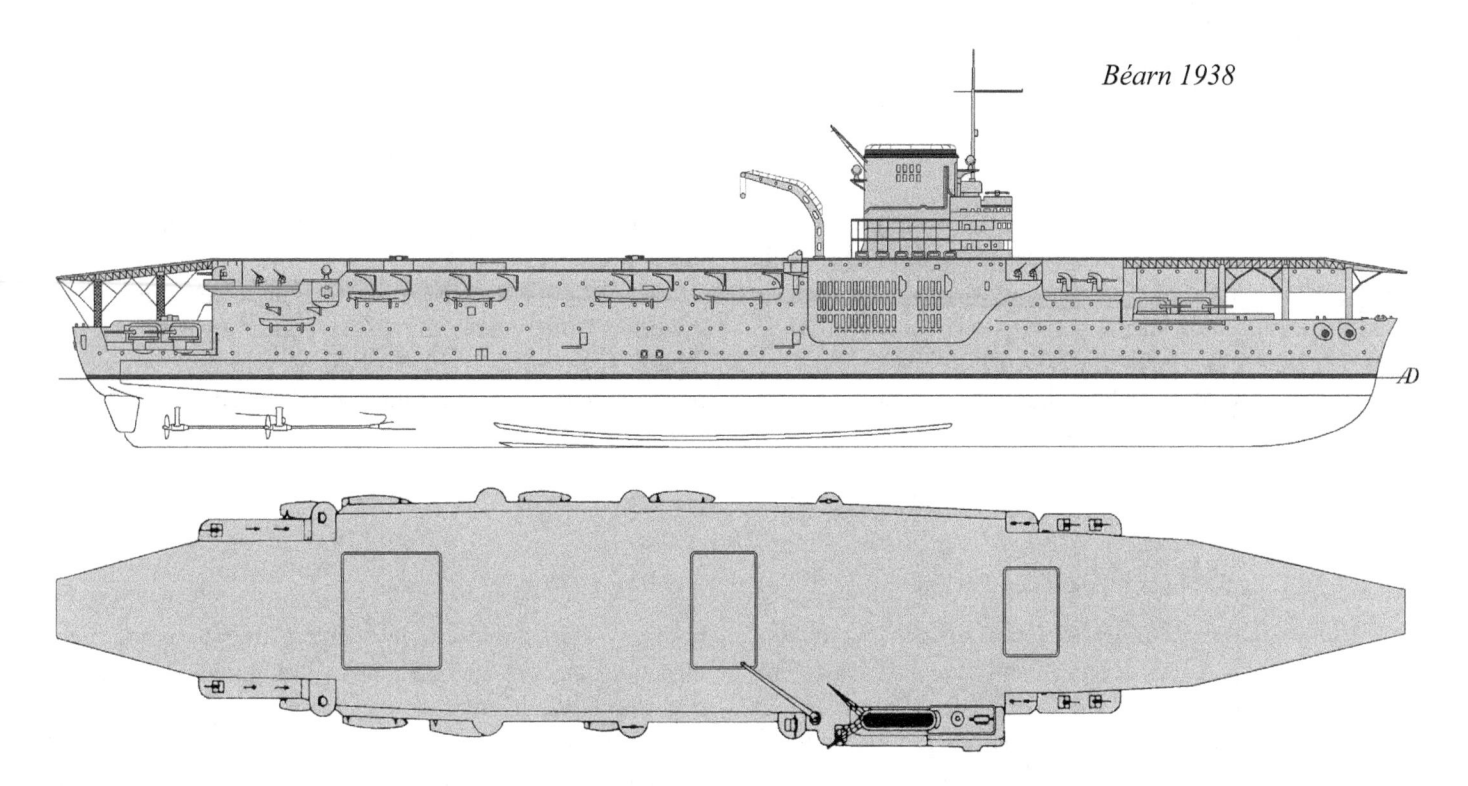

Béarn 1938

22146/28400t, 182.6x31.0x9.3m, 2st+2vte(4)/6b, 22500+15000=37500hp, 21.5kts, 2160t oil, 7000(10) nm, 865p; belt 80, decks 24+24+60, casemates 70-24; 8 x 1 – 155/50 M1920, 6 x 1 – 75/50 M1924, 8 x 1 – 37/50 M1925, 12 x 1 – 8 MG, 4 – 550 TT (beam), 40 aircraft (Wib.74, Wib.75, D.373, D.376 fighters, PL.7 torpedo bombers, PL.10, PL.101 reconnaissance planes, CAMS.37 amphibians).

9.1939- 20 D.373, 5 PL.7; Early 1940- 40 LN.401 and V-156-F.

Flight deck: 180.0x27.0m, hangars: 124.5x19.5 (upper) and 98.0x18.0 (lower)m, 3 elevators (15.3x15.7m fore and amidships, 8.2x12.2m aft), 328.000l aviation petrol.

Laid down as battleship of *Normandie* class. To follow decisions of Washington Naval Conference she was rebuilt to aircraft carrier. Works were begun in August 1923. Battle value of the ship was sharply reduced by insufficient area of a flight deck that ensured simultaneous usage of no more than 10-12 airplanes. By the end of 1930th *Béarn* was unique aircraft carrier with torpedo tubes (according to some sources, they were removed only late 1939), and was considered too slow for operations with a fleet. In 1939 decision to convert her to seaplane tender with preservation of possibility of basing of wheeled airplanes was accepted.

80mm main belt had 83m length. Flight, upper hangar, and lower hangar decks were protected with 24, 24 and 60-28mm armor respectively. 155mm guns were installed in casemates with 70mm armor.

(Autumn 1943 - 3.1945): ship was converted to aircraft

Béarn 1928

Béarn 1945

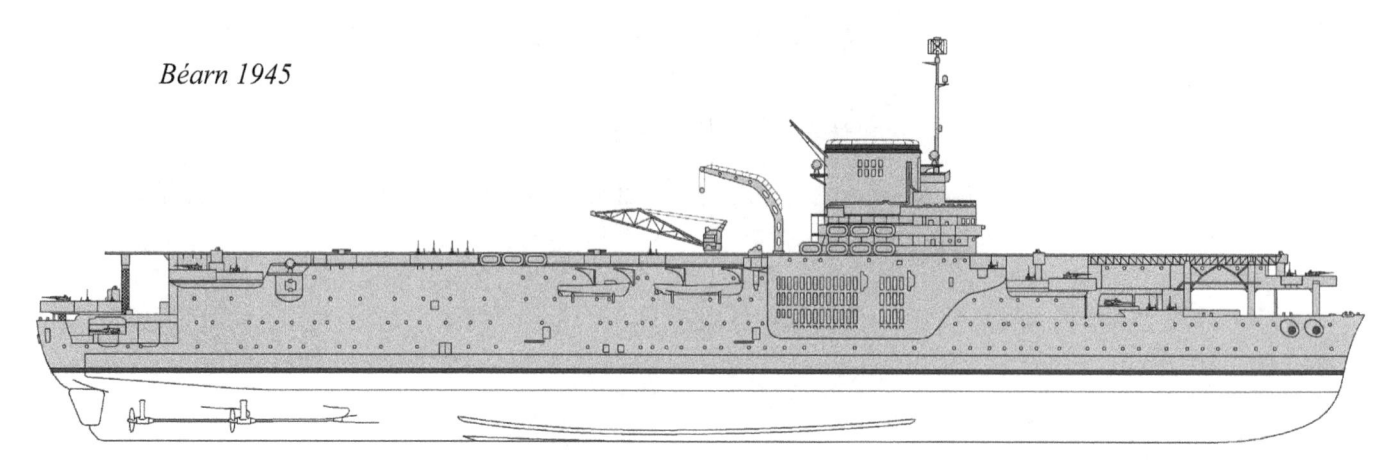

transport, flight deck was shortened, its breadth rose to 35.2m, fuel stowage was increased to 4500t, midship elevator was removed. Complement was 651. Radars were installed. Fully new artillery consisted of 4 x 1 - 127/38 Mk 12, 6 x 4 - 40/56 Bofors, 26 x 1 - 20/70 Oerlikon.

At the time of armistice signing *Béarn* was at Fort-de-France (Martinique) and under the agreement was disarmed 1.5.1942.

30.6.1943 Government of Martinique recognized the Algerian Government and *Béarn* passed to the USA for repair. Since autumn of 1943 till March 1945 works on her conversion to aircraft transport proceeded.

JOFFRE class aircraft carriers

Joffre (A C de St-Nazaire, Penhoët, 26.11.1938// - BU on the stocks 6.1940)

18000/20000t, 236.0x34.5x6.6m, 4gst/8b, 125000hp, 33kts, 1251p; belt 105, deck 70-37; 4 x 2 – 130/45 M1932, 4 x 2 – 37/50 M1933, 7 x 4 – 13.2 MG, 40 aircraft (15 D.790 fighters, 25 Br.810 torpedo bombers).

Flight deck: 200.0x28.0m. Upper (195x20.8x5.0m) and lower (79.2x15.6x4.4m) hangars. Two elevators, no catapults.

Building of two aircraft carriers was provided by the 1938 Programme.

Ships should have two hangars; flight deck was shifted to the port side and was equipped with two elevators and nine arrested gears. Basing of 15 fighters and 25 torpedo bombers was supposed. It is interesting to mark, that torpedo bombers should be twin-engined. Length of flight deck was insufficient, and island superstructure was disproportionate massive and long.

When the war begun, *Joffre* was 25%-ready and later broken up on the slipway. *Painlevé* was only ordered to A C de St-Nazaire, Penhoët, but never begun.

105mm main belt protected machinery spaces, magazines, and petrol tanks, 37mm main deck was connected to its upper edge. Thickness of main deck was increased to 70mm over magazines. There was 45-25mm longitudinal torpedo bulkhead.

DIXMUDE escort aircraft carrier

Dixmude (ex-Biter, ex-BAVG3, ex-Rio Parana) (Sun SB, Chester, USA / Atlantic Basin Iron Wks, USA, 28.12.1939/18.12.1940/(1.5.1942)/9.4.1945 - aircraft transport 1949, accommodation ship 1960)

12850/15300t, 150.0x23.7x7.8m, 4d(1), 8500hp, 16.5kts, 1308t diesel oil + 1097t cargo oil, 15000(15)nm, 555p; 3 x 1 – 102/45 QF Mk V, (4 x 2 + 11 x 1) – 20/70 Oerlikon, 15 aircraft (Seafire fighters); Type 79B, Type 272 radars.

1945- 15 Seafire.

Flight deck: 134.7x23.7m, hangar: 57.9x14.3x4.88m. 1 elevator (12.8x10.4m, 5.4t), 1 catapult H-II (3.2t plane was launched at 113km/h). Aircraft fuel stowage 164000l.

Former British escort aircraft carrier of *Archer* class, received from the USA under lend-lease. Early 1945 she was returned to the USA which transferred her to France. Converted from hull of transport ship of standard type C3. The stability was ensured with a concrete ballast (1930t). Besides, holding of 1000t of a water-ballast was recommended. Ship had no armor or underwater protection.

FRANCE

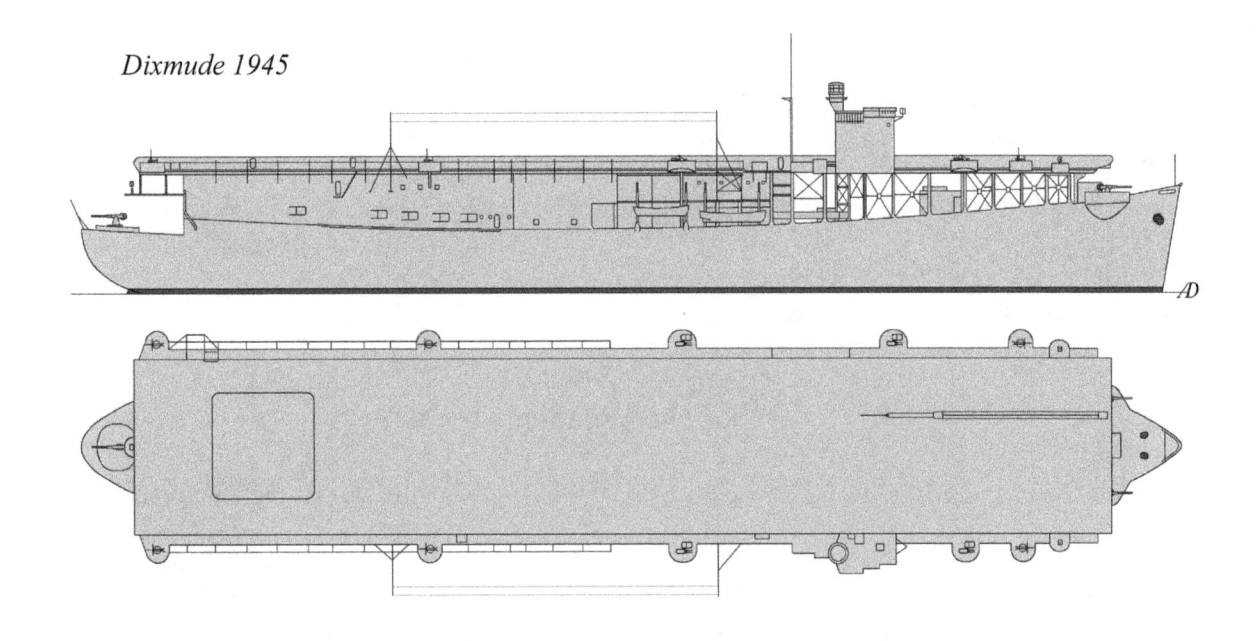

Dixmude 1945

COMMANDANT TESTE seaplane tender

Commandant Teste (F C de la Gironde, Bordeaux, 6.9.1927/12.4.1929/18.4.1932 - scuttled 27.11.1942)

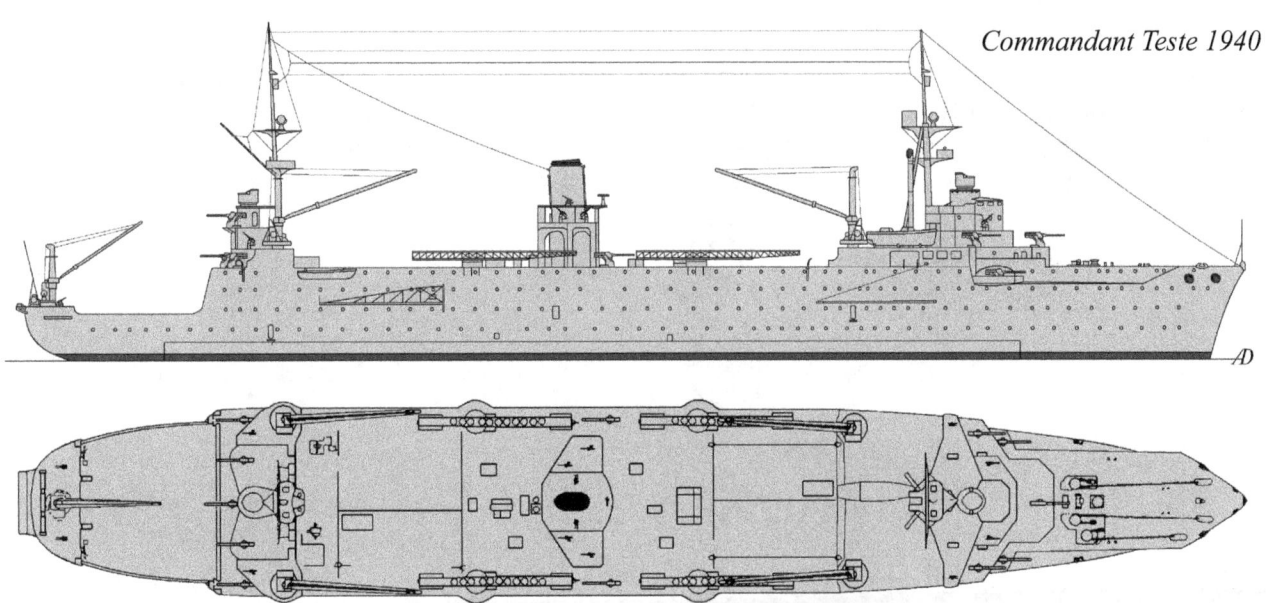

Commandant Teste 1940

10000/11500t, 167.0x27.0x6.9m, 2gst/4b, 21000hp, 20.5kts, 720t coal + 290t oil, 6000(10)nm, 644p; belt 50, deck 36, CT 80; 12 x 1 – 100/45 M1927, 8 x 1 – 37/50 M1925, 6 x 2 – 13.2 MG, 4 catapults, 26 seaplanes (12 PL.15 torpedo bombers, 14 GL.813 reconnaissance seaplanes).

1937- 12 PL.15, 12 GL.810/811; 12.1938- 6 Laté 298, 7 Loire 130; 9.1939- 6 L.N.210 (not embarked), 12 Laté 298, 7 Loire 130

Commandant Teste

Hangar: 84x27x7m, 5 5-12t cranes.

Built under the 1926 Programme and should serve as an aircraft transport, seaplane carrier with the limited repair capacities and seaplane depot ship for battleships and cruisers. The largest seaplane carrier built in Europe. Launch of seaplanes was ensured by 4 catapults, arresting was provided by a towed canopy.

Main 50mm belt protected most part of the length from CT to stern hangar deck. Armoured 36mm deck covered only machinery. CT had 80mm sides.

After defeat of France *Commandant Teste* remained under the control of Vichy Government. She was scuttled at Toulon 27.11.1942, salvaged by Italians 1.5.1943, then captured by Germans and 19.8.1944 sunk by Allied aircraft. In 1945 ship was again salvaged; but plans of conversion to training aircraft carrier or personnel transport were not realized.

SANS SOUCI class seaplane tenders

Sans Souci (A C de la Loire, St. Nazaire, 1938/28.11.1940/(11.1942) - completed as German escort SG3 (ex-Jupiter, ex-Uranus))
La Pérouse (ex-Sans Pareil) (A C de la Loire, St. Nazaire, 1939/28.11.1940/(9.1943)/5.1947 - completed as German escort SG4 (ex-Saturn, ex-Merkur), returned 5.1945, commissioned as survey vessel / aviso, stricken 1969)
Beautemps Beaupré (ex-Sans Peur) (A C de St. Nazaire – Penhoët, 1940/2.10.1940/(8.1942)/5.1947 - completed as German escort SG1 (ex-Merkur, ex-Jupiter), returned 5.1945, commissioned as survey vessel / aviso, stricken 1969)
Sans Reproche (A C de St. Nazaire – Penhoët, 1938/30.10.1940/(9.1942)/ - completed as German escort SG2 (ex-Uranus, ex-Saturn))

1372/1760t, 95.0x11.8x3.2m, 2d, 4200hp, 18kts, 256t diesel oil, 12000(10)nm; 1 x 1 – 75/50 M1927, seaplanes.

These seaplane tenders were captured by German troops in St. Nazaire on the stocks in June 1940 on various readiness stages. It was originally planned to complete them as air defense and fighter direction ships (Flügsicherungsschiffe) under names *Uranus, Saturnus, Jupiter* and *Merkur*. In February 1941, control over building was transferred to German ministry of aviation, however in April 1942 the control was returned to Kriegsmarine, and ex-depot ships were completed as fast escorts (Schnelle Geleitboote) *SG1-4*. They were armed with German artillery, purposed mostly on AA role. During service hull weakness and bad seaworthiness came to light. After war two survived *SG1* and *SG4* were returned to France and after repair commissioned as "Avisos Hydrographiques" ("aviso / survey ships") but in 1950 received numbers with F- prefixes, as frigates.

Cruisers

DUQUESNE class heavy cruisers

Duquesne (Arsenal de Brest, 30.10.1924/17.12.1925/6.12.1927 - FNFL 6.1943, depot ship late 1948)
Tourville (Arsenal de Lorient, 4.3.1925/24.8.1926/1.12.1928 - FNFL 6.1943, accommodation ship late 1948)

Tourville 1929

10000/12200t, 191.0x19.0x6.3m, 4gst/9b, 120000hp, 33.7kts, 1820t oil, 5500(13)nm, 605p; magazines 30, deck 24-22, turrets 30, CT 30; 4 x 2 – 203/50 M1924, 8 x 1 – 75/50 M1924, 8 x 1 – 37/50 M1925, 4 x 2 – 13.2 MG, 2 x 3 – 550 TT, 1 catapult, 1 seaplane (Loire 130).

Built under the 1924 Programme. First French "Washington" cruisers. Increased variant of *Duguay Trouin* class with improved hull form. Intended for long-distance scouting and operations on trade

FRANCE

Duquesne 1939

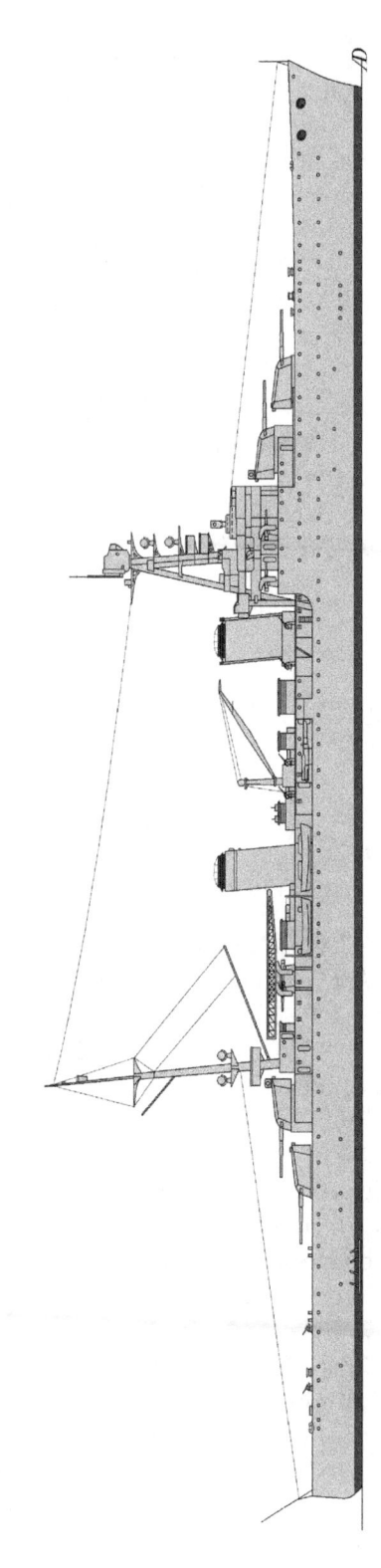

Tourville 1945

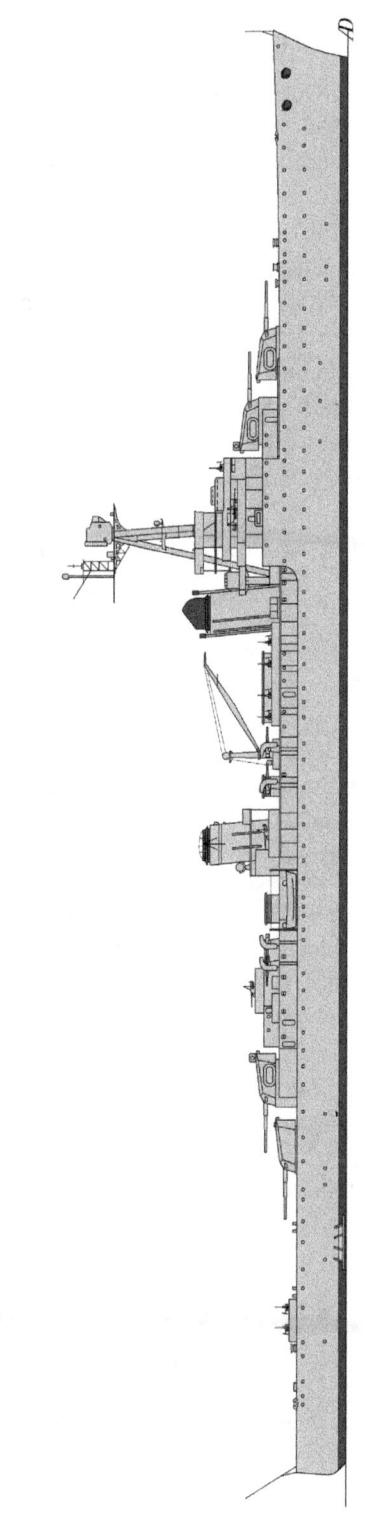

communications, first of all colonials. According to the task cruisers should exceed on speed all possible opponents (British and US light cruisers), and their armament should ensure the superiority over light and auxiliary merchant cruisers. Proceeding from tasks weakness of their armor protection (weight of armor was only 430t) was not a significant lack. Practically they had no underwater protection, only thickened longitudinal bulkheads abreast machinery.

Both ships during trials reached designed speed. *Duquesne* on 4hour trials developed overall speed 34.12kts at 131770hp (maximum speed was 35.3kts), and *Tourville* during 6hour trials signed 33.22kts overall at 126900hp (maximum speed was 34.13kts). Cruisers were characterized as well seaworthy and handy ships: 30kts speed they easily was made at half power of main machinery.

In 1930s variants of conversion to light aircraft carriers were studied. It was supposed, that in new quality they could carry 12-14 aircraft. Three variants of design from four provided preservation of fore or aft turret pairs. Detailed design study was refused in favor of real aircraft carrier of *Joffre* class.

Magazines and steering gear had box-shaped 30mm protection. Outer transverse bulkheads of engine spaces had 20mm thickness. Machinery was additionally protected with 14 - 12-mm torpedo bulkhead. Main deck had 24-22mm thickness, turrets had 30mm protection, CT had 30mm sides.

Late 1930s, both: + 2 x 2 - 13.2 MG.

In July 1940 as a part of Force "X" both cruisers were disarmed at Alexandria but remained under the French control. In May 1943 they came over to the side of Gaullist Algerian Government and joined FNFL 24.6.1943. *Tourville* in 1944-1945 was used as personnel transport.

DUQUESNE class heavy cruisers

Suffren (Arsenal de Brest, 17.4.1926/3.5.1927/1.1.1930 - hulk 12.1962)
Colbert (Arsenal de Brest, 12.6.1927/20.4.1928/4.3.1931 - scuttled 27.11.1942)
Foch (Arsenal de Brest, 21.6.1928/24.4.1929/15.9.1931 - scuttled 27.11.1942)
Dupleix (Arsenal de Brest, 14.11.1929/9.10.1930/20.7.1932 - scuttled 27.11.1942)

10000/12928(*Suffren*)-13103(*Colbert*)-13429(*Foch*)-13407(*Dupleix*)t, 196.0x20.0x7.3m(*Suffren*) or 194.2x19.4x7.3m(*Colbert*) or 194.2x19.3x7.5m(*Foch*) or 194.0x19.3x7.2m(*Dupleix*), 3gst/8b(*Suffren, Colbert*) or 3gst/6b(*Foch, Dupleix*), 90000hp, 32kts, 1700t oil + 640t coal (*Suffren, Colbert*) or 2620t oil (*Foch*) or 2585t oil (*Dupleix*), 4600(15)(*Suffren, Colbert*)-5300(15)(*Foch, Dupleix*)nm, 602-605p; belt 50 (*Suffren, Colbert*) or torpedo bulkhead 54-40 (*Foch*) or 60-20 (*Dupleix*), decks 25+18 (*Suffren*) or 22-20 + 18 (other), turrets 30, CT 30; 4 x 2 – 203/50 M1924, 8 x 1 – 90/50 M1926 (*Colbert, Foch, Dupleix*), 8 x 1 – 75/50 M1927 (*Suffren*), 8 (*Suffren*) or 6 x 1 – 37/50 M1925, 4 x 4 – 13.2 MG (*Dupleix*), 2 x 3 – 550 TT, 2 catapults, 2 (*Suffren*) or 3 seaplanes (all 2 Loire 130).

Built under 1925-1928 Programmes, development of the previous class with strengthened protection, differed by exclusively good seagoing capacities. Cruisers a little differed among themselves. *Suffren* and *Colbert* had two coal-burning boilers and their protection of engine rooms and aft boiler rooms was strengthened by 2m-wide bunkers.

Last two ships of class had internal armored belt and, accordingly, lost a longitudinal armored bulkhead. Armor weight for *Suffren* was 951t, for *Colbert* and *Foch* 1374t, and for *Dupleix* 1533t. Weaker torpedo armament since the second ship of class became a payment for strengthened protection. *Colbert, Foch,* and *Dupleix* had only two triple TTs instead of four on *Suffren*. In 1933 *Suffren* lost additional pair of TT banks.

On trials they reached from 32.51 (*Suffren*) to 33.06 (*Colbert*) knots.

50mm armor belt with 2.56m height protected

Suffren 1931

FRANCE

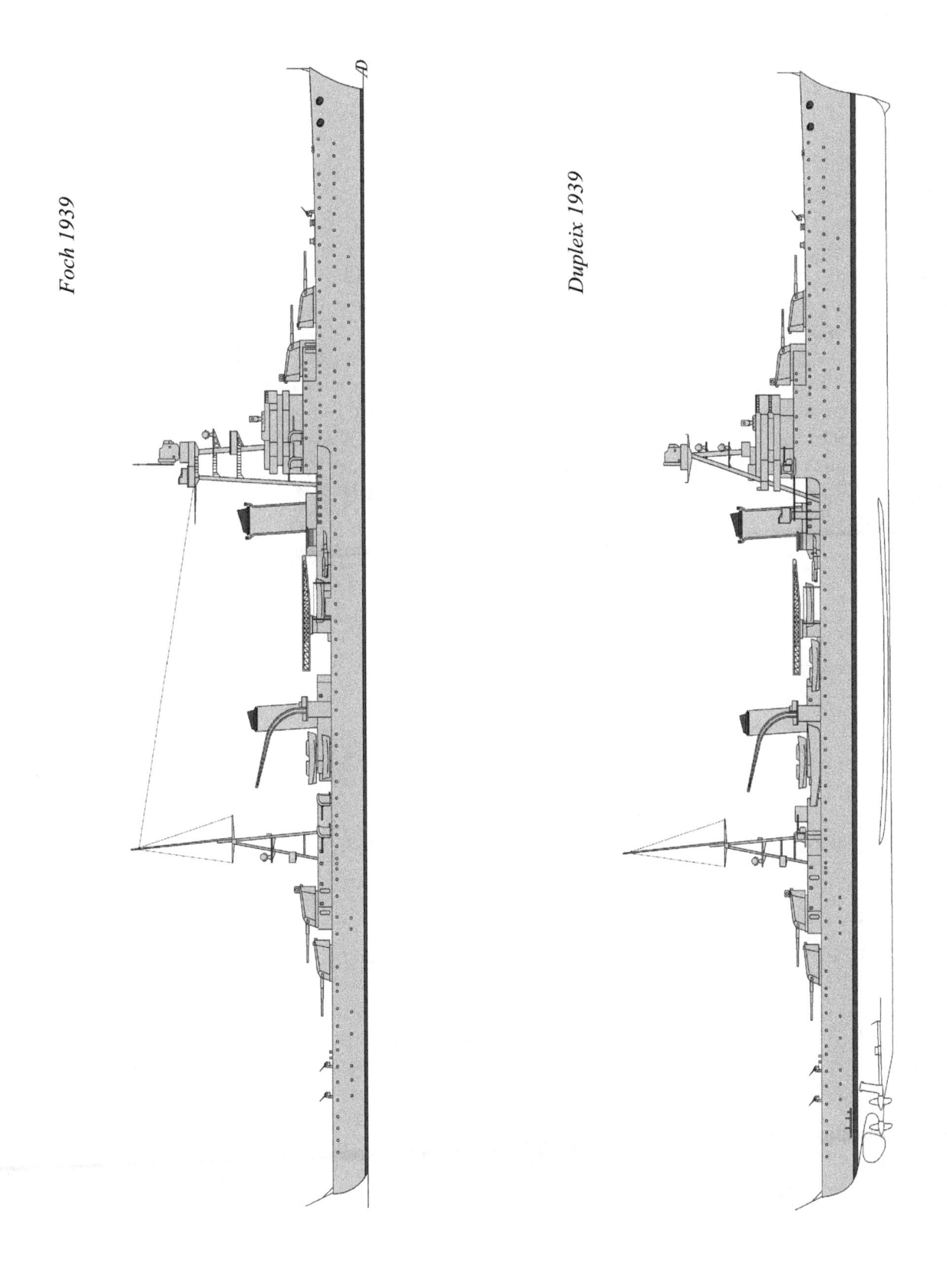

Foch 1939

Dupleix 1939

machinery spaces on *Suffren* and *Colbert*. *Foch* had 54mm longitudinal bulkhead with 5.5-6.1m height, connected abreast aft machinery spaces to double bottom with 40mm lower part. On *Dupleix* that bulkhead was 60mm-thick and 5.5-6.1m high, its part abreast aft machinery was doubled, consisting of two 40-20mm layers, and was connected to double bottom. Upper deck amidships was 25mm on first pair and 22mm (with 20mm small area near centerline) on the second pair, main deck had 18mm thickness (Main deck of *Dupleix* between armored longitudinal bulkheads had 30mm thickness). Magazines had box-shaped protection with 50mm (first pair) or 54mm (second pair) longitudinal bulkheads and 20mm transverse bulkheads and crowns. Steering gear compartment on *Foch* and *Dupleix* had 26-18mm protection. Turrets and CT had 30mm protection.

Late 1930s, *Suffren, Colbert, Foch*: + 3 x 4 - 13.2 MG. 1941-1942, *Colbert*: + 6 x 1 - 37/50 M1925, (4 x 4 + 2 x 2) - 13.2 MG, 4 x 1 – 8 MG. 1941-1942, *Foch*: + 4 x 2 - 37/50 M1933, (4 x 4 + 2 x 2) - 13.2 MG, 7 x 1 – 8 MG. 1941-1942, *Dupleix*: + 4 x 2 - 37/50 M1933, (4 x 4 + 2 x 2) - 13.2 MG, 3 x 1 – 8 MG.

Mid-1942, *Colbert*: + Sadire radar.

Mid-1945, *Suffren*: - 8 x 1 - 37/50, 2 x 3 - 550 TT, catapults, seaplanes; + 8 x 1 - 40/56 Bofors, 20 x 1 - 20/70 Oerlikon, SA, SF radars.

Suffren in July 1940 was disarmed at Alexandria and 30.5.1943 came over to the side of Gaullist Government in Algeria.

Other ships remained under control of Vichy. *Colbert, Foch,* and *Dupleix* were scuttled 27.11.1942 at Toulon. *Foch* and *Dupleix* were salvaged by Italians in April and July 1943 respectively, but never repaired. Former was broken up; latter was sunk by Allied aircraft in 1944.

ALGÉRIE heavy cruiser

Algérie (Arsenal de Brest, 19.3.1931/21.5.1932/15.9.1934 - scuttled 27.11.1942)

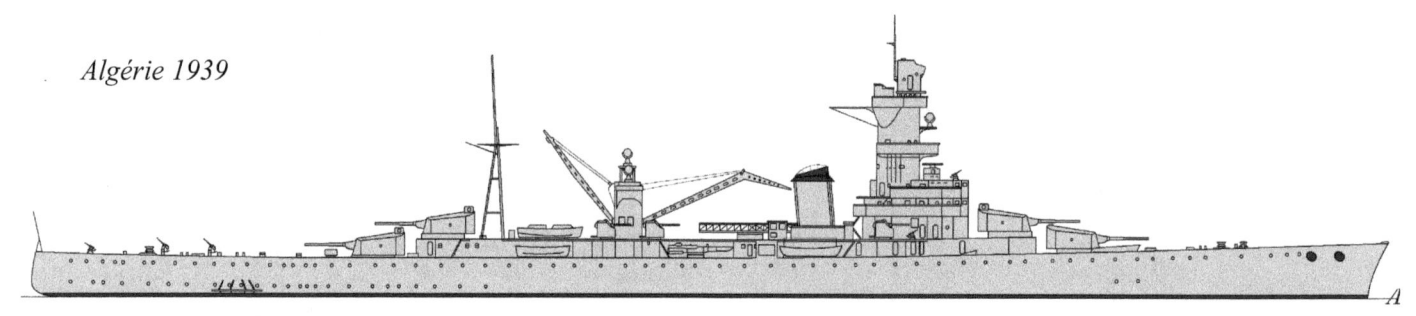

Algérie 1939

Algérie 1939

10109/13461t, 186.2x20.0x6.2m, 4gst/6b, 84000hp, 31kts, 3186t oil, 8700(15)nm, 616p; belt 110, deck 80-30, turrets 100-70, CT 100; 4 x 2 – 203/55 M1931, 6 x 2 – 100/45 M1930, 4 x 1 – 37/50 M1925, 4 x 4 – 13.2 MG, 2 x 3 – 550 TT, 1 catapult, 3 seaplanes (2 Loire 130).

Last and strongest French heavy cruiser, built under the 1930 Programme, often was considered as best heavy cruiser in Europe.

Designed as opponent for Italian cruisers of *Zara* class. Differed from predecessors by jump in protection: armor weight was increased more than by 1000t. Despite decrease in power of machinery in comparison with *Suffren* class, thanks to successful hull lines speed was not decreased. The special consideration in the design was given to horizontal and underwater protection: longitudinal bulkheads were connected to armor deck and stretched between barbettes of end turrets. Depth of underwater protection reached 5.1m. Practically for the first time in world practice heavy cruiser received adequate protection for armament and ammunition. The weight of protection reached 2657t. Stressing differences from earlier "tins", she sometimes called as an armored cruiser (croiser protegé).

Algérie 1942

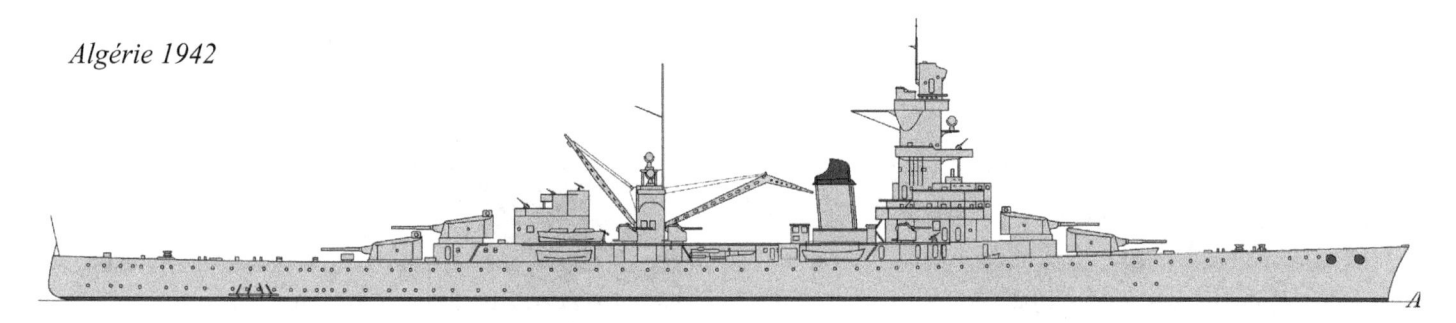

Algérie made serious impact on later design of the German cruisers of *Admiral Hipper* class. At the same time, she exceeded German ship on fire power, keeping immunity on distances between 18000 and 26000m. From contemporaries, cruiser differed by flush-deck hull with raised ship ends, that was uncharacteristic for French shipbuilding.

Algérie became first large French ship with fire control system mounted on a tower mast, she was the first received twin 100mm AA mounts. Only one catapult took place on the port side. Besides, starboard TT was installed by 2 m aft, than port one.

110mm main belt had 4.46-3.76m height abreast machinery and fore magazines, its height was decreased to 2.45m abreast aft magazines. This belt was closed with 70mm bulkheads, 70mm bulkhead separated machinery spaces and aft magazines. Thickness of side plating above the belt was 22mm. 40mm torpedo bulkhead extended between end barbettes, torpedo protection consisted of 3 compartments and was 5.1m deep. Main deck was 80mm between torpedo bulkheads and 30mm between these bulkheads and side plating (its thickness over fore magazines was 80mm from side to side). Upper deck was 22mm. Turrets had 100mm faces, 70mm sides and crowns and 85-50mm rears. CT had 100mmm sides.

1.1940: - 4 x 1 - 37/50; + 4 x 2 - 37/50 M1933.
Summer 1941: + 4 x 1 - 13.2 MG.
April 1942: + Sadire radar. 8.1942: - catapult with seaplanes; + new radar.

Algérie was destroyed by crew at Toulon 27.11.1942. The fire onboard lasted till November 29th. 18.3.1943 she was salvaged by Italians and broken up.

DUGUAY TROUIN class light cruisers

Duguay Trouin (Arsenal de Brest, 4.8.1922/14.8.1923/10.9.1926 - FNFL 7.1943, stricken 3.1952)
Lamotte-Picquet (Arsenal de Lorient, 17.1.1923/21.3.1924/1.10.1926 - training hulk 9.1942, sunk 12.1.1945)
Primaguet (Arsenal de Brest, 10.8.1923/21.5.1924/1.9.1926 - beached 8.11.1942)

7249/9350t, 181.6x17.2x5.2m, 4gst/8b, 100000hp, 33kts, 1500t oil, 4500(15)nm, 578p; deck 20, turrets 25, CT 25; 4 x 2 – 155/50 M1920, 4 x 1 – 75/50 M1922, 6 x 2 – 13.2 MG, 4 x 3 – 550 TT (24), 1 catapult, 2 seaplanes (2 GL.832) (*Duguay Trouin, Primaguet*) or (2 Po.452) (*Lamotte-Picquet*).

First large ships built in France after First World War, built under the 1922 Programme. They became first-ever light cruisers with artillery placed in superfiring closed turrets. Practically had no serious armor protection. Partly its absence was indemnified by the double bottom and presence of 16 transverse bulkheads. Differed with strong torpedo armament.

On trials all reached designed speed at full load. Differed with good seaworthiness, to lacks it is possible to refer short endurance, especially on the high speed.

Magazines and steering gear had box-shaped 20mm protection. There was no belt, hull was protected by only 20mm deck. Turrets and CT had 25mm protection.

Duguay Trouin 1943

Primauguet 1939

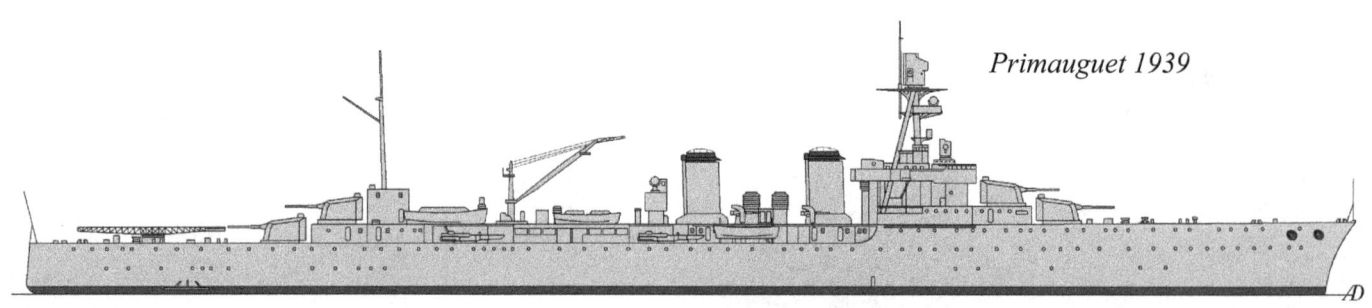

1937, *Primaguet*: - 6 x 2 - 13.2 MG; + 2 x 1 - 25/60 M1938, 4 x 4 - 13.2 MG.

1942, *Primaguet*: - 2 x 3 - 550 TT

10.1943, *Duguay Trouin*: - 4 x 2 - 13.2 MG, 4 x 3 - 550 TT, catapult with seaplanes; + 2 x 1 - 13.2 MG.

1.1944, *Duguay Trouin*: - 2 x 2 - 13.2 MG; + 6 x 1 - 40/56 Bofors, 20 x 1 - 20/70 Oerlikon, 2 x 1 - 13.2 MG, SF-1 radar.

Late 1945, *Duguay Trouin*: - 2 x 1 - 20/70, 2 x 1 - 13.2 MG; + SA radar.

Duguay Trouin was a part of Force "X" and was disarmed at Alexandria in July 1940, since July 1943 served with the Allies. *Lamotte-Picquet* was the largest French ship in IndoChina. She was laid up at Saigon in September 1942 and was used as training hulk. Cruiser was bombed in Cam Ranh Bay by USN carrier aircraft (TF38.2) 12.1.1945. *Primauguet* also remained under the control of Vichy. During Allied landing to Casablanca she was hard damaged by gunfire of US cruisers and SBD carrier diving bombers, ran aground and became a total loss.

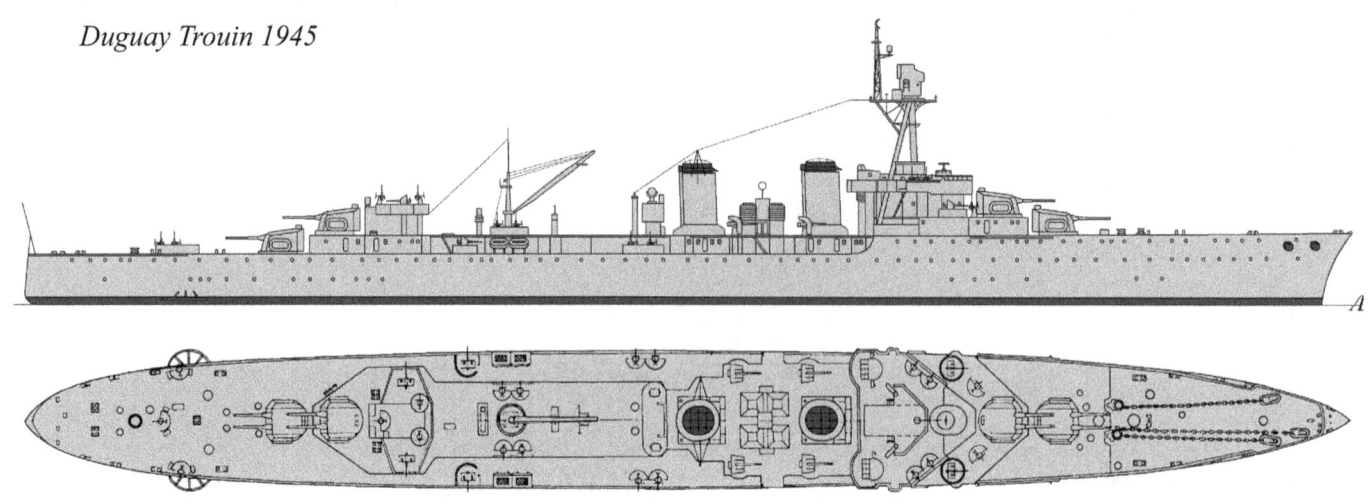

Duguay Trouin 1945

JEANNE D'ARC training cruiser

Jeanne d'Arc (A C de la Loire et Penhoët, St-Nazaire, 31.8.1928/14.2.1930/14.9.1931 - FNFL 6.1943, stricken 7.1964)

Jeanne d'Arc 1935

6496/8950t, 170.0x17.7x6.4m, 2gst/4b, 32500hp, 25kts, 1400t oil, 5200(11)nm, 506p+176cadets; magazines 20, turrets 25, CT 25; 4 x 2 – 155/50 M1920, 4 x 1 – 75/50 M1927, 2 x 1 – 37/50 M1925, 4 x 2 – 13.2 MG, 2 x 1 – 550 TT, 2 seaplanes (2 Loire 130).

Built under 1927 Programme. Purpose built training ship for midshipmen. To cruisers this ship was referred on formal characteristics, as displacement and artillery caliber. On 3hour trials she reached 27.03kts at 39000hp.

Magazines had 20mm box-shaped protection. Turrets

FRANCE

Jeanne d'Arc 1937

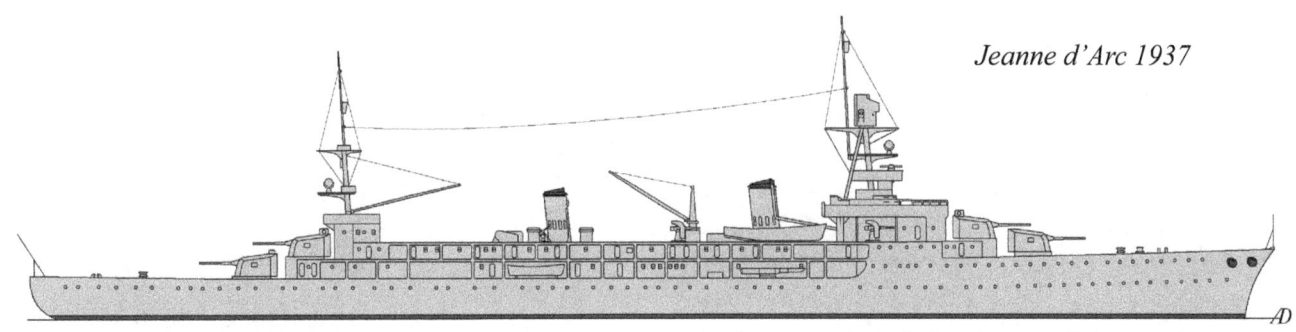

and CT had 25mm protection.
 1.1942: + 6 x 1 - 12.7 MG.
 9.1943: - 2 x 1 - 37/50, 4 x 2 - 13.2 MG, 6 x 1 - 12.7 MG, 2 x 1 - 550 TT; + 6 x 1 - 40/56 Bofors, 20 x 1 - 20/70 Oerlikon, SF radar.
 5.1944: - 2 x 1 - 20/70; + 4 x 1 - 40/56 Bofors.

At the time of armistice *Jeanne d'Arc* was in Martinique. Under the agreement of 1.5.1942 she was disarmed. After 3.6.1943 Government of Martinique recognized the Algerian Government, cruiser passed to the USA for repair and was armed again in September.

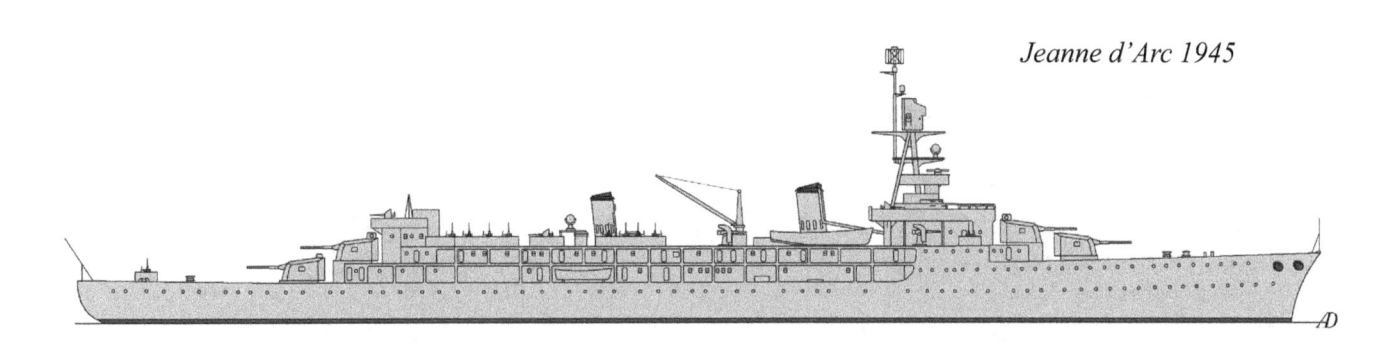

Jeanne d'Arc 1945

ÉMILE BERTIN light cruiser-minelayer

Émile Bertin (A C de la Loire et Penhoët, St-Nazaire, 18.8.1931/9.5.1933/28.1.1935 - FNFL 6.1943, stricken 10.1959)

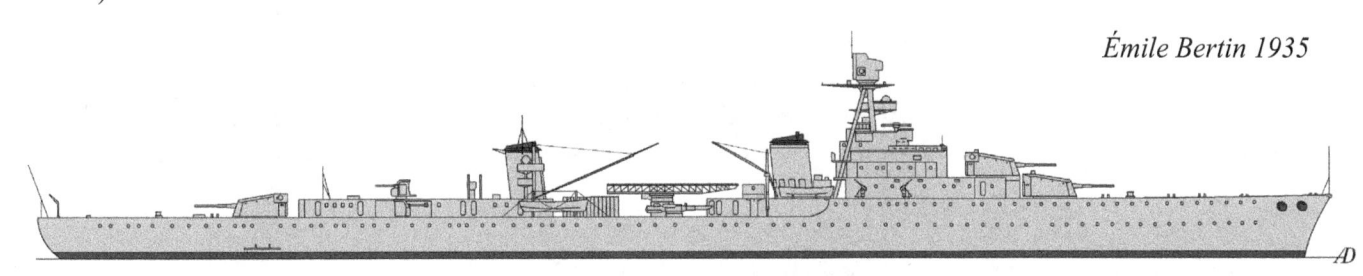

Émile Bertin 1935

5886/8480t, 177.0x16.0x6.6m, 4gst/6b, 102000hp, 34kts, 1360t oil, 3600(15)nm, 567p; magazines 30, deck 20, CT 25; 3 x 3 – 152/55 M1930, 1 x 2 – 90/50 M1930, 2 x 1 – 90/50 M1926, 4 x 2 – 37/50 M1933, 4 x 2 – 13.2 MG, 2 x 3 – 550 TT, 1 catapult, 2 seaplanes (2 GL.832), 200 mines (overloaded).
 Built under the 1927 Programme. Originally it was supposed to create an advanced cruiser-minelayer on the base of *Pluton*, but in ultimate variant minelaying abilities were faded into the background.

Émile Bertin

Émile Bertin 1945

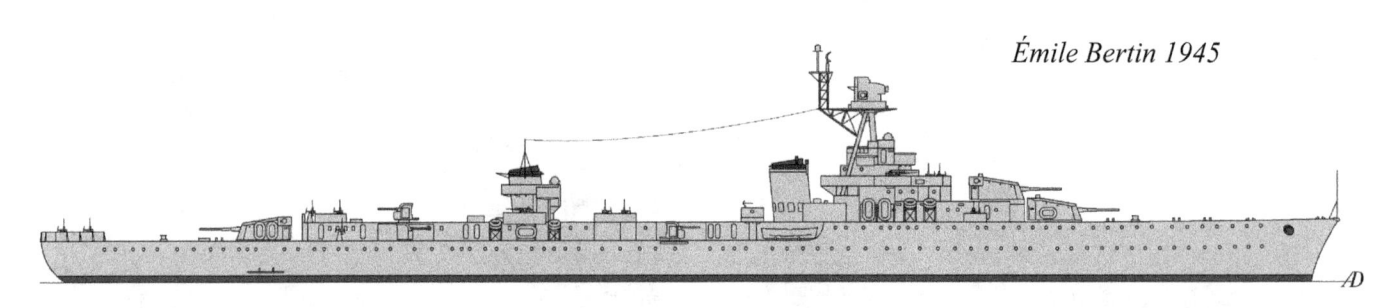

First in the French Navy *Émil Bertin* received triple 152mm turrets. The construction appeared too light, and in 1935 hull under turrets was strengthened. On trials cruiser reached 39.66kts at 137908hp.

Magazines had 30mm box-shaped protection. Turrets had no armor. Deck had 20mm protection, CT had 25mm sides.

12.1943: - 4 x 2 - 37/50, 4 x 2 - 13.2 MG, 2 x 3 - 500 TT, catapult with seaplanes; + 2 x 2 - 90/50 M1930, 4 x 4 - 40/56 Bofors, 20 x 1 - 20/70 Oerlikon, SA, SF radars.

1945: + Type 284, Type 285 radars.

At the time of armistice *Émil Bertin* was in Martinique. Under the agreement of 1.5.1942 she was disarmed. Later, in June 1943, Government of Martinique recognized Gaullist Algerian Government, and cruiser passed to the USA for repair.

LA GALISSONNIÈRE class light cruisers

La Galissonnière (Arsenal de Lorient, 15.12.1931/18.11.1933/1.4.1936 - scuttled 27.11.1942)
Jean de Vienne (Arsenal de Brest, 20.12.1931/31.7.1935/10.2.1937 - scuttled 27.11.1942)
Marseillaise (A C de la Loire, St-Nazaire, 23.10.1933/17.7.1935/10.10.1937 - scuttled 27.11.1942)
Gloire (F C de la Gironde, Bordeaux, 13.11.1933/28.9.1935/15.11.1937 - FNFL 1.1943, stricken 1.1958)
Montcalm (F C de la Méditerranée, La Seyne, 15.11.1933/26.10.1935/15.11.1937 - FNFL 1.1943, accommodation ship 1959)
Georges Leygues (A C de la Loire et Penhoët, St-Nazaire, 21.9.1933/24.3.1936/15.11.1937 - FNFL 1.1943, stricken 11.1959)

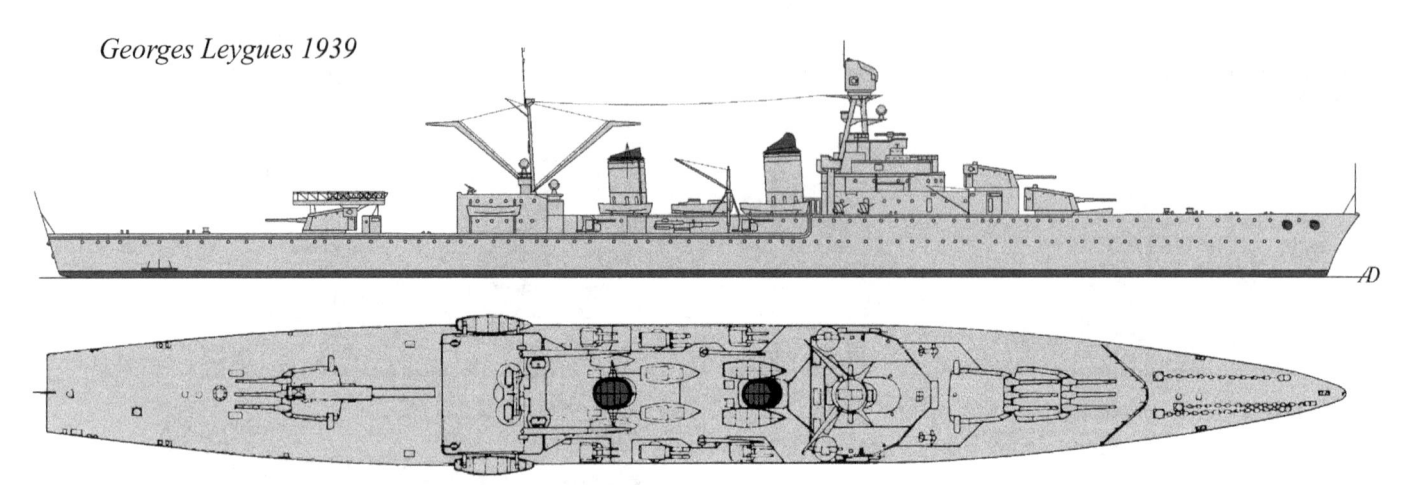

Georges Leygues 1939

7600/9100t, 179.5x17.5x5.4m, 2gst/4b, 84000hp, 31kts, 1569t oil, 5500(18)nm, 540p; belt 105, deck 38, turrets 100-50, CT 95-50; 3 x 3 – 152/55 M1930, 4 x 2 – 90/50 M1930, 4 x 2 – 13.2 MG, 2 x 2 – 550 TT, 1 catapult, 4 (*La Galissonnière*) or 3 seaplanes (2 Loire 130).

Built under 1931 (first two) and 1932 (others) Programmes. Became the answer to occurrence of Italian light cruisers of *Raimondo Montecuccoli* and *Duca d`Aosta* classes with armored belts.

They presented development of *Émile Bertin* and distinguished by much stronger protection at some decrease of contract speed. However, Italy did similarly. Accepted armor ensured practically absolute ballistic

FRANCE 33

protection against 152mm shells on expected fire distances. At the expense of machinery power decrease it was possible to make it more compact and designers could place in the hull 20mm longitudinal anti-torpedo bulkhead, notably having raised protection of the ships.

Despite the "stated" 31kts speed, on trials all cruisers exceeded it and shown from 34.98 to 35.42kts. Endurance remained rather small.

It is necessary to mark strong (at the time of designing) antiaircraft artillery of large caliber. The torpedo armament consisted of only 4 tubes look a little weakened. It is necessary to mark, that TTs were installed so, that the starboard mount "looked" ahead, and port mount was directed astern. For simplification of arresting seaplanes ships received a towed landing canopy. For the given design, the hangar for 2 seaplanes with double doors, fitted in an aft superstructure was characteristic. 2 more planes could be stored openly. Besides, release of a stern for operations with seaplanes became feature of external appearance of these cruisers. A catapult arrangement on main turret for late 1930th was unusually enough.

On set of characteristics ships of this class presented almost ideal pre-war light cruiser.

20mm torpedo bulkhead protected the hull between end barbettes. Main 105mm belt protected machinery and command center under main deck, it was about by 2m narrower abreast magazines. Transverse bulkheads had 60mm thickness between main deck and upper platform and 20mm between upper platform and double bottom. They were placed forward of barbette No1, between command center and barbette No2, between machinery spaces and barbette No3 and aft of barbette No3. Belt was closed with 38mm main deck. Steering gear compartment had 38mm crown, 26mm sides and 20mm transverse bulkheads. Turrets had 100mm faces, 50mm sides and crowns and 40mm rears. Barbettes had 95mm protection over upper deck and 70mm between main and upper decks. CT had 95mm sides and 50mm roof and had communication tube with 45mm armor.

Early 1941, *La Galissonière, Jean de Vienne, Gloire,*

Gloire 1944

Georges Leygues: + 1 x 2 - 25/60 M1938, 2 x 2 - 13.2 MG.

8.1941, *La Galissonière, Jean de Vienne, Marseillaise*: + 1 x 2 - 37/50 M1933

7.1943, *Montcalm*: - 6 x 2 - 13.2 MG, catapult with seaplanes; + 6 x 4 - 40/56 Bofors, 16 x 1 - 20/70 Oerlikon, SA, SF radars, full displacement increased to 10850 t, maximal speed was up to 32 kts. 11.1943, *Gloire, Georges Leygues*: - 1 x 2 - 25/60, 6 x 2 - 13.2 MG, catapult with seaplanes; + 6 x 4 - 40/56 Bofors, 16 x 1 - 20/70 Oerlikon, SA, SF radars.

La Galissonnière and *Jean de Vienne* were scuttled at Toulon 27.11.1942. Both were salvaged by Italians 9.3.1943 and 18.2.1943 respectively and received names *FR12* and *FR11*. Incomplete ships in September 1943 again were captured by Germans. They were sunk by US aircraft 18.8.1944 and 24.11.1943 respectively. *Marseillaise* was fired by crew at Toulon 27.11.1942. After a long-term fire cruiser became not subject to repair.

In May 1943 *Gloire, Montcalm* and *Georges Leygues* came over to the side of Allies.

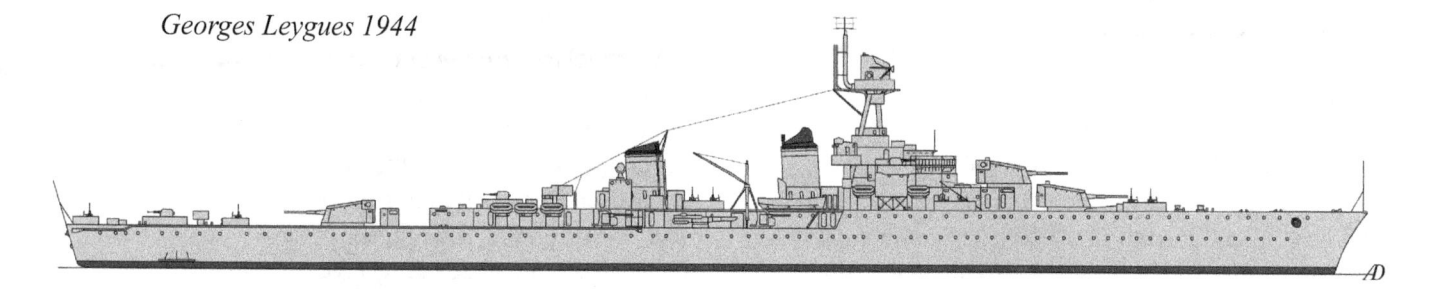

Georges Leygues 1944

DE GRASSE class light cruisers

De Grasse (Arsenal de Lorient, 28.8.1939/11.9.1946/3.9.1956 - stricken 1.1974)

As designed: 8000(std)t, 176.3x18.0x5.5m, 2gst/4b, 110000hp, 33kts, 540p; belt 100, deck 38, turrets 100-50, CT 95-50; 3 x 3 – 152/55 M1930, 3 x 2 – 100/45 M1933, 5 x 1 – 25/60 M1938, (1 x 4 + 2 x 2) – 13.2 MG, 2 x 3 – 550 TT, 2 catapults, 4 seaplanes (Loire 130).

De Grasse as completed: 9380/12350t, 188.3x21.5x5.5m, 2gst/4b, 105000hp, 33kts, 6000(18)nm, 950p; belt 100, torpedo bulkhead 20, bulkheads 60-20, deck 38; 8 x 2 – 127/54 M1948, 10 x 2 – 57/60 M1951; DRBV-20A, DRBV-11, DRBI-10, 4 DRBC-11, 4 DRBC-30 radars.

Improved *La Galissoniére*, *De Grasse* was ordered in 1937, *Châteaurenault* (F C de la Méditerranée, La Seyne) and *Guichen* (F C de la Gironde, Bordeaux) in 1938. They were designed faster than original, with strengthened AA artillery and aviation equipment arranged amidships. Only lead ship was laid down and completed after war under modified design, later ships were never laid down.

Torpedo bulkhead protected the hull between end barbettes. Main 100mm belt protected machinery and command center under main deck, it was about 2m narrower abreast magazines. Transverse bulkheads had 60mm thickness between main deck and upper platform and 20mm between upper platform and double bottom. They were placed forward of barbette No1, between command center and barbette No2s, between machinery spaces and aft magazines and aft of barbette No3. Belt was closed with 38mm main deck. Steering gear compartment had 38mm crown, 26mm sides and 20mm transverse bulkheads. Turrets had 100mm faces, 50mm sides and crowns and 40mm rears. Barbettes had 95mm protection over upper deck and 70mm between main and upper decks. CT had 95mm sides and 50mm roof and had communication tube with 45mm armor.

PLUTON cruiser-minelayer

Pluton (Arsenal de Lorient, 16.4.1928/10.4.1929/1.10.1931 - TS, internal explosion 18.9.1939)

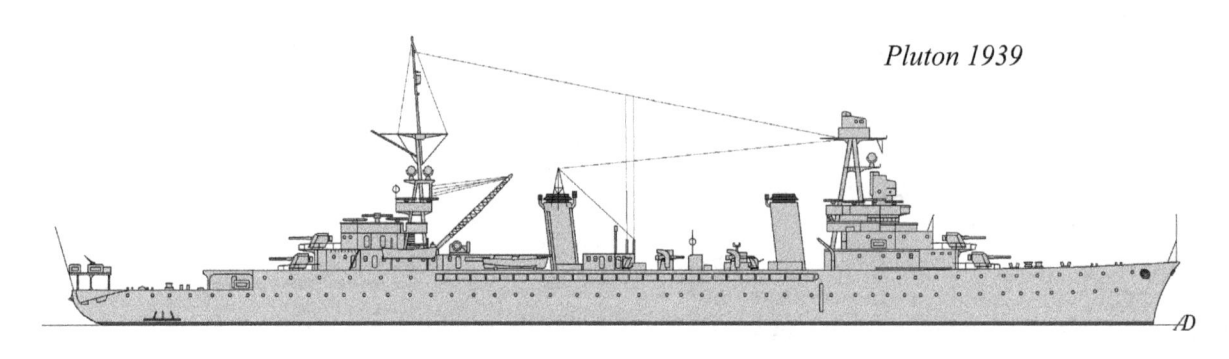

Pluton 1939

4773/6500t, 152.5x15.6x5.2m, 2gst/4b, 57000hp, 30kts, 1200t oil, 4510(14)nm, 424p; shields 20; 4 x 1 – 139/40 M1927, 4 x 1 – 75/50 M1927, 2 x 1 – 47/50 M1885, 2 x 1 – 37/50 M1925, 6 x 2 – 13.2 MG, 290 mines.

Built under the 1925 Programme, designed on the sample of British *Adventure* as minelayer for 250 mines and personnel transport for 1000 troops with armament. Armament consisted of 2 single 203mm and 2 single 138mm guns was originally supposed. However, in this case ship would be considered as "A" class (heavy) cruiser which number was limited by treaties.

Only guns had light splinter protection.

As minelayer *Pluton* practically was not used. 24.10.1932-27.4.1933 she passed conversion to gunnery TS. Many rangefinders for cadet training were installed. Since June 1940 ship should become ultimately training ship and been renamed *La Tour D'Auvergne*. Though, she (contrary to a popular belief) did not manage to receive it. *Pluton* was lost at Casablanca 18.9.1939 as result of internal explosion and following 18hour fire.

Armed merchant cruisers

X01 Aramis (1932/9.1939, 17537grt, 165.4ppx21.2x8.7m, 17kts, 8 x 1 - 139/45, 2 x 1 - 75/35, 2 x 1 – 37/50 - paid off 8.1940); **X04 Koutoubia** (1931/9.1939, 8790grt, 135.2ppx17.8x7.3m, 16.5kts, 8 x 1 - 139/45, 1 x 1 – 37/50, 2 x 1 – 25/60 - paid off 9.1940); **X05 Ville d'Oran** (1936/9.1939, 10172grt, 140.8ppx19.3x6.6m, 21kts, 5 x 1 - 139/45 - paid off 10.1940); **X06 El Mansour** (1933/10.1939, 5818grt, 121.7ppx16.4x5.5m, 21.5kts, 7 x 1 - 139/45, 2 x 1 - 75/35 - paid off 10.1940); **X07 Victor Schoelcher**, 11.1941- **Bougainville** (1939/9.1939, 4504grt, 114.5ppx15.8x5.9m, 17kts, 7 x 1 - 139/45, 2 x 1 - 75/35, 2 x 1 – 37/50 - paid off 10.1940, re-commissioned 11.1941, sunk 6.5.1942); **X10 Colombie** (1931/11.1939, 13390grt, 155.2ppx20.4x8.0m, 16kts, 7 x 1 - 149/45, 2 x 1 - 75/35, 2 x 1 – 37/50, 35 DC - paid off 9.1940); **X11 Charles Plumier** (1939/9.1939, 4504grt, 114.5ppx15.8x5.9m, 17kts, 7 x 1 - 149/45, 2 x 1 - 75/35, 2 x 1 – 37/50 - paid off 10.1940); **X17 El Djezair** (1934/10.1939, 5818grt, 121.5ppx16.4x5.5m, 21.5kts, 7 x 1 - 139/45, 2 x 1 - 75/35 - paid off 10.1940); **X18 El Kantara** (1932/9.1939, 5079grt, 116.3x16.4x5.7m, 20.5kts, 7 x 1 - 139/45, 2 x 1 - 75/35 - paid off 10.1940); **X19 Barfleur** (1938/11.1939, 3259grt, 102.6ppx13.9x5.8m, 16kts, 7 x 1 - 149/45, 2 x 1 - 75/35, 2 x 1 – 37/50 - armed transport X2 1944); **X20 Quercy** (1937/9.1939, 3100grt, 98.5ppx13.9x5.7m, 15.5kts, 7 x 1 - 139/45, 2 x 1 - 75/35, 2 x 1 – 37/50 (1941: 3 x 1 - 139/45, 4 x 2 – 37/50) - paid off 11.1940, re-commissioned 1941, armed transport 1944); **X21 Estérel** (1938/10.1939, 3100grt, 98.5ppx13.9x5.7m, 15.5kts, 7 x 1 - 139/45, 2 x 1 - 75/35, 2 x 1 – 37/50 - paid off 11.1940); *X22 Mexique* (1915/10.1939, 12000grt, 166.6ppx19.5m, 16kts - conversion cancelled 11.1939); **X1 Cap des Palmes** (1935/1941, 3081grt, 100.6ppx13.4x5.2m, 17.5kts - 2 x 1 - 90/50 - returned 1947)

Aramis prewar

Cap des Palmes as AMC

Former passenger liners and fast refrigerators converted to AMCs.

1941, *Quercy*: was rearmed with 3 x 1 - 139/40, 8 x 1 - 37/50, 10 x 1 - 13.2 MG.

1943, *Cap des Palmes* was rearmed with 2 x 1 - 152/45, 2 x 1 - 76/45, 8 x 1 - 20/70, 2 x 3 - 533 TT, 4 DCT. 1943, *Barfleur*: - 5 x 1 - 149/45, 2 x 1 - 37/50; + 6 x 1 - 20/70. 1943, *Quercy*: - 2 x 1 - 139/40, 6 x 1 - 37/50, 10 x 1 - 13.2 MG; + 8 x 1 - 20/70.

Aramis was laid up in Indochina in August 1940, later captured by Japanese and sunk by USN submarine *Rasher*. *El Mansour* was paid off in October 1940, later captured by Italians, renamed *Anagni* and scuttled at Marseilles in August 1944. *Bougainville* was sunk 6.5.1942 at Diego Suarez by British aircraft. *El Djezair* was paid off in October 1940, later captured by Germans, transferred by them to Italians as *Cassino*, re-captured by Germans in 1943 and sunk 25.6.1944 by Allied aircraft. *El Kantara* was paid off in October 1940, later captured by Italians as *Aquino* and sunk by Allied aircraft 2.4.1943. *Estérel* was paid off in November 1940, later captured by Germans and ran aground after being attacked by British submarine *Shakespeare*.

Destroyers and torpedo boats

CHACAL class large destroyers

Jaguar (Arsenal de Lorient, 8.1922/17.11.1923/6.1926 - sunk 23.5.1940); **Panthère** (Arsenal de Lorient, 12.1922/27.10.1924/11.1926 - scuttled 27.11.1942); **Léopard** (A C de la Loire, St-Nazaire, 8.1923/29.9.1924/10.1927 - captured by British 3.7.1940, FNFL 8.1940, wrecked 27.5.1943); **Lynx** (A C de la Loire, St-Nazaire, 1.1923/24.2.1924/8.1927 - scuttled 27.11.1942); **Chacal** (A C de St-Nazaire-Penhoët, 8.1923/27.9.1924/6.1926 - sunk 24.5.1940); **Tigre** (A C de Bretagne, Nantes, 9.1923/2.8.1924/12.1925 - scuttled 27.11.1942, salvaged by Italians (FR23), returned 10.1943, BU 1954)

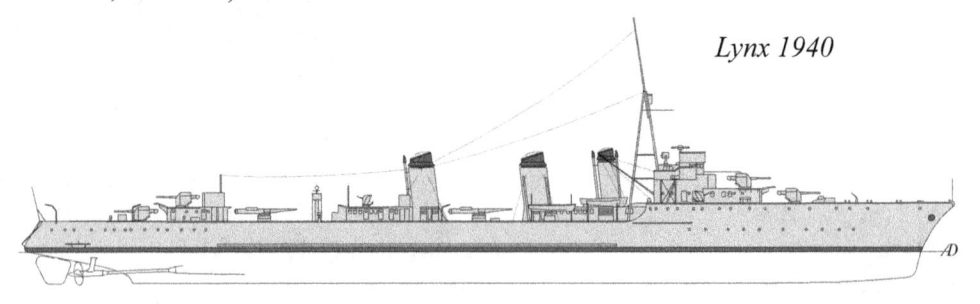

Lynx 1940

2126/2950-3050t, 126.8x11.3x4.1m, 2gst/5b, 50000hp, 35.5kts, 530t oil, 2900(16)nm, 195p; 5 x 1 – 130/40 M1919, 2 x 1 – 75/50 M1922, 2 x 3 – 550 TT, 4 DCT, 2 DCR (46).

Built under the 1922 Programme. First series of super-destroyers built for the French Navy. Intended for operations against Italian scouts and British destroyer leaders. Should fulfil also functions of small cruisers.

Usage of the longitudinal hull framing became their feature. Firing rate of main guns was only 4-5 shots/min that was obviously insufficiently for destroyers. Too high outline profile that facilitated detection of the ships was criticized also and led to an increase in windage when maneuvering.

By beginning of war ships made no more than 31kts. The maneuverability lack on high speed besides, came to light. The spring of 1940 considered a question of conversion of this class ships to AA ships with twin 100mm gun mounts.

1939, all: - 1 x 1 - 130/40 (No 3), 2 x 1 - 75/50; + 4 x 2 - 13.2 MG. 1939-1940, *Jaguar, Léopard, Lynx, Chacal, Tigre*: + Type 123 sonar.

1940, *Léopard*: + 1 x 1 - 102/45 QF Mk V, 1 x 1 - 40/39 pompom, 6 x 1 - 7.7 MG, DC stowage increased to 52.

3.1942, *Léopard*: 1 boiler with fore funnel was removed, 100t of permanent ballast were added. Fuel stowage was increased to 780t, maximal speed was 31.5kts; - 4 x 2 - 13.2 MG, 5 x 1 - 7.7 MG; + 2 x 1 - 40/39 pompom, 4 x 1 - 20/70 Oerlikon, 4 DCT, radar.

Late 1943, *Tigre*: - 4 x 2 - 13.2 MG, 1 x 3 - 550 TT; + 2 x 1 - 40/56 Bofors, 10 x 1 - 20/70 Oerlikon.

4.1944, *Tigre*: 1 boiler with fore funnel was removed, 100t of permanent ballast were added. Fuel stowage was increased to 745t, maximal speed was 28.5kts; + 4 DCT, radars.

Jaguar on the night of 23.5.1940 at Dunkirk was hard damaged by German MTBs *S21* and *S23* and ran aground. Abandoned ship was destroyed by German aircraft. *Panthère, Tigre* and *Lynx* were scuttled 27.11.1942 at Toulon. *Panthère* was salvaged by Italians and received name *FR22*. She was never commissioned and 9.9.1943 scuttled by Italians at La Spezia. *Lynx* was salvaged by Germans and broken up. *Tigre* was salvaged by Italians and under name *FR23* was commissioned as personnel transport. After capitulation of Italy 28.9.1943 she returned to France and served as tender. *Léopard* 3.7.1940 at Portsmouth was captured by British and 31.8.1940 transferred to FNFL. 27.5.1943 she ran aground at Bengasi; it was not possible to salvage her. *Chacal* 24.5.1940 was sunk by German Ju 87 diving bombers at Boulogne.

Panthère 1927

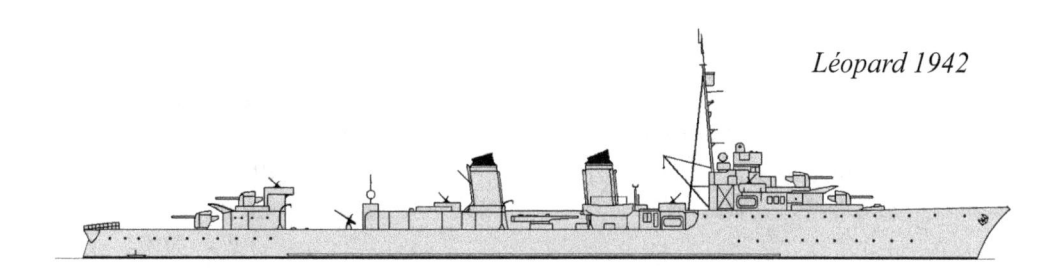

FRANCE

Léopard 1942

GUÉPARD class large destroyers

Guépard (Arsenal de Lorient, 3.1927/19.4.1928/8.1929 - scuttled 27.11.1942); **Bison** (Arsenal de Lorient, 3.1927/29.10.1928/10.1930 - sunk 3.5.1940); **Valmy** (A C de St-Nazaire-Penhoët, 5.1927/19.5.1928/1.1930 - scuttled 27.11.1942); **Verdun** (A C de la Loire, St-Nazaire, 8.1927/4.7.1928/4.1930 - scuttled 27.11.1942); **Lion** (A C de France, Dunkerque, 7.1927/5.8.1929/2.1931 - scuttled 27.11.1942); **Vauban** (A C de France, Dunkerque, 3.1929/1.2.1930/2.1931 - scuttled 27.11.1942)

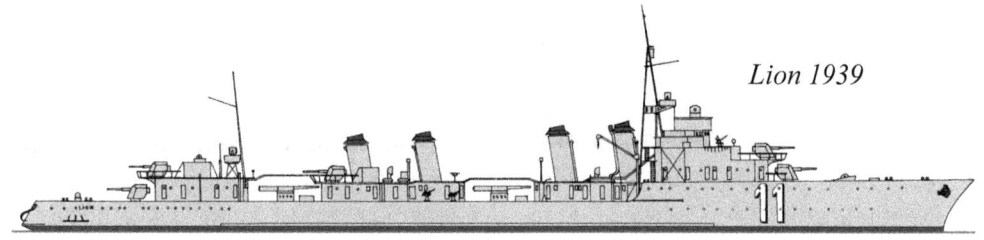

Lion 1939

2436/3200t, 130.2x11.8x4.7m, 2gst/4b, 64000hp, 35.5kts, 572t oil, 3450(14.5)nm, 230p; 5 x 1 – 139/40 M1923, 4 x 1 – 37/50 M1925, 2 x 2 – 13.2 MG, 2 x 3 – 550 TT, 2 DCR (32).

Built under 1925 (3 ships) and 1926 (3 ships) Programmes. First series of 2400ton "four-funnelers". Eighteen ships were built under close designs and had rare (and archaic) for 1930th years four-funnel outline profile. Reconnaissance, operations on trade lines (protection of own and breaking of enemy trade), fighting against enemy light forces and support of the own were assumed to them. Originally ships differed by weakness of fire control system (only 1 rangefinder). Only in 1935 the second rangefinder was installed.

Insufficient firing rate of main guns (5-6rpm) and low muzzle velocity was considered as the basic lack. Originally destroyers carried 4 DCTs, but in 1932 they were removed for stability raise. Weakness of ASW armament was not considered as a significant lack - ships did not intend for anti-submarine service. They appeared quite good seaworthy boats. By beginning of WWII most ships could keep 37kts speed at full load. First two ships belonged to Group 'A', next ships to slightly differed group 'B'.

1939, *Bison*: + sonar.
1941, *Guépard, Valmy*: - 1 x 3 - 550 TT; + 1 x 2 - 37/50 M1933, 2 x 1 - 13.2 MG. 1941, *Verdun*: + 1 x 2 - 37/50 M1933, 2 x 1 - 13.2 MG.

Bison on night of 8.2.1939 collided with light cruiser *Georges Leygues* and lost fore end to the main gun No2. It is curious, that the gun together with its crew appeared on cruiser's forecastle. Destroyer was commissioned again before the war. 3.5.1940 during evacuation of Allied troops from Namsos (Norway) *Bison* was sunk by German diving bombers. All other ships of this class were scuttled at Toulon 27.11.1942. *Guépard, Lion, Verdun* and *Valmy* were salvaged by Italians, but were never repaired. *Guépard* was again sunk by Allied aircraft in March 1944. *Lion* received Italian name *FR21* and 9.9.1943 was scuttled at Genoa after capitulation of Italy. *Valmy* received name *FR24*, in September 1943 she was captured by Germans and scuttled by them at Genoa 24.4.1945.

Bison prewar

AIGLE class large destroyers

Aigle (A C de France, Dunkerque, 10.1928/19.2.1931/11.1932 - scuttled 27.11.1942); **Gerfaut** (A C de Bretagne, Nantes, 5.1929/14.6.1930/3.1932 - scuttled 27.11.1942); **Albatros** (A C de la Loire, St-Nazaire, 1.1929/27.6.1930/1.1932 - BU 9.1959); **Vautour** (F C de la Méditerranée, La Seyne, 2.1929/28.8.1930/6.1932 - scuttled 27.11.1942); **Épervier** (Arsenal de Lorient, 8.1930/14.8.1931/5.1934 - beached 9.11.1942); **Milan** (Arsenal de Lorient, 12.1930/13.10.1931/5.1934 - beached 8.11.1942)

Épervier 1941

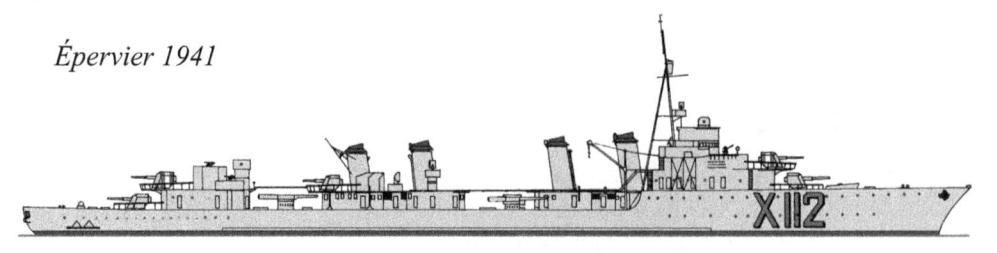

2441/3410t, 128.5-129.3(*Épervier, Milan*)x11.8x5.0m, 2gst/4b, 64000-68000(*Épervier, Milan*)hp, 36kts, 580t oil, 3650(18)nm, 230p; 5 x 1 – 139/40 M1927, 4 x 1 – 37/50 M1925, 2 x 2 – 13.2 MG, 2 x 3 or (1 x 3 + 2 x 2) (*Épervier, Milan*) – 550 TT, 4 DCT (*Épervier, Milan*), 2 DCR (44), 20 mines (*Épervier, Milan*).

Built under the 1927 Programme, the second series of "four-funnelers", a little differing from *Guépard* class. First four ships belonged to group 'C'. Last two ships of 'D' group were re-ordered under the special Programme and had machinery with raised steam parameters. Installation of different boiler types on these two ships was undertaken for their comparison. As consequence of the raised

Épervier prewar

profitability of a new machinery the endurance was increased. Leaders of 'D' group appeared also faster. So, *Milan* reached 41.94kts on trials instead of 41.2kts of *Gerfaut*.

There were also some external differences between ships of 'C' and 'D' groups, new stern and superstructures form concerned to the most significant. Main M1927 guns with increased firing rate (theoretically to 12-15 shots/min) became the basic difference from the first classes. For the first time in the French Navy 'D' group ships can carry mines.

Early 1940, *Vautour, Gerfaut*; 1942, *Albatros*: + sonar.

1940-1942, *Aigle*: + 1 x 2 - 37/50 M1933. 1940-1942, *Gerfaut, Albatros, Vautour*: + 1 x 2 - 37/50 M1933, 2 x 1 - 13.2 MG.

1941, *Épervier, Milan*: + 1 x 2 - 37/50 M1933, 2 x 1 - 37/50 M1925, 2 x 1 - 13.2 MG.

Three ships were scuttled at Toulon 27.11.1942; they were salvaged, but were never repaired, and between November 1943 till March 1944 were sunk by Allied aircraft. *Milan* and *Épervier* 8.11.1942 during Allied landing at Casablanca and Oran were hard damaged by gunfire of British and US ships and ran aground next day.

Albatros was also damaged at Casablanca and ran aground. After war she was repaired and converted to tender assigned to gunnery school, she had her fore boilers and funnels removed, speed being reduced to 24kts.

Albatros 1942

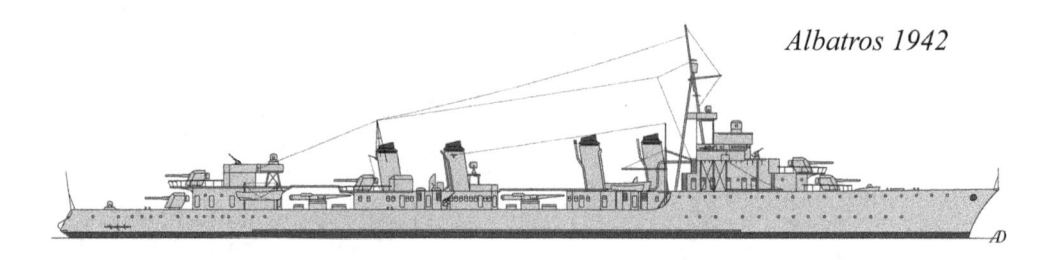

FRANCE

VAUQUELIN class large destroyers

Vauquelin (A C de France, Dunkerque, 3.1930/29.3.1931/3.1934 - scuttled 27.11.1942); **Cassard** (A C de Bretagne, Nantes, 4.1930/8.11.1931/10.1933 - scuttled 27.11.1942); **Maillé Brézé** (A C de St-Nazaire-Penhoët, 10.1930/9.11.1931/4.1934 - blew up 30.4.1940); **Kersaint** (A C de la Loire, St-Nazaire, 9.1930/14.11.1931/1.1934 - scuttled 27.11.1942); **Tartu** (A C de la Loire, St-Nazaire, 9.1930/7.12.1931/2.1933 - scuttled 27.11.1942); **Chevalier Paul** (F C de la Méditerranée, La Seyne, 2.1931/21.3.1932/8.1934 - sunk 16.6.1941)

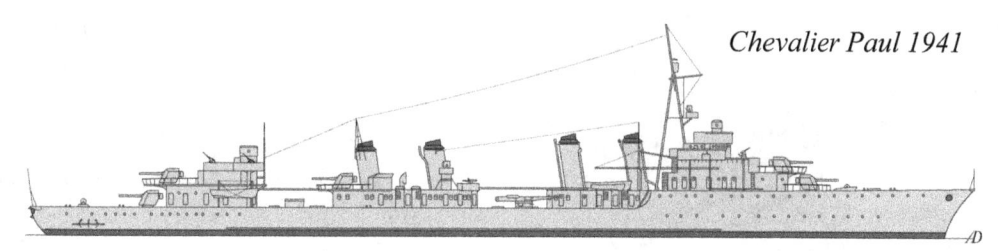

Chevalier Paul 1941

2441/3140t, 129.3x11.8x5.0m, 2gst/4b, 64000hp, 36kts, 585t oil, 3650(18)nm, 230p; 5 x 1 – 139/40 M1927, 4 x 1 – 37/50 M1925, 2 x 2 – 13.2 MG, (1 x 3 + 2 x 2) – 550 TT, 4 DCT, 2 DCR (44), 50 mines.

Built under 1928 (3 ships) and 1929 (3 ships) Programmes. Third and last series of "four-funnelers" ("E" group). On trials they reached for the short time from 39.83 (*Chevalier Paul*) to 42.85 (*Cassard*) knots. Welding was used at first time in the French Navy during building of these ships.

1940, *Chevalier Paul*: - 1 x 3 - 550 TT, 2 x 1 - 37/50; + 1 x 2 - 37/50 M1933, 2 x 1 - 13.2 MG. 1940, *Vauquelin, Tartu*: + Type 123 sonar.

1941, *Vauquelin*: + 1 x 2 - 37/50 M1933, 2 x 1 - 13.2 MG. 1941, *Cassard, Tartu*: - 2 x 1 - 37/50; + 1 x 2 - 37/50 M1933, 2 x 1 - 13.2 MG. 1941, *Kersaint*: + 1 x 2 - 37/50 M1933, 3 x 1 - 25/60 M1938, 2 x 1 - 13.2 MG.

Maillé Brézé 30.4.1940 was lost at Greenock on Clyde (UK). One of torpedo tubes was spontaneously discharged, explosion and a fire followed. During campaign off Syria 16.6.1941 *Chevalier Paul* was attacked by five British torpedo bombers off Latakia and received one torpedo hit to boiler room, she lost speed and sank. 22.6.1941 at Beirut *Vauquelin* was damaged by British aircraft. Remaining destroyers were scuttled at Toulon 27.11.1942 and never salvaged.

Chevalier Paul 1934

LE FANTASQUE class large destroyers

Le Malin (F C de la Méditerranée, La Seyne, 11.1931/17.8.1933/5.1936 - FNFL 2.1943, hulk 1956); **Le Terrible** (CNF, Caen, 12.1931/30.11.1933/4.1935 - FNFL 1.1943, school ship 1957); **L'Indomptable** (F C de la Méditerranée, La Seyne, 1.1932/7.12.1933/2.1936 - scuttled 27.11.1942); **L'Audacieux** (Arsenal de Lorient, 11.1931/15.3.1934/11.1935 - sunk 7.5.1943); **Le Fantasque** (Arsenal de Lorient, 11.1931/15.3.1934/3.1936 - FNFL 1.1943, stricken 5.1957); **Le Triomphant** (A C de France, Dunkerque, 8.1931/16.4.1934/5.1936 - captured by British 3.7.1940, FNFL 8.1940, stricken 12.1954)

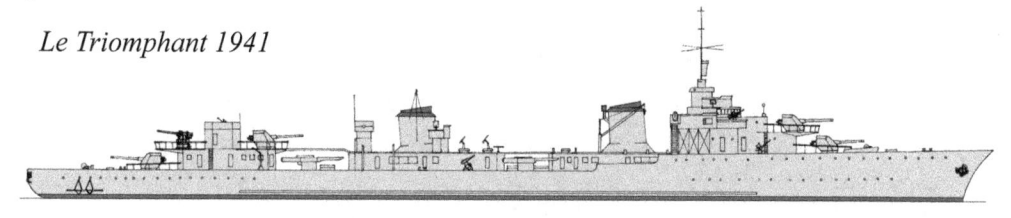

Le Triomphant 1941

Le Triomphant 1944

2569/3380t, 132.4x12.5x5.0m, 2gst/4b, 74000hp, 37kts, 580t oil, 3000(14)nm, 210p; 5 x 1 – 139/50 M1929, 2 x 2 – 37/50 M1933, 2 x 2 – 13.2 MG, 3 x 3 – 550 TT, 2 DCR (16), 50 mines.

Built under the 1930 Programme. Last "full" (6 ships) class of French super-destroyers - became top of their development. In this class designers reached optimum (from their point of views) combination of speed qualities and fire power at comprehensible displacement. Though the endurance remained "Mediterranean" and was insufficient for operations in the ocean.

They notably differed from predecessors outwardly: with typical "cruiser-destroyer" outline profile with two funnels. Introduction of new main guns (M1929) became the basic difference from the previous class, for the first time, destroyers received centralized fire control system for main guns with computer. Side salvo weighed about 200kg, twice more than of British destroyers. Placing of three main guns astern and engine and boiler rooms shifted aft led to 2m trim astern on full speed. On trials all made over 40kts speed. *Le Fantasque* was slowest (42.71kt), and the record of speed not broken till now for large surface ships belongs to *Le Terrible* (45.03kts).

"Champion" differed from colleagues a little by propeller shaft knees. Probably, that it influenced speed characteristics. Speed qualities were kept till the end of service: in the end of war overloaded ships easily made 37kts.

Autumn 1940, *Le Triomphant*: - 1 x 1 - 139/50 (No 4); + 1 x 1 - 102/45 QF Mk V, 2 x 1 - 40/39 pompom, (1 x 4 + 2 x 2 + 2 x 1) - 12.7 MG, Type 123 sonar.

1941, *L`Indomptable*: + 3 x 2 - 37/50 M1933.

1942, *Le Triomphant*: + 7 x 1 - 20/70 Oerlikon.

4.1944, *Le Fantasque, Le Terrible*: - 2 x 2 - 37/50, 2 x 2 - 13.2 MG, 1 x 3 - 550 TT; + (1 x 4 + 2 x 1) - 40/56 Bofors, 8 x 1 - 20/70 Oerlikon, radars, sonar, fuel stowage was 730t. 4.1944, *Le Malin*: - 2 x 2 - 37/50, 2 x 2 - 13.2 MG, 1 x 3 - 550 TT; + (1 x 4 + 2 x 1) - 40/56 Bofors, 10 x 1 - 20/70 Oerlikon, radars, sonar, fuel stowage was 730t

3.1945, *Le Triomphant*: - 1 x 1 - 102/45, 2 x 1 - 40/39, 2 x 2 - 37/50, 2 x 2 - 13.2 MG, (1 x 4 + 2 x 2 + 2 x 1) - 12.7 MG, 1 x 3 - 550 TT; + 1 x 1 - 139/50 M1929, 3 x 2 - 40/56 Bofors, 10 x 1 - 20/70 Oerlikon, radars, fuel stowage was 730t.

In January 1943 *Le Fantasque* and *Le Terrible* passed to the USA. A little bit later *Le Malin* and *Le Triomphant* joined them. After repair ships were classified as light cruisers.

L'Audacieux 23.9.1940 was damaged by gunfire of Australian heavy cruiser *Australia*, strong fire begun, and ship ran aground. Later she was towed for repair to Bizerte and sunk by Allied bombers during Tunisia campaign 7.5.1943. *Le Malin* was hard damaged at Casablanca during Allied landing. 25.12.1944 as result of collision at Naples *Le Malin* lost her fore hull part till main gun No1 (repair was completed already after war), and boiler room was flooded on *Le Terrible*. *Le Triomphant* 3.7.1940 was captured by British and already 28.8.1940 transferred to FNFL. *L'Indomptable* was scuttled at Toulon 27.11.1942. Germans salvaged her and formally enlisted as fast escort *SG9*. She was never commissioned and 7.3.1944 again sunk by Allied aircraft. Parts of her hull were used during repair of *Le Malin*.

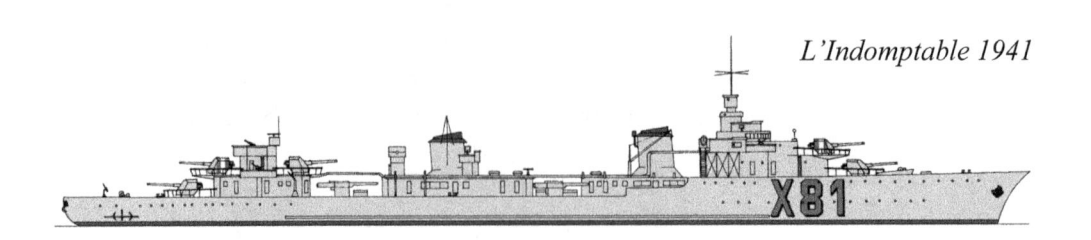

L'Indomptable 1941

FRANCE

MOGADOR class large destroyers

Volta (A C de Bretagne, Nantes, 12.1934/26.11.1936/3.1939 - scuttled 27.11.1942); **Mogador** (Arsenal de Lorient, 12.1934/9.6.1937/8.1938 - scuttled 27.11.1942)

2884/4018t, 137.5x12.7x4.6m, 2gst/4b, 92000hp, 39kts, 710t oil, 4200(15)nm, 264p; 4 x 2 – 139/50 M1934, 2 x 2 – 37/50 M1933, 2 x 2 – 13.2 MG, (2 x 3 + 2 x 2) – 550 TT, 2 DCT, 2 DCR, 40 mines.

Built under 1932 and 1934 Programmes. Logical end of evolution of French super-destroyers, ultimately approached with light cruisers. Steam temperature and pressure increase (to 350° and 27atm) became feature of the design. On sea trials they reached almost 44kts. (*Mogador* 43.45kts and *Volta* 42.88kts). Placing of main guns in twin turrets was characteristic. However, these too complicated and whimsical mounts considerably reduced battle value of the ships. Real firing rate of main guns made half of designed one, and fire power was received even less, than of previous ships.

Kléber class (*Kléber, Desaix, Marceau* and *Hoche*) should become the further development of this design. Their characteristics were assumed close to *Mogador*, but with increased endurance and much strengthened AA artillery. In last variant of the design (on 1.6.1940) following data was provided: 3750/4180t; 137.5x13.0x4.7m; 850t of oil, 3600(30)nm(kts); 4 x 2 - 139/45, 2 x 2 - 100/45, 4 x 2 - 13.2 MGs, 2 x 3 - 550TT. Building of this class was never begun.

Volta 1939

Late 1940, *Mogador*: - 1 x 2 - 139/50; + 2 x 2 - 37/50 M1933.

1941, *Mogador*: + 8 x 1 - 13.2 MG. 1941, *Volta*: + 2 x 1 - 37/50 M1925, 2 x 1 - 25/60 M1938, 8 x 1 - 13.2 MG.

At Mers-el-Kebir *Mogador* received hit of 15" shell and after detonation of own depth charges lost a stern. During repair destroyed turret No4 was replaced with turret No3, and 2 twin 37mm MGs were installed on its place.

Mogador and *Volta* were scuttled at Toulon 27.11.1942. They were salvaged by Italians in April-May 1943 and broken up.

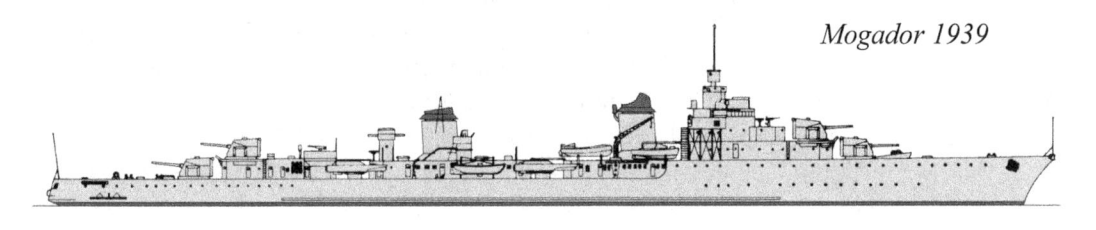

Mogador 1939

ENSEIGNE GABOLDE destroyer

Enseigne Gabolde (Normand, Le Havre, 6.1914/23.4.1921/1923 - stricken 1938)

835/950t, 83.6x8.2x3.1m, 2gst/4b, 20000hp, 31kts, 196t oil, 1300(14)nm, 80p; 3 x 1 – 100/45 M1893, 1 x 1 – 75/35 M1897, 2 x 2 – 550 TT, 2 DCR (10).

Enlarged version of 800-tonner. Laid down under 1913 Programme as third *Mécanicien Principal Lestin* class destroyer but completed after war under modified design with more powerful geared turbines (instead of direct drive on previous ships) and strengthened armament.

Enseigne Gabolde

SIMOUN class destroyers

Simoun (A C de St-Nazaire-Penhoët, 8.1923/3.6.1924/4.1926 - sold 2.1950); **Siroco** (A C de St-Nazaire-Penhoët, 3.1924/3.10.1925/7.1927 - sunk 31.5.1940); **Tempête** (A C Dubigeon, Nantes, 12.1923/22.2.1925/9.1926 - BU 2.1950); **Bourrasque** (A C de France, Dunkerque, 11.1923/5.8.1925/9.1926 - sunk 30.5.1940); **Orage** (CNF, Caen, 8.1923/30.8.1924/12.1926 - sunk 23.5.1940); **Ouragan** (CNF, Caen, 4.1923/6.12.1924/1.1927 - captured by UK 3.7.1940, to Poland (Ouragan), returned 4.1941, sold 4.1949); **Cyclone** (F C de la Méditerranée, Le Havre, 9.1923/24.1.1925/6.1928 - scuttled 18.6.1940); **Mistral** (F C de la Méditerranée, Le Havre, 11.1923/6.6.1925/6.1927 - to UK 7.1940-5.1945 (Mistral), BU 2.1950); **Trombe** (F C de la Gironde, Bordeaux, 3.1923/29.12.1925/10.1927 - scuttled 27.11.1942, to Italy (FR31), returned 10.1943, BU 2.1950); **Tramontane** (F C de la Gironde, Bordeaux, 6.1923/29.11.1924/10.1927 - beached 8.11.1942); **Typhon** (F C de la Gironde, Bordeaux, 9.1923/22.5.1924/6.1928 - scuttled 9.11.1942); **Tornade** (Dyle et Baccalan, Bordeaux, 4.1923/13.3.1925/5.1928 - sunk 8.11.1942)

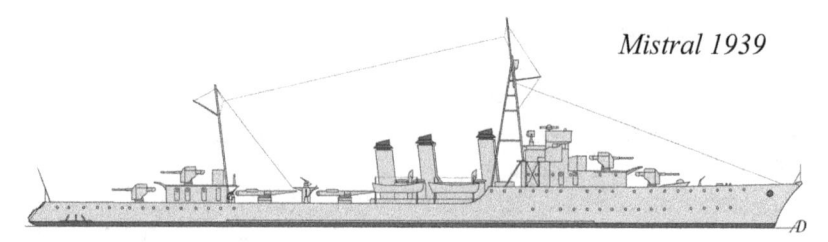

Mistral 1939

1319/1900t, 105.8x9.6x4.3m, 2gst/3b, 33000hp, 33kts, 345t oil, 2150(14)nm, 142p; 4 x 1 – 130/40 M1919, 2 x 1 – 37/50 M1925, 2 x 2 – 13.2 MG, 2 x 3 – 550 TT, 2 DCT, 2 DCR (32).

First interwar "standard" destroyers of French Navy were built under the 1922 Programme. They were outlined among the ships-contemporaries with an archaic three-funnel outline profile. At the time of laying down they carried strongest artillery in the world though its value was considerably decreased by low firing rate. Absence of sonar appeared a serious lack. Speed characteristics appeared rather mediocre: no more than 30kts at full displacement and by beginning of war ships reached only 28-29kts.

1939-1940, all: + Type 123 sonar.
1941-1942, *Tornade*: + 1 x 1 - 25/60 M1938, 2 x 2 - 13.2 MG. 1941-1942, *Tramontane*: - 1 x 3 - 550 TT; + 1 x 1 - 25/60 M1938, 2 x 2 - 13.2 MG. 1941-1942, *Typhon*: - 2 x 3 - 550 TT; + 1 x 1 - 25/60 M1938, 2 x 2 - 13.2 MG, 1 x 2 - 550 TT.
1943, *Simoun*: - 1 x 1 - 130/40, 2 x 1 - 37/50, 2 x 2 - 13.2 MG, 1 x 3 - 550 TT; + 1 x 1 - 40/56 Bofors, 6 x 1 - 20/70 Oerlikon, radars. 1943, *Tempête*: - 1 x 1 - 130/40, 2 x 1 - 37/50, 2 x 2 - 13.2 MG, 1 x 3 - 550 TT; + 1 x 1 - 40/56 Bofors, 8 x 1 - 20/70 Oerlikon, radars. 1943, *Ouragan*; 1945, *Mistral*: - 4 x 1 - 130/40, 2 x 1 - 37/50, 2 x 2 - 13.2 MG, 1 x 3 - 550 TT; + 4 x 1 - 120/45 QF Mk IX, 1 x 1 - 76/40 12pdr 12cwt QF, 3 x 1 - 20/70 Oerlikon, Type 291 radar.

Early 1944, *Simoun*: - 1 x 3 - 550 TT.

Bourrasque 29.5.1940 was mined off Ostend and sunk by German coastal guns off Nieuwpoort. *Cyclone* 31.5.1940 at Dunkirk was damaged by German MTB *S24* and lost fore end. 18.6.1940 she was blown up in dock at Brest during the approach of German troops. *Mistral* 3.7.1940 was captured by British at Plymouth (though she was partly scuttled by crew during capture). Till 1944 she was used as TS and then laid up into reserve. *Orage* in the evening 23.5.1940 was damaged by German aircraft off Boulogne and sank at next day morning. *Ouragan* 3.7.1940 was captured by British at Portsmouth. 18.7.1940-30.4.1941 she served under Polish flag but was never fully commissioned. Some time she served as TS and then was laid up into reserve. In 1943 she was returned to France, but never commissioned by French Navy again. *Siroco* on the night of 31.5.1940 at Dunkirk was hard damaged by German MTBs *S23* and *S26* and sunk by German aircraft in the morning. During Allied landing in the North Africa in November 1942 off Oran *Tornade* and *Tramontane* were sunk by gunfire of British ships (*Tornade* was sunk by cruiser *Aurora* and sloop *Calpe* and *Tramontane* beached being damaged by *Aurora*), and damaged *Typhon* was

Simoun prewar

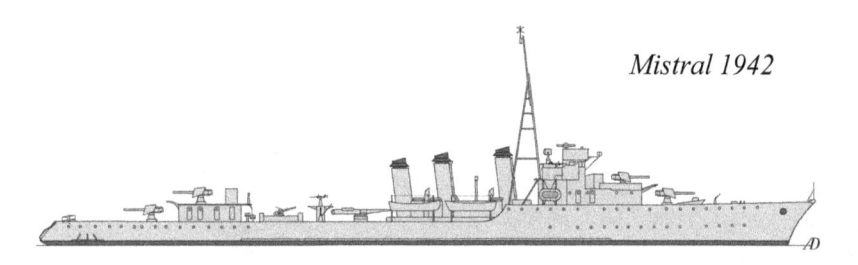

FRANCE 43

Mistral 1942

scuttled by crew at Oran. *Trombe* was scuttled at Toulon 27.11.1942, but salvaged by Italians. She received name *FR23*. After capitulation of Italy 28.10.1943 she was returned to France. 16.4.1945 off San Remo she was hard damaged by torpedo from German MTB.

L'ADROIT class destroyers

L'Adroit (A C de France, Dunkerque, 5.1925/1.4.1927/7.1929 - sunk 21.5.1940); **L'Alcyon** (F C de la Gironde, Bordeaux, 2.1925/26.6.1926/7.1929 - FNFL late 1942, sold 6.1952); **Le Mars** (CNF, Caen, 7.1925/28.8.1926/1.1928 - scuttled 27.11.1942); **Le Fortune** (CNF, Caen, 9.1925/15.11.1926/7.1928 - FNFL late 1942, sold 8.1950); **La Palme** (A C Dubigeon, Nantes, 5.1925/30.6.1926/2.1928 - scuttled 27.11.1942); **La Railleuse** (A C Dubigeon, Nantes, 7.1925/9.9.1926/2.1928 - explosion 24.3.1940); **Brestois** (Dyle et Baccalan, Bordeaux, 5.1926/18.5.1927/6.1928 - sunk 8.11.1942); **Boulonnais** (CNF, Caen, 5.1926/1.6.1927/6.1928 - sunk 8.11.1942); **Basque** (A C de la Seine-Maritime, Le Trait, 9.1926/25.5.1929/3.1931 - FNFL late 1942, sold 12.1952); **Le Bordelais** (F C de la Gironde, Bordeaux, 11.1926/23.5.1928/4.1930 - scuttled 27.11.1942); **Forbin** (F C de la Méditerranée, Le Havre, 6.1927/17.7.1928/5.1930 - FNFL late 1942, sold 11.1952); **Frondeur** (CNF, Caen, 11.1927/20.6.1929/10.1931 - sunk 8.11.1942); **Fougueux** (A C de Bretagne, Nantes, 9.1927/4.8.1928/6.1930 - sunk 8.11.1942); **Le Foudroyant** (Dyle et Baccalan, Bordeaux, 7.1927/24.4.1929/10.1930 - sunk 1.6.1940)

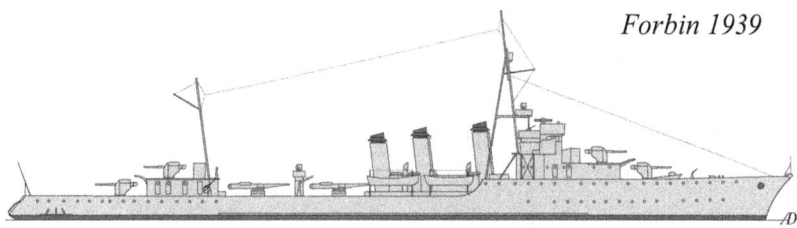

Forbin 1939

1378/2000t, 107.2x9.8x4.3m, 2gst/3b, 34000hp, 33kts, 340t oil, 2150(14)nm, 142p; 4 x 1 – 130/40 M1924, 1 x 1 – 75/50 M1924, 2 x 1 – 8 MG, 2 x 3 – 550 TT, 2 DCT, 2 DCR (32).

Built under 1924 (6 ships), 1925 (4 ships) and 1926 (4 ships) Programmes. Main guns were differed by complexity in maintenance and insufficient firing rate. By the beginning of war ships reached no more than 28-29kts. In 1940 for stability increase they lost main gun No3 or (less often) No4.

Late 1930s, all: - 1 x 1 - 75/50, 2 x 1 – 8 MG; + 2 x 1 - 37/50 M1925, 2 x 2 - 13.2 MG.

1940, all survived: - 1 x 1 - 130/40.

1943, *L'Alcyon, Le Fortune, Basque, Forbin*: - 1 x 3 - 550 TT; + 1 x 1 - 40/56 Bofors, (4 - 6) x 1 - 20/70 Oerlikon, radars, sonar.

La Railleuse was lost at Casablanca 24.3.1940 after spontaneous explosion of torpedoes in fore TT. *L'Adroit* and *Le Foudroyant* were sunk by German aircraft off Dunkirk 21.5.1940 and 1.6.1940 respectively.

Boulonnais, Fougueux, Brestois, Frondeur were sunk during Allied landing at Casablanca by gunfire of Allied ships and carrier aircraft 8.11.1942. Three ships, *Le Mars, La Palme* and *Le Bordelais*, were scuttled at Toulon 27.11.1942, later salvaged by Germans and scrapped.

Le Fortune, Basque and *Forbin* since June 1940 till July 1943 as a part of Force "X" laid disarmed at Alexandria.

L'Adroit prewar

LE HARDI class destroyers

Le Hardi (A C de la Loire, Nantes, 5.1936/4.5.1938/6.1940 - scuttled 27.11.1942); **Fleuret**, 4.1941- **Le Foudroyant** (F C de la Méditerranée, La Seyne, 8.1936/28.7.1938/6.1940 - scuttled 27.11.1942); **Epée**, 4.1941- **L'Adroit** (F C de la Méditerranée, La Seyne, 10.1936/26.10.1938/6.1940 - scuttled 27.11.1942); **Casque** (F C de la Méditerranée, La Seyne, 11.1936/2.11.1938/6.1940 - scuttled 27.11.1942); *Lansquenet* (F C de la Gironde, Bordeaux, 12.1936/20.5.1939/ - scuttled incomplete 27.11.1942); **Mameluk** (A C de la Loire, Nantes, 1.1937/18.2.1939/6.1940 - scuttled 27.11.1942); **Le Corsaire**, 4.1941- **Sirocco** (F C de la Méditerranée, La Seyne, 3.1938/14.11.1939/7.1941 - scuttled 27.11.1942); *Le Filibustier*, 4.1941- **Bison** (F C de la Méditerranée, La Seyne, 3.1938/14.12.1939/ - scuttled incomplete 27.11.1942); *L'Intrépide* (F C de la Méditerranée, La Seyne, 8.1939/26.6.1941/ - abandoned incomplete 4.1941); *Le Téméraire* (F C de la Méditerranée, La Seyne 8.1939/7.11.1941/ - abandoned incomplete 11.1941); *L'Aventurier* (F C de la Gironde, Bordeaux, 8.1939/20.4.1947/ - BU incomplete 5.1960); *L`Opiniâtre* (F C de la Gironde, Bordeaux, 8.1939// - abandoned 7.1943)

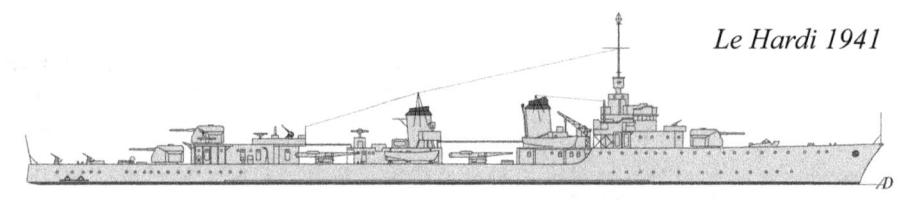

Le Hardi 1941

Completed ships: 1772/2577t, 117.2x11.1x4.2m, 2gst/4b, 58000hp, 37kts, 470t oil, 1900(25)nm, 187p; 3 x 2 – 130/45 M1935, 2 x 1 – 37/50 M1925, 2 x 2 – 13.2 MG, (1 x 3 + 2 x 2) – 550 TT, 1 DCR (8), 1 Ginocchio towed AS torpedo.

Incomplete ships: 2215/2929t, 118.6(pp)x11.9x4.2m, 2gst/4b, 62000hp, 35kts, 470t oil; 3 x 2 – 130/45 M1935, 2 x 2 – 13.2 MG, 2 x 3 – 533 TT.

Built under 1932 (1 ship), 1935 (2 ships), 1936 (4 ships) and 1937 (2 ships) Programmes. Destroyers of this class were created as escorts for new fast battleships of *Dunkerque* class. Ships of previous classes could not solve this task, as did not reach necessary speed. Besides, it was required to strengthen their antiaircraft armament considerably. At the same time, their ASW and AA possibilities remained obviously insufficient. Semi-automatic main guns were like secondary guns of *Dunkerque* and were mounted in turrets. Insufficient elevation angle (no more than 30°) excluded their usage in air defense.

Le Foudroyant, L'Adroit, Cyclone, Sirocco and *Bison* were named *Fleuret, L'Epée, Lansquenet, Le Corsaire* and *Le Flibustier* before 1.4.1941. Four of them were renamed into memory of destroyers lost in a beginning of war.

Le Hardi

Last four ships of 1938 and 1939 Programmes (*L'Intrépide, L'Opiniâtre, Le Téméraire* of 1938 Programme and *L'Aventurier* of 1939 Programme), remained on slipways, should be built under modified design and in certain degree represented analogue of British AA cruisers with heavy antiaircraft guns. It was supposed to equip destroyers of this subgroup with DP main guns of new model. Thus, small caliber AA armament should be limited by MGs, and torpedo armament should be decreased to 6 tubes. ASW armament should be absent. Changes in the design led to appreciable growth of displacement (to 2180/2882t and dimensions (118.2ppx11x8x4.2m) and despite increase in machinery power to 62000hp fall of speed from 37 to 35kts was expected. Works on them were begun in August 1939, but no one was completed, and *L'Opiniâtre* was never officially laid down.

As the ships were commissioned in wartime (also after an armistice), many of their characteristics it was not possible to check up in practice. Though it is known, that *Le Hardi* on trials shown 39.09kts speed. After commission, the antiaircraft artillery was strengthened. Late 1940, all: - 2 x 1 - 37/50; + 1 x 2 - 37/50 M1933, 2 x 2 - 13.2 MG, 5 x 1 - 8 MG.

Fleuret and *L'Epée* participated in attack of Gibraltar 24-25.9.1940. However, because of technical defects they appeared disabled.

All eight completed ships (*Lansquenet* and *Bison* were almost completed in June 1940 and passed to Toulon under their own power) were scuttled at Toulon 27.11.1942. Soon they were salvaged by Italians,

FRANCE

but *Mameluck* and *Casque* were recognized as not subjects to repair. Remaining ships received names *FR37 (Le Hardi), FR36 (Le Foudroyant), FR33 (L'Adroit), FR34 (Le Cyclone), FR32 (Sirocco)* and *FR35 (Bison)*. In September 1943 after capitulation of Italy Germans captured these ships, but no one of them was commissioned. All destroyers were scuttled by Germans: *FR37* and *FR34* 24.4.1945 and *FR32* 28.10.1944 at Genoa; *FR35* and *FR36* in August 1944 at Toulon.

Only *FR33* was returned to France, but she was never repaired.

LA MELPOMÈNE class light destroyers (torpedo boats)

La Melpomène (A C de Bretagne, Nantes, 12.1933/24.1.1935/11.1936 - captured by British 3.7.1940, to Netherlands 8.1940, FNFL 1.1941, to United Kingdom 10.1942, returned 9.1943, sold 5.1950); **La Pomone** (A C de la Loire, Nantes, 11.1933/25.1.1935/12.1936 - captured by Germans 8.12.1942, to Italy (FR42)); **La Flore** (A C de Bretagne, Nantes, 3.1934/5.3.1935/11.1936 - captured by British 3.7.1940, FNFL 8.1940, sold 8.1950); **L'Iphigénie** (A C de la Loire, Nantes, 12.1933/18.4.1935/11.1936 - captured by Germans 8.12.1942, to Italy (FR43)); **La Bayonnaise** (C Maritimes du Sud Ouest, Bordeaux, 10.1934/28.1.1936/4.1938 - scuttled 27.11.1942); **Bombarde** (A C de la Loire, Nantes, 2.1935/23.3.1936/8.1937 - captured by Germans 8.12.1942, to Italy (FR41)); **L'Incomprise** (A C de la Seine-Maritime, Le Trait, 10.1934/14.4.1936/3.1938 - captured by British 3.7.1940, FNFL 8.1940, sold 8.1950); **La Poursuivante** (A C de France, Dunkerque, 8.1934/4.8.1936/11.1937 - scuttled 27.11.1942); **La Cordelière** (A C Augustin-Normand, Le Havre, 8.1934/9.9.1936/12.1937 - captured by British 3.7.1940, FNFL 8.1940, sold 2.1950); **Baliste** (A C de France, Dunkerque, 9.1934/17.3.1937/5.1938 - scuttled 27.11.1942); **Branlebas** (A C Augustin-Normand, Le Havre, 8.1934/12.4.1937/3.1938 - captured by British 3.7.1940, FNFL 8.1940, foundered 14.12.1940); **Bouclier** (A C de la Seine-Maritime, Le Trait, 10.1934/9.8.1937/8.1938 - captured by British 3.7.1940, to Netherlands 8.1940, FNFL 1.1941, sold 8.1950)

680/895t, 80.7x8.0x3.1m, 2gst/2b, 22000hp, 34.5kts, 170t oil, 1000(20)nm, 105p; 2 x 1 – 100/45 M1932, 2 x 2 – 13.2 MG, 1 x 2 – 550 TT, 1 DCR, 1 Ginocchio towed AS torpedo.

Building of escorts for Mediterranean Sea armed with two 75mm guns and 4 400mm TTs was originally assumed.

These ships were built under 1931 (8 ships) and 1932 (4 ships) Programmes. Boats had exclusive manoeuvrability, but so disgusting stability and obviously insufficient seaworthiness.

1941, *Branlebas*: + 2 x 1 - 40/39 pompom.
1943, *La Melpomène, L'Incomprise, Bouclier, La Flore, La Cordelière*: - 1 x 1 - 100/45; + 3 x 1 - 40/39 pompom, 2 x 1 - 20/70 Oerlikon, radars.

After battle of Dunkirk *L'Incomprise, Bouclier, Branlebas, La Flore, La Melpomène* and *La Cordelière* were captured by British 3.7.1940. *La Melpomène* after four-month service under the FNFL flag (September-December 1940) was laid up into reserve. Since 15.10.1942 till September 1943 she served as TS under British flag. Then she was again laid up into reserve. *Bouclier* 31.8.1940-12.1.1941 was transferred to Dutch Navy, but never commissioned by Dutch and transferred again to FNFL. She was used as TS before she was laid up into reserve in 1944. *L'Incomprise, La*

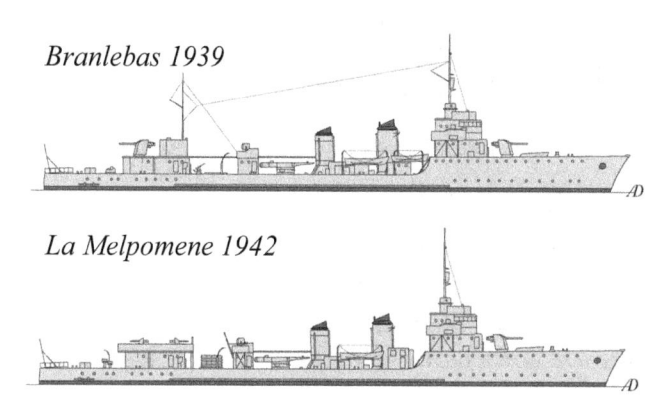

Branlebas 1939

La Melpomene 1942

Flore and *La Cordelière* sometime were listed in the FNFL, but never really commissioned. *Branlebas* with British crew served as escort. 14.12.1940 she was lost during a storm at southern coast of England. Other ships remained at Hartlepool and were returned to France in 1945.

8.12.1942 Germans captured at Bizerte *Bombarde, L'Iphigénie* and *La Pomone*. 28.12.1942-5.4.1943 ships were under the Italian control under

La Pomone 1937

names *FR41*, *FR43* and *FR42*, respectively. 5-7.4.1943 torpedo boats again were transferred to Germans and originally classified as escorts. Since 15.5.1943 they were re-classified as torpedo boats and received names *TA9*, *TA11* and *TA10*. Germans removed TTs, installed radar and strengthened AA artillery to 2 single 37mm, 1 quadruple and 10 single 20mm MGs. *TA9* since 27.9.1943 was laid up into reserve at Toulon and 23.8.1944 was sunk by US aircraft. *TA11* was destroyed by Italian tanks and ships at Piombino (Elba Island) during capitulation of Italy in September 1943. *TA10* became unique ship of this class which shared in operations under German flag. 23.9.1943 at Rhodes she was hard damaged in battle against British destroyer *Eclipse* and in four days scuttled by crew.

La Bayonnaise, *Baliste* and *La Poursuivante* were scuttled at Toulon 27.11.1942 and salvaged by Italians. First two were supposed to be repaired and they received names *FR44* and *FR45*, respectively. After capitulation of Italy 9.9.1943 ships were captured by Germans and received names *TA13* and *TA12*. They were never commissioned. Disabled *TA13* was scuttled 25.8.1944, and *TA12* was destroyed by bombs of US aircraft at Toulon 24.11.1943.

LE FIER class light destroyers (torpedo boats)

Le Fier (A C de Bretagne, Nantes, 1.1939/12.3.1940/ - incomplete to Germany (TA1), scuttled incomplete 11.8.1944); *L'Agile* (A C de Bretagne, Nantes, 4.1939/23.5.1940/ - incomplete to Germany (TA2), sunk incomplete 6.9.1943); *L'Entreprenant* (A C de la Loire, Nantes, 1.1939/25.5.1940/ - incomplete to Germany (TA4), sunk incomplete 6.9.1943); *Le Farouche* (A C de la Loire, Nantes, 4.1939/19.10.1940/ - incomplete to Germany (TA5), scuttled incomplete 11.8.1944); *L'Alsacien* (A C de la Loire, Nantes, 4.1939/1942/ - incomplete to Germany (TA3), BU incomplete 1944); *Le Corse* (A C de la Loire, Nantes, 1.1940/4.4.1942/ - incomplete to Germany (TA6), scuttled incomplete 11.8.1944); *Le Breton* (A C de la Loire, Nantes, 1.1940// - incomplete to Germany, BU 6.1940)

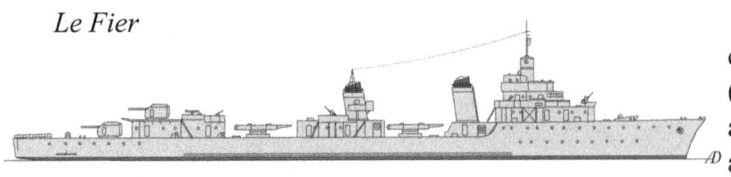

Le Fier

1010/1337t, 95.0x9.4x3.3m, 2gst/3b, 30800hp, 33kts, 290t oil, 2000(10)nm, 136p; 2 x 2 – 100/45 M1933, 4 x 2 – 13.2 MG, 2 x 2 – 550 TT, 2 DCR.
Built under 1937 (4 ships) and 1938 (3 ships) Programmes. 5 more boats were ordered under additional 1938b Programme and two under the 1938c Programme. 7 ships were laid down only. Building of *Le Breton* (she was laid down in January 1940), *Le Tunisien*, *Le Normand*, *Le Parisien*, *Le Provencal*, *Le Saintongeais*, *Le Nicois* and *Le Savoyard* was cancelled.

Boats presented development of previous class with correction of its lacks. They should carry DP main guns (for the first time on French torpedo ships) at aft end, and AA MGs should be grouped at fore end. Besides, armor protection of gun mounts, bridge and deck became a novelty.

Germans tried to complete the ships, but no one was finished. Under German flag characteristic of ships should change a little. Displacement was supposed about 1087/1443t, and dimensions should be 93.2x9.2x3.9m; armament consisted of 3x1 105mm guns at aft end, 2 single 37mm and 9 single 20mm MGs and 2 triple 533mm TT. Almost ready *TA2* was sunk by US aircraft, as well as *TA4*. Parts of *TA3* were used for completion of sister ships. *TA1*, *TA5* and *TA6* were scuttled by Germans at departure from Nantes.

No 295 class torpedo boats

similar No 339 1920

A C de la Loire, Nantes: N° 349 (1906)
Arsenal de Toulon: N° 369 (1908)
Discarded: N° 349 (1937)
Lost: N° 369 (1942)
100/104t, 38.0x4.4x1.9m, 1vte/2b, 2000(*No349*)-1800(*No369*)hp, 26kts, 2000(10)nm, 23p; 1 x 1 – 75/35 N1897, 1 – 450 TT (bow).
Ancient pre-WWI torpedo boats of '38-m type'. *N° 369* was scuttled at Toulon 27.11.1942.

Submarines

SURCOUF submarine cruiser

Surcouf (Arsenal de Cherbourg, 12.1927/18.10.1929/5.1934 - captured by United Kingdom 3.7.1940, FNFL 9.1940, collision 18.2.1942)

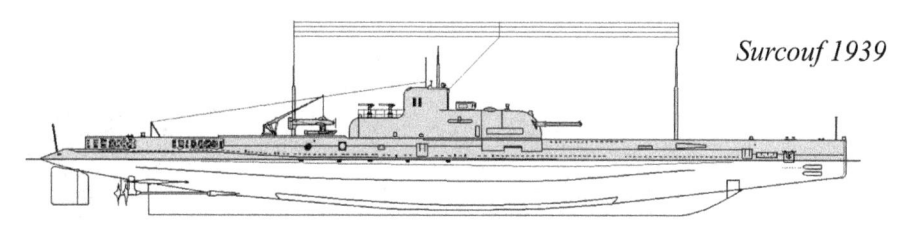

Surcouf 1939

3250/4304t, 110.0x9.0x7.3m, 2d/2em, 7600/3400hp, 18.5/10kts, 306t diesel oil, 10000(10)/70(4.5)nm, 118p, 80m; 1 x 2 – 203/50 M1924, 2 x 1 – 37/50 M1925, 2 x 2 – 13.2 MG, 8 – 550 TT (4 bow, 1 x 4 ext, 14), 1 x 4 – 400 TT (ext, 8), 1 seaplane (MB.411); hydrophone.

Under other data, TTs were placed so: 4 bow 550mm TT with 8 torpedoes and 2 triple trainable mounts with one middle 550mm tube and two side 400mm tubes.

Design "Q5", built under the 1926 Programme. To beginning of WWII *Surcouf* was the largest submarine in the world and carried artillery of biggest caliber resolved by Washington Treaty. Strictly speaking, corresponding article of treaty was adjusted under *Surcouf* (and British *X1*). *Surcouf* was intended for long-term (up to 90 days) ocean cruising on enemy communications, first of all British, with usage of torpedoes and artillery. There was a special accommodation for prisoned crewmen from sunken vessels. Main role was assigned to artillery. To it promoted both strong gun armament, and big diving time of a submarine cruiser (up to 2min). *Surcouf* carried folding reconnaissance seaplane Besson MB.411 in hangar. She was unique submarine with possibility of reloading of trainable external TTs (the truth, only being surfaced). Design represented substantially an experimental pattern and did not received development. With it handicapped both Treaties limitations, and absence of intelligent concept of usage of such submarines: during war. Machinery appeared insufficiently reliable. Already 18.10.1939, after two campaigns, the cruiser should be undergoing major repair.

1942: - 2 x 2 - 13.2 MG; + 2 x 2 - 12.7 MG.

In June 1940 under one diesel submarine passed to Plymouth, where 3.7.1940 she was captured by British (4 crewmen were lost in firing). 15.9.1940 she was transferred to FNFL. Assumed conversion to transport (in particular, for supply of Malta) had not taken place, basically for political reasons. *Surcouf* was considered lost in collision with US s/s *Thomson Lykes* in Gulf of Mexico 18.2.1942.

Surcouf prewar

LAGRANGE class 1st class submarines

Laplace (Arsenal de Rochefort, 11.1913/12.8.1919/12.1923 - stricken 4.1939); **Regnault** (Arsenal de Toulon, 11.1913/25.6.1924/10.1924 - stricken 4.1938)

Lagrange 1920s

920/1318t, 75.2x6.3x3.6m, 2d/2em, 2600/1640hp, 16.5/11kts, 4300(10)/125(5)nm, 47p, 50m; 2 x 1 – 75/35 M1897, 8 – 450 TT (2 bow, 4 inboard, 2 external cradles, 10)

Largest French submarines of WWI-era, improved *Dupuy de Lôme* class.

ex-German RENÉ AUDRY 1st class submarine minelayer

René Audry (ex-U119) (Vulcan, Hamburg, Germany, 1916/4.4.1918/(6.1918)/11.1918 - stricken 10.1937)

1164/1512t, 81.5x7.4x4.2m, 2d/2em, 2400/1200hp, 14.7/7kts, 217t diesel oil, 13900(8)/35(4.5)nm, 40p, 75m; 1 x 1 – 149/42 TK C/16, 4 – 500 TT (bow, 14), 42 mines + 30 mines in deck stowage.

German submarine cruiser-minelayer of UE II type, requisitioned after WWI.

REQUIN class 1st class submarines

Requin (Arsenal de Cherbourg, 6.1922/19.7.1924/5.1926 - captured by Germany 8.12.1942, to Italy (FR113)); **Souffleur** (Arsenal de Cherbourg, 10.1922/1.10.1924/8.1926 - sunk 25.6.1941); **Morse** (Arsenal de Cherbourg, 2.1923/11.11.1925/2.1928 - sunk 16.6.1940); **Narval** (Arsenal de Cherbourg, 3.1923/9.5.1925/7.1926 - FNFL 6.1940, sunk 15.12.1940); **Marsouin** (Arsenal de Brest, 11.1922/27.12.1924/9.1927 - FNFL 11.1942, BU 2.1946); **Dauphin** (Arsenal de Toulon, 12.1922/2.4.1925/11.1927 - captured by Germany 8.12.1942, to Italy (FR115)); **Caïman** (Arsenal de Cherbourg, 8.1924/3.3.1927/2.1928 - scuttled 27.11.1942); **Phoque** (Arsenal de Brest, 5.1924/16.3.1926/5.1928 - captured by Germany 8.12.1942, to Italy (FR111)); **Espadon** (Arsenal de Toulon, 10.1923/29.5.1926/12.1927 - captured by Germany 8.12.1942, to Italy (FR114))

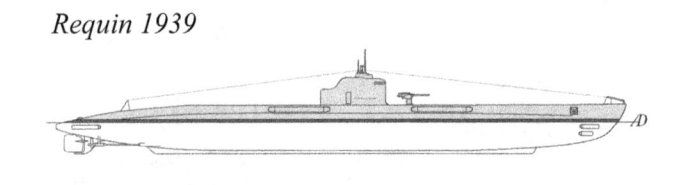

Requin 1939

1150/1441t, 78.3x6.8x5.1m, 2d/2em, 2900/1800hp, 15/9kts, 167t diesel oil, 6650(10)/105(5)nm, 51p, 80m; 1 x 1 – 100/45 M1917, 2 x 1 – 8 MG, 10 – 550 TT (4 bow, 2 stern, 2 x 2 ext, 16)

Project "C4". 1922 (first six boats) and 1923 (last 3 boats) Programmes. First French interwar ocean-going submarines. During their designing experience of study of requisitioned German boats was used. Bad maneuverability and low surface speed concerned to lacks. They were intended for service in colonies, operations on communications and reconnaissance. Double-hulled. In 1935-1937 all submarines of the class passed major refit with full machinery replacing.

M. b. 1943 - 1944, *Marsouin*: - 2 x 1 – 8 MG; + 1 x 1 - 20/70 Oerlikon.

Morse was 16.6.1940 lost at Sfax (Tunisia) on a mine or (under Italian version) was sunk by Italian submarine *Durbo*. *Souffleur* was sunk by British submarine *Parthian* 25.6.1941 off Beirut during Syrian campaign. *Narval* after armistice 26.6.1940 passed to Malta and joined Allies. She was lost at coast of Tunisia 15-19.12.1940 on a mine or sunk by Italian destroyer *Curtatone* or 7.1.1941 by Italian torpedo boat *Clio*. *Requin* was captured by Germans at Bizerte 8.12.1942 and transferred to Italians. She was named *FR113*, but never commissioned and blown up by Italians at Genoa 9.9.1943. *Dauphin* was captured by Germans at Bizerte 8.12.1942 and transferred to Italians. She was named *FR115*, but never commissioned. She was again captured by Germans and scuttled by them at Puzzoli (Italy) 15.9.1943. *Espadon* was captured by Germans at Bizerte 8.12.1942 and transferred to Italians. She was

FRANCE

named *FR114*, but never commissioned. She was again captured by Germans and scuttled by them at Castellamare (Italy) 13.9.1943. *Phoque* was captured by Germans at Bizerte 8.12.1942 and transferred to Italians. She was commissioned as *FR111* and sunk in the first route by Allied aircraft off Syracuse (Sicily) 28.2.1943. *Caïman* was scuttled at Toulon 27.11.1942. Later she was salvaged by Italians and again sunk by Allied aircraft 11.3.1944.

Marsouin left from Toulon to Algiers and joined Allies. Early 1944 she was laid up to reserve.

Souffleur 1926

REDOUTABLE class 1st class submarines

1st series
Redoutable (Arsenal de Cherbourg, 7.1925/24.2.1928/7.1931 - scuttled 27.11.1942); **Vengeur** (Arsenal de Cherbourg, 1.1926/1.9.1928/8.1931 - scuttled 27.11.1942); **Pascal** (Arsenal de Brest, 6.1926/19.7.1928/9.1931 - scuttled 27.11.1942); **Pasteur** (Arsenal de Brest, 7.1926/19.8.1928/9.1932 - scuttled 18.6.1940); **Henri Poincaré** (Arsenal de Lorient, 3.1927/10.4.1929/12.1931 - scuttled 27.11.1942); **Poncelet** (Arsenal de Lorient, 3.1927/10.4.1929/9.1932 - scuttled 8.11.1940); **Archimède** (CNF, Caen, 8.1927/6.9.1930/12.1932 - FNFL 11.1942, sold 2.1952); **Fresnel** (A C de St-Nazaire-Penhoët, 7.1927/8.6.1929/2.1932 - scuttled 27.11.1942); **Monge** (F C de la Méditerranée, La Seyne, 9.1927/25.6.1929/6.1932 - sunk 8.5.1942); **Achille** (Arsenal de Brest, 9.1928/28.5.1930/6.1933 - scuttled 18.6.1940); **Ajax** (Arsenal de Brest, 9.1928/28.5.1930/2.1934 - sunk 24.9.1940); **Actéon** (A C de la Loire, Nantes, 7.1927/10.4.1929/12.1931 - sunk 8.11.1942); **Achéron** (A C de la Loire, Nantes, 9.1927/6.8.1929/2.1932 - scuttled 27.11.1942); **Argo** (A C Dubigeon, Nantes, 8.1927/11.4.1929/2.1933 - FNFL 1.1943, sold 4.1946); **Persée** (CNF, Caen, 4.1929/23.5.1931/2.1933 - sunk 23.9.1940); **Protée** (F C de la Méditerranée, La Seyne, 10.1928/31.7.1930/11.1932 - FNFL 1.1943, sunk 29.12.1943); **Pégase** (A C de la Loire, Nantes, 9.1928/28.6.1930/6.1932 - paid off 9.1941, BU 1944), **Phénix** (A C Dubigeon, Nantes, 11.1928/12.4.1930/10.1932 - lost 15.6.1939)
2nd series
L'Espoir (Arsenal de Cherbourg, 8.1929/18.7.1931/2.1934 - scuttled 27.11.1942); **Le Glorieux** (A C de St-Nazaire-Penhoët, 2.1930/29.11.1932/6.1934 - FNFL 12.1942, sold 10.1952); **Le Centaure** (Arsenal de Brest, 8.1930/14.10.1932/1.1935 - FNFL 1.1943, sold 6.1952); **Le Héros** (Arsenal de Brest, 8.1930/14.10.1932/9.1934 - sunk 7.5.1942); **Le Conquérant** (A C de la Loire, Nantes, 8.1930/26.6.1934/9.1936 - sunk 13.11.1942); **Le Tonnant** (F C de la Méditerranée, La Seyne, 1.1931/15.12.1934/6.1937 - scuttled 15.11.1942)
3rd series
Agosta (Arsenal de Cherbourg, 2.1932/30.4.1934/2.1937 - scuttled 18.6.1940); **Bévéziers** (Arsenal de Cherbourg, 4.1932/14.10.1935/6.1937 - sunk 5.5.1942); **Ouessant** (Arsenal de Cherbourg, 4.1932/30.11.1936/2.1937 - scuttled 18.6.1940); **Sidi-Ferruch** (Arsenal de Cherbourg, 1.1932/9.7.1937/1.1939 - sunk 11.11.1942); **Sfax** (A C de la Loire, Nantes, 7.1931/6.12.1934/9.1936 - sunk 19.12.1940); **Casabianca** (A C de la Loire, Nantes, 3.1931/7.2.1935/1.1937 - FNFL 12.1942, sold 2.1952)

1570/2084t, 92.3x8.2x4.7m, 2d/2em, 6000(1st series)-7200(2nd series)-8000(3rd series)/2000hp, 17(1st series)-19(2nd series)-20(3rd series)/10kts, 95t diesel oil, 10000(10)/100(5)nm, 61p, 80m; 1 x 1 – 100/45 M1925, 1 x 2 – 13.2 MG, 9 – 550 TT (4 bow, 1 x 3 ext, 1 x 2 ext in quadruple two-caliber TT bank), 11), 2 – 400 TT (1 x 2 ext in quadruple two-caliber TT bank, 2); hydrophone.

Formally concerned to two designs: first two to "M5" and other to "1500ton" "M6". Built under 1924 (2

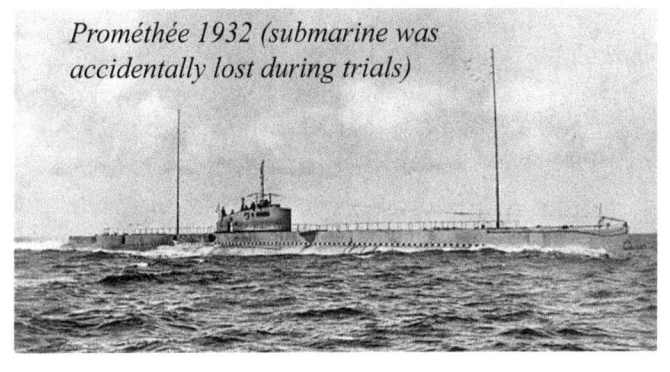

Prométhée 1932 (submarine was accidentally lost during trials)

Casabianca 1940

Archimède 1943

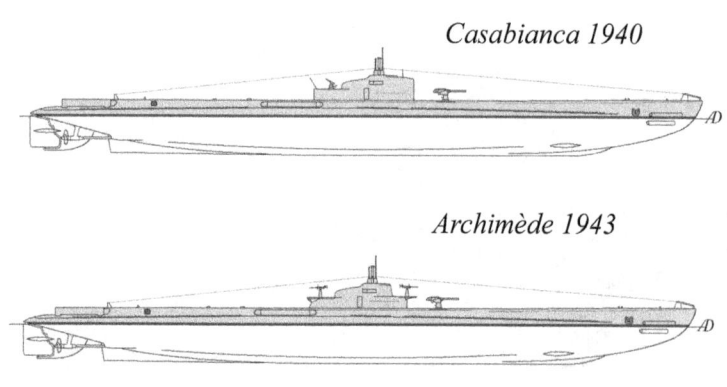

boats), 1925 (7 boats), 1926 (5 boats), 1927 (3 boats), 1928-1929 (6 boats) and 1930 (6 boats) Programmes.

During building minor alterations were brought into the design. Basically, they concerned a machinery. So, boats of first series (first 17 submarines) had 6000hp diesels and made 17kts surfaced. Submarines of the second series (6 submarines) had 7200hp diesels and reached 19kts surfaced. 6 submarines of third series reached 20kts with 8000hp diesels. Double-hulled. They were successful ships, proved to be seaworthy and handy enough, had high surface speed. At the same time, to the WWII time, diving time was too long (45-50sec). In 1941 ballast tanks were partly converted for storage of additional fuel oil. It allowed to increase surface endurance to 10000nm.

1941, some survived: maximal fuel stowage was 108 t.

1942, some survived: - 1 x (2 - 550, 2 - 400) TT; + 1 x 3 - 550 TT (maximal torpedo stowage was 12). 1942-1943, some survived: - 1 x 2 - 13.2 MG; + 2 x 1 - 20/70 Oerlikon.

1944, *Archimède, Le Glorieux, Le Centaure*; 1945, *Casabianca*: + presumably SD, SJ radars, WDA, JP sonars.

Phénix was accidentally lost 15.6.1939 off Cam Ranh.

During annexation of Gabon by Gaullists *Poncelet* tried to show resistance but was damaged by British sloop *Milford* at Libreville and scuttled 8.11.1940. Four submarines (*Pasteur, Achille, Agosta* and *Ouessant*) were in summer 1940 under repair at Brest; they were blown up 18.6.1940 in base to avoid capture by German troops. 7 more boats were scuttled at Toulon 27.11.1942 (*Redoutable, Vengeur, Pascal, Fresnel, Henri Poincaré, Achéron, L'Espoire*). *Redoutable, Pascal* and *Henri Poincaré* were salvaged by Italians, but were sunk by Allied aircraft 11.3.1944, 23.3.1944 and 9.9.1944 respectively. There is also a version of scuttling of them by Italians. Two submarines were lost in September 1940 during attack of Dakar by British and FNFL forces. *Ajax* became victim of British destroyer *Fortune* 24.9.1940, and *Persée* was sunk by destroyers *Foresight* and *Inglefield* 23.9.1940. Three more submarines were lost at Diego Suarez during occupancy of Madagascar by British in May 1942. *Monge* was sunk by British destroyer *Active* 8.5.1942, *Le Héros* was sunk by air group of British aircraft carrier *Illustrious* 7.5.1942, and *Bévéziers* was sunk by air group of *Illustrious* directly in harbor of Diego Suarez 5.5.1942. Four submarines were lost during operations in the North Africa. *Le Conquérant* was sunk by US aircraft off Villa Cisneros (Morocco) 13.11.1942. *Actéon* was sunk at Oran 8.11.1942 by British destroyer *Westcott*. *Sidi Ferruch* was sunk 11.11.1942 by US carrier aircraft off Casablanca. *Le Tonnant* received heavy damages as result of air attacks but managed to break into Spanish waters and ran aground at Cadiz 15.11.1942. *Sfax* was torpedoed by German submarine *U37* off Casablanca (Morocco) 19.12.1940. *Protée* was a part of "X" Force and was disarmed at Alexandria. In 1943 she joined Allies and was lost on a mine at Toulon 29.12.1943.

Pégase based in Indochina. In September 1941 she was disarmed at Saigon and later cannibalized for spares.

Casabianca and *Le Glorieux* left to Allies from Toulon (to Algiers and Oran respectively). *Archimède* also in 1942 left to Allies.

ROLAND MORILLOT class 1st class submarines

Roland Morillot (Arsenal de Cherbourg, 1.1937/19.6.1940/ - scuttled 19.6.1940); *La Praya* (Arsenal de Cherbourg, 3.1938// - destroyed on the stocks 19.6.1940); *La Martinique* (Arsenal de Cherbourg, 9.1938// - destroyed on the stocks 19.6.1940); *La Guadeloupe* (A C Dubigeon, Nantes, 6.1940// - abandoned 6.1940); *La Réunion* (Arsenal de Cherbourg, 6.1940// - abandoned 6.1940)

1810/2417t, 102.5x8.3x4.6m, 2d/2em, 12000/2300hp, 22/9.5kts, 178t diesel oil, 4400(10)/85(5)nm, 70p, 100m; 1 x 1 – 100/34 M1936, 1 x 2 – 13.2 MG, 10 – 550 TT (4 bow, 1 x 4 ext, 1 x 2 ext (in quadruple two-caliber TT bank), 20-21); 2 – 400 TT (1 x 2 in quadruple two-caliber TT bank, 2); hydrophone.

Project "Z2", improved version of the *Redoutable*. Placing of 85t of fuel oil in ballast tanks became the

FRANCE

Roland Morillot

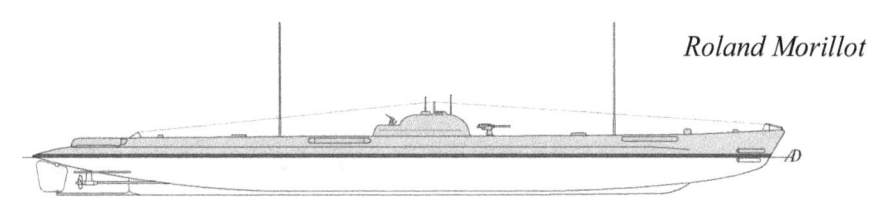

basic improvement. Built under 1934 (1 boat), 1937 (1 boat) and 1938 (3 boats) Programmes. 8 more boats were ordered under the 1940 Programme. Two of them, *Île de France* and *Île de Ré*, were begun in April. Following submarines were named but never laid down: *La Guadeloupe*, *Île de Yeu* and *La Réunion*. It was supposed to order three more boats, but they never received names.

Incomplete submarines were blown up on slipways 19.6.1940 before occupancy of Cherbourg by Germans. Earlier that day *Roland Morillot* was launched.

Ex-German JEAN CORRE 2nd class submarine

Jean Corre (ex-UB155) (Vulcan, Hamburg, Germany, 1917/26.10.1918/(2.1919)/3.1919 - stricken 10.1937)

539/656t, 55.5x5.8x3.9m, 2d/2em, 1060/788hp, 13.5/7.5kts, 71t diesel oil, 7120(6)/50(4)nm, 34p, 75p; 1 x 1 – 105/42 Ubts C/16, 5 – 500 TT (4 bow, 1 stern, 10).

German submarine of UB III type, requisitioned after WWI.

SIRÈNE class 2nd class submarine

Sirène (A C de la Loire, Nantes, 11.1923/6.8.1925/3.1927 - scuttled 27.11.1942); **Naïade** (A C de la Loire, Nantes, 11.1923/20.10.1925/5.1927 - scuttled 27.11.1942); **Galathée** (A C de la Loire, Nantes, 2.1924/18.12.1925/5.1927 - scuttled 27.11.1942); **Nymphe** (A C de la Loire, Nantes, 1923/1.4.1926/6.1927 - BU 1938)

609/757t, 64.0x5.2x4.3m, 2d/2em, 1300/1000hp, 14/7.5kts, 60t diesel oil, 3500(7.5)/75(5)nm, 41p, 80m; 1 x 1 – 75/35 M1925, 2 x 1 – 8 MG, 7 – 550 TT (2 bow, 2 ext bow, 1 ext stern, 1 x 2 ext, 13).

First series of "600ton" submarines, built under 1922 Programme. Loire-Simonot type. Successful medium submarines which were well enough armed and maneuverable. Narrowness of internal compartments was considered as a lack, but at fortnight endurance it was not of great importance. *Galatée* on trials reached 14.3kts. She became fastest submarine of "600ton" class.

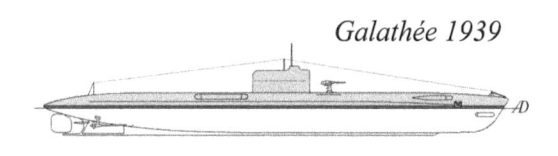

Galathée 1939

Nymphe was broken up for unknown reason in 1938.

All three survived submarines were scuttled at Toulon 27.11.1942. Later they were salvaged by Italians and Germans and lost under Allied air bombs; the first 24.11.1943 became *Naïade*, *Sirène* followed in February 1943 and *Galatée* in June 1944.

ARIANE class 2nd class submarine

Ariane (A C Augustin-Normand, Le Havre, 2.1923/6.8.1925/9.1929 - scuttled 9.11.1942); **Eurydice** (A C Augustin-Normand, Le Havre, 7.1923/31.5.1927/9.1929 - scuttled 27.11.1942); **Danaé** (A C Augustin-Normand, Le Havre, 2.1923/11.9.1927/11.1929 - scuttled 9.11.1942)

Ariane 1930

626/787t, 66.0x6.2x4.1m, 2d/2em, 1250/1000hp, 14/7.5kts, 60t diesel oil, 3500(7.5)/75(5)nm, 41p, 80m; 1 x 1 – 75/35 M1925, 2 x 1 – 8 MG, 7 – 550 TT (2 bow, 2 ext bow, 1 ext stern, 1 x 2 ext, 13)

Normand-Fenaux type. Built under the 1922 Programme and generally presented variant of *Sirène* class. These submarines were considered as the most successful variant of "600ton" boats.

Disabled *Ariane* and *Danaé* were destroyed by crews at Oran 9.11.1942 before occupancy of base by Allies. *Eurydice* was salvaged by Italians but sunk again by Allied aircraft 22.6.1944. *Eurydice* was scuttled at Toulon 27.11.1942.

CIRCÉ class 2nd class submarine

Circé (Schneider, Chalon-sur-Saône, 1.1924/29.10.1925/6.1929 - captured by Germany 8.12.1942, to Italy (FR117)); **Calypso** (Schneider, Chalon-sur-Saône, 2.1923/15.1.1926/6.1929 - captured by Germany 8.12.1942); **Thétis** (Schneider, Chalon-sur-Saône, 7.1923/30.6.1927/6.1929 - scuttled 27.11.1942); **Doris** (Schneider, Chalon-sur-Saône, 7.1923/25.11.1927/5.1928 - sunk 9.5.1940)

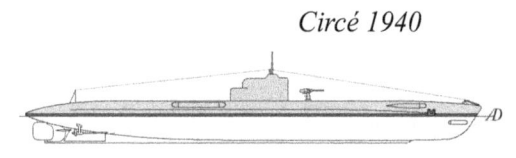

Circé 1940

615/776t, 62.5x6.2x4.0m, 2d/2em, 1250/1000hp, 14/7.5kts, 60t diesel oil, 3500(7.5)/75(5)nm, 41p, 80m; 1 x 1 – 75/35 M1925, 2 x 1 – 8 MG, 7 – 550 TT (2 bow, 2 ext bow, 1 ext stern, 1 x 2 ext, 13).

Schneider-Laubeuf type. Built under the 1922 Programme. Variant of *Sirène* design.

Doris after diesel incapacitation was sunk 9.5.1940 by German submarine *U9* off Dutch coast. *Circé* and *Calypso* were captured by Germans at Bizerte 8.12.1942 and transferred to Italians, but they never been commissioned again. *Circé* was renamed *FR117* and scuttled during Italian retreat 6.5.1943. *Calypso* was destroyed by Allied air bombs 30.1.1943. *Thétis* was scuttled at Toulon 27.11.1942.

SAPHIR class submarine minelayers

Saphir (Arsenal de Toulon, 11.1925/20.12.1928/9.1930 - captured by Germany 8.12.1942, to Italy (FR112)); **Turquoise** (Arsenal de Toulon, 10.1926/16.5.1929/9.1930 - captured by Germany 8.12.1942, to Italy (FR116)); **Nautilus** (Arsenal de Toulon, 8.1927/21.3.1930/7.1931 - captured by Germany 8.12.1942, to Italy); **Rubis** (Arsenal de Toulon, 4.1929/30.9.1931/4.1933 - FNFL 7.1940, stricken 4.1949); **Diamant** (Arsenal de Toulon, 7.1930/18.5.1933/6.1934 - scuttled 27.11.1942); **Perle** (Arsenal de Toulon, 7.1931/30.7.1935/3.1937 - FNFL 7.1940, sunk 8.7.1944)

Diamant prewar

761/925t, 65.9x7.2x4.3m, 2d/2em, 1300/1000hp, 12/9kts, 75t diesel oil, 7000(7.5)/80(4)nm, 42p, 80m; 1 x 1 – 75/35 M1928, 1 x 2 – 13.2 MG, 3 – 550 TT (2 bow, 1 x 1 in triple two-caliber TT bank, 5), 2 – 400 TT (1 x 2 in triple two-caliber TT bank, 2), 32 mines.

Project "Q6". 1925 (2 submarines) and 1926-1929 (4 subs) Programmes. Perhaps, the most successful submarines of French Navy. Double-hulled, mines were stored in vertical tubes out of a pressure hull.

M. b. 1943-1944, *Rubis, Perle*: - 1 x 2 - 13.2 MG; + 1 x 1 - 20/70 Oerlikon.

FRANCE

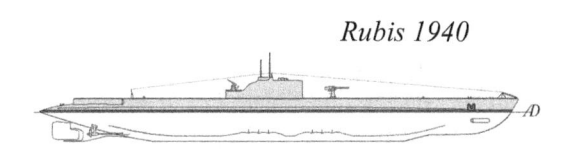

Rubis in July 1940 came over to the side of De Gaulle. *Diamant* was scuttled at Toulon 27.11.1942. She was salvaged by Germans and sunk again in 1944 by US air bombs. *Perle* was erroneously sunk by US aircraft in Atlantic 8.7.1944. Remaining submarines were disarmed at Bizerte, where 8.12.1942 they were captured by Germans. Later they were transferred to Italians, and then again captured by Germans. *Saphir* was renamed *FR112* and disarmed at Genoa, 15.9.1943 she

Rubis 1940

was blown up by Germans at Naples. Two more submarines did not departure Bizerte. *Turquoise*, renamed *FR116*, was scuttled there 6.5.1943, and *Nautilus* was sunk by Allied aircraft 31.1.1943.

ARGONAUTE class 2nd class submarines

Argonaute (Schneider, Chalon-sur-Saône, 4.1928/23.5.1929/6.1932 - sunk 8.11.1942); **Aréthuse** (Schneider, Chalon-sur-Saône, 4.1928/8.8.1929/7.1933 - FNFL 12.1942, sold 3.1946); **Atalante** (Schneider, Chalon-sur-Saône, 1.1929/5.8.1930/9.1934 - FNFL 12.1942, sold 3.1946); **La Vestale** (Schneider, Chalon-sur-Saône, 1.1930/25.5.1932/8.1934 - FNFL 12.1942, sold 8.1946); **La Sultane** (Schneider, Chalon-sur-Saône, 1.1930/5.8.1932/5.1935 - FNFL 12.1942, sold 12.1946)

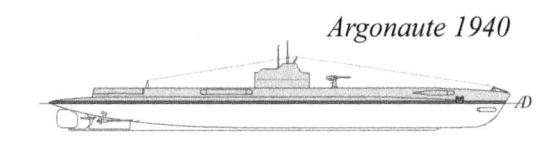

630/798t, 63.4x6.4x4.2m, 2d/2em, 1300/1000hp, 14/9kts, 39t diesel oil, 4000(10)/82(5)nm, 41p, 80m; 1 x 1 – 75/35 M1928, 1 x 1 – 8 MG, 6 – 550 TT (3 bow, 1 ext stern, 1 x 2 ext, 7), 2 – 400 TT (1 x 2 ext, 2); hydrophone.

Built under 1926 (2 boats), 1927 (1 boat) and 1929 (2 boats) Programmes. These "630-ton" boats became development of "600-ton" submarine of 1922 Programme. Underwater maneuverability was improved a little. As well as boats of the previous group, these submarines were built by different yards and had insignificant differences. *Argonaute* class submarines belonged to

Argonaute 1940

Schneider-Laubeuf design.

M. b. 1943 - 1944, all survived: - 1 x 1 – 8 MG; + 1 x 1 - 20/70 Oerlikon.

Argonaute was sunk at Oran by British destroyers *Ashanti* and *Westcott* 8.11.1942. *Aréthuse*, *Atalante* and *La Vestale* in 1944 were laid up into reserve.

DIANE class 2nd class submarines

Diane (A C Augustin-Normand, Le Havre, 4.1927/13.5.1930/9.1932 - scuttled 9.11.1942); **Méduse** (A C Augustin-Normand, Le Havre, 4.1927/26.8.1930/9.1932 - beached 10.11.1942); **Antiope** (A C de la Seine-Maritime, Le Trait, 3.1928/19.8.1930/10.1932 - FNFL 12.1942, sold 4.1946); **Amphitrite** (A C Augustin-Normand, Le Havre, 1.1928/20.12.1930/6.1933 - sunk 8.11.1942); **Amazone** (A C de la Seine-Maritime, Le Trait, 11.1928/28.12.1931/10.1933 - FNFL 12.1942, sold 4.1946); **Orphée** (A C Augustin-Normand, Le Havre, 11.1928/10.11.1931/6.1933 - FNFL 12.1942, sold 4.1946); **Oréade** (A C de la Seine-Maritime, Le Trait, 11.1928/23.5.1932/12.1933 - sunk 8.11.1942); **La Sibylle** (A C de la Seine-Maritime, Le Trait, 1.1930/28.1.1932/12.1934 - sunk 11.11.1942); **La Psyché** (A C Augustin-Normand, Le Havre, 1.1930/4.8.1932/12.1933 - sunk 8.11.1942)

651/807t, 64.4x6.2x4.3m, 2d/2em, 1400/1000hp, 14/9kts, 39t diesel oil, 4000(10)/82(5)nm, 41p, 80m; 1 x 1 – 75/35 M1928, 1 x 1 – 8 MG, 6 – 550 TT (3 bow, 1 ext aft, 1 x 2 ext, 7), 2 – 400 TT (1 x 2 ext, 2); hydrophone.

Built under 1926 (2 submarines), 1927 (3), 1928 (2 boats) and 1929 (2 boats) Programmes. Normand-Fenaux variant of "630ton" submarine.

M. b. 1943 - 1944, all survived: - 1 x 1 – 8 MG; + 1 x

Diane-class submarine

1 - 20/70 Oerlikon.

Six boats of this class were lost during Allied landing in the North Africa in November 1942. *Diane* was destroyed by crew at Oran 9.11.1942 before occupancy of base by Allies. *Méduse* was damaged by aircraft and ran aground 10.11.1942 off Mazagon (Morocco). *Amphitrite*, *Oréade* and *La Psyché* were sunk by gunfire of Allied ships and carrier aircraft at Casablanca (Morocco) 8.11.1942. *La Sybille* was lost off Casablanca 11.11.1942. French considered her as lost on a mine, but loss of submarine from torpedoes of German submarine *U173* is more probable.

Antiope, *Amazone* and *Orphée* in 1944 were laid up into reserve.

ORION class 2nd class submarines

Orion (A C de la Loire, Nantes, 11.1928/21.4.1931/7.1932 - FNFL 6.1940, BU 4.1943); **Ondine** (A C Dubigeon, Nantes, 11.1928/4.5.1931/7.1932 - FNFL 6.1940, BU 4.1943)

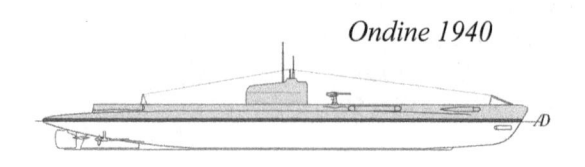

Ondine 1940

656/822t, 66.8x6.2x4.4m, 2d/2em, 1400/1000hp, 14/9kts, 39t diesel oil, 4000(10)/82(5)nm, 41p, 80m; 1 x 1 - 75/35 M1928, 1 x 1 - 8 MG, 6 - 550 TT (3 bow, 1 ext aft, 1 x 2 ext, 7), 2 - 400 TT (1 x 2 ext, 2); hydrophone.

Built under the 1928 Programme. Loire-Dubigeon variant of "630ton" boats.

In June 1940 both were withdrawn to Britain. Both boats were captured by British 3.7.1940 and in view of a strong deterioration were cannibalized for spares for *Junon* and *Minerve*.

MINERVE class 2nd class submarines

Minerve (Arsenal de Cherbourg, 8.1931/23.10.1934/9.1936 - FNFL 6.1940, wrecked 19.9.1945); **Junon** (A C Augustin-Normand, Le Havre, 6.1932/15.9.1935/9.1937 - FNFL 6.1940, sold 12.1954); **Vénus** (A C de la Seine-Maritime, Le Trait, 6.1932/6.4.1935/11.1936 - scuttled 27.11.1942); **Iris** (A C Dubigeon, Nantes, 7.1932/23.9.1934/9.1936 - interned 12.1942, returned 5.1945, sold 2.1950); **Pallas** (A C Augustin-Normand, Le Havre, 10.1936/25.8.1938/8.1939 - scuttled 9.11.1942); **Cérès** (A C de la Seine-Maritime, Le Trait, 8.1936/9.12.1938/7.1939 - scuttled 9.11.1942)

Junon under FNFL flag

Junon 1940

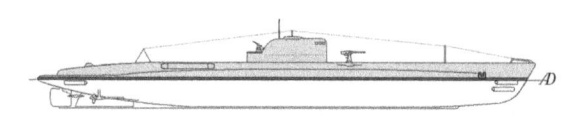

662/856t, 68.1x5.6x4.0m, 2d/2em, 1800/1230hp, 14.5/9kts, 51t diesel oil, 2000(10)/85(5)nm, 42p, 80m; 1 x 1 - 75/35 M1928, 2 x 1 - 13.2 MG, 6 - 550 TT (4 bow, 2 aft, 6), 1 x 3 - 400 TT (ext, 3); hydrophone.

Project "T2". 1930 (4 submarines) and 1936 (2 submarines) Programmes. First series of "standard" submarines. The design was grounded on drawings of "630ton" boats, since them there was a withdrawal from practice of ordering of ship design to private yards in favor of standardization.

M. b. 1943-1944, all survived: - 2 x 1 - 13.2 MG; + 1 x 1 - 20/70 Oerlikon.

1944, *Junon*: + radar, sonar.

Damaged *Iris* escaped from Toulon in November 1942 and was interned at Barcelona till the end of war (later she was transferred to Cartagena). *Junon* and *Minerve* in June 1940 withdrawn to Britain and later came over to the side of "Free France".

Cérès and *Pallas* were scuttled at Oran 9.11.1942 during Allied landing in the North Africa. Later they were salvaged but never commissioned again. *Minerve* 10.10.1943 was hard damaged in La Manche as result of erroneous attack of patrol Canadian B-24 bomber and laid up into reserve. After war, 19.9.1945, she was lost in navigating accident off British coast.

AURORE class 2nd class submarines

Aurore (Arsenal de Toulon, 9.1936/26.7.1939/6.1940 - scuttled 27.11.1942); ***La Créole*** (A C Augustin-Normand, Le Havre, 8.1938/8.6.1940-8.5.1946 (2nd time)/4.1949 – stricken 4.1962); *La Bayadère* (A C Augustin-Normand, Le Havre, 12.1937// - BU on slip 6.1940); *La Favorite* (A C de la Seine-Maritime, Le Trait, 12.1937/12.9.1942/(11.1942) - incomplete to Germany (UF2)); ***L'Africaine*** (A C dc la Seine-Maritime, Le Trait, 9.1938/7.12.1946/12.1949 – stricken 2.1963); ***L'Astrée*** (A C Dubigeon, Nantes, 11.1939/4.5.1946/4.1949 – stricken 11.1965); ***L'Andromède*** (A C Dubigeon, Nantes, 4.1940/17.11.1949/4.1953 – stricken 8.1965); *L'Antigone* (Schneider, Chalon-sur-Saône, 11.1938// - abandoned 1940); *L'Andromaque* (A C de la Seine-Maritime, Le Trait, 11.1938// - abandoned 1940); ***L'Artémis*** (A C Augustin-Normand, Le Havre, 1.1940/28.7.1942/2.1954 – stricken 11.1965); *L'Armide* (A C de la Seine-Maritime, Le Trait, 5.1939// - abandoned 1940); *L'Hermione* (A C Augustin-Normand, Le Havre, 2.1940// - abandoned 1940); *La Gorgone* (A C Augustin-Normand, Le Havre, 3.1940// - abandoned 1940); *La Clorinde* (A C Dubigeon, Nantes, 3.1940/8.7.1943/ - cancelled 1940); *La Cornélie* (A C Dubigeon, Nantes, 5.1940// - cancelled 1940)

As designed: 893/1170t, 73.5x6.5x4.2m, 2d/2em, 3000/1400hp, 14.5/9kts, 101t diesel oil, 5600(10)/80(5)nm, 44p, 100m; 1 x 1 – 100/34 M1936, 2 x 1 – 13.2 MG, 9 – 550 TT (4 bow, 2 aft, 1 x 3 ext, 10-11); hydrophone.

As completed postwar: 970/1250t, 73.5x6.5x4.2m, 2d/2em, 3000/1400hp, 15.5/9.3-10.3(*L'Andromède, L'Artémis*)kts, 101t diesel oil, 8800(10)/80(5)nm, 62p, 100m; 1 x 1 – 88/45 SK C/35 (*La Créole, L'Africaine, L'Astrée*), 2 x 1 – 20/65 C/38 (*La Créole, L'Africaine, L'Astrée*), 10 – 550 TT (4 bow, 4 amidships, 2 aft, 10-11); radar, sonar.

Project "Y3". 1934 (lead ship), 1937 (4 boats) and 1938 (10 boats) Programmes. One more design developing "630ton" type. The basic differences consisted in increase of diving depth to 100m and strengthened armament. It is necessary to mark transition to uniform torpedo caliber.

Only lead *Aurore* was commissioned before armistice. Incomplete *La Créole* was towed to Britain. *L`Andromède* was captured by Germans. Both boats were completed only after war. *L`Africaine, La Favorite* and *L`Astrée* also were captured by Germans; they received names *UF1, UF2* and *UF3* respectively.

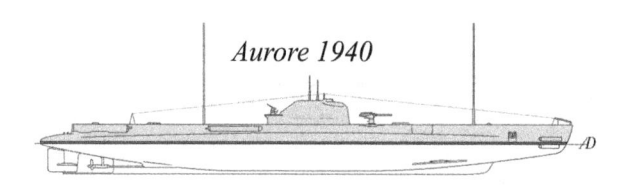

Aurore 1940

Only *UF2* was commissioned, served as training submarine, and sunk by Allied aircraft at Gdynia 5.7.1944.

Remaining incomplete submarines were blown up on slipways in June 1940.

After war 5 incomplete submarines were completed under modified design. 3 submarines (*La Créole, L`Africaine* and *L`Astrée*) received German 88mm gun and 10 TTs instead of original 9. Submarines had 4 internal bow and two internal stern tubes and external tubes installed in pairs fwd and aft of the fin. *L`Andromède* and *L`Artémise* were more redesigned, they received also newly designed fin with snorkel. *L`Artémise* was commissioned with new fire control system destined for new *Narval* class.

Aurore was scuttled by crew at Toulon 27.11.1942.

EMERAUDE class submarine minelayers

Emeraude (Arsenal de Toulon, 5.1938// - demolished on the slipway 23.6.1940); *L'Agate* (Schneider, Chalon-sur-Saône, 7.1939// - demolished on the slipway 23.6.1940); *Le Corail* (Schneider, Chalon-sur-Saône, 9.1939// - demolished on the slipway 23.6.1940); *L'Escarmouche* (Schneider, Chalon-sur-Saône, 9.1939// - demolished on the slipway 23.6.1940)

862/1119t, 72.7x7.4x4.1m, 2d/2em, 2000/1270hp, 15/9kts, 76t diesel oil, 5600(12)/90(4)nm, 43p, 100m; 1 x 1 – 100/34 M1936, 1 x 2 – 13.2 MG, 4 – 550 TT (bow, 4), 40 mines; hydrophone.

Project "V2". Built under 1937 (lead ship) and 1938 Programmes. Development of *Saphir*. According to some information, only *Emeraude* was begun. All were blown up on slipways.

Ex-British CURIE submarine

Curie (ex-Vox) (Vickers-Armstrong, Barrow, UK, 12.1942/23.1.1943/5.1943 - to United Kingdom 9.1946 (P67))

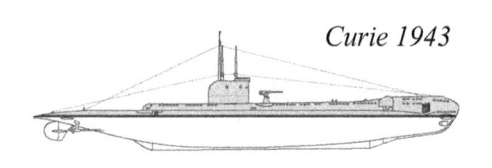

Curie 1943

646/732t, 60.0x4.9x4.7m, 2dg,2em, 615/825hp, 11.2/10kts, 55t diesel oil, 4050(10)/nm, 33p, 60m; 1 x 1 – 76/45 20cwt QF, 4 – 533 TT (bow, 8 torpedoes or 6 mines); Type 291W radar, Type 129, Type 138 sonars.

Ex-British submarine of 'U short hull' class, transferred to France at day of completion.

Ex-British DORIS class submarines

Doris (ex-Vineyard) (Vickers-Armstrong, Barrow, UK, 1943/8.5.1944/8.1944 - to United Kingdom 1947 (Vineyard));
Morse (ex-Vortex) (Vickers-Armstrong, Barrow, UK, 1943/19.8.1944/11.1944 - to Denmark 1947 (Sælen))

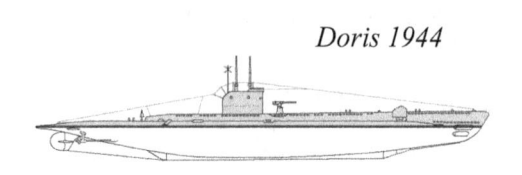

Doris 1944

658-662/740t, 62.3x4.9x4.7m, 2dg.2em, 615/825hp, 11.2/10kts, 55t diesel oil, 4700(10)/30(9)nm, 33p, 90m; 1 x 1 – 76/45 20cwt QF, 2 x 1 – 20/70 Oerlikon, 4 – 533 TT (bow, 8 torpedoes or 6 mines); Type 267QW radar, Type 129, Type 138 sonars.

Ex-British submarines of 'U class (long hull)' transferred to France at days of completion.

Ex-Italian NARVAL submarine

Narval (ex-P714, ex-Bronzo) (Tosi, Taranto, Italy, 12.1940/28.9.1941/(1.1942)/1.1944 - TS, sold 1.1949)

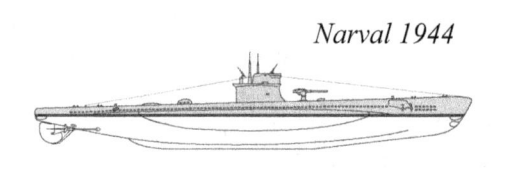

Narval 1944

697/850t, 60.2x6.4x4.8m, 2d/2em, 1400/800hp, 14.7/7.7kts, 78t diesel oil, 2300(14)/80(4)nm, 45p, 80m; 1 x 1 – 100/47 M1938, 2 x 1 – 13.2 MG, 4 – 533 TT (bow, 8).

Italian submarine of *Acciaio* class was captured by British minesweepers *Boston, Cromarty, Poole* and *Seeham* 12.7.1943. Transferred to FNFL 29.1.1944.

Ex-German BOUAN submarine

Bouan (ex-U510) (Deutsche Werft, Hamburg, Germany, 11.1940/4.9.1941/(11.1941)/5.1945 - BU 1958)

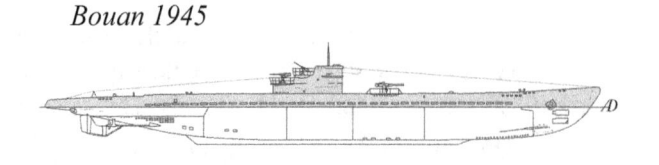

Bouan 1945

1120/1232t, 76.8x6.8x4.7m, 2d/2em, 4400/1000hp, 18.2/7.3kts, 208t diesel oil, 13450(10)/63(4)nm, 48p, 100p; 1 x 1 – 37/69 FlaK M/42, 2 x 2 – 20/65 C/38, 6 – 533 TT (4 bow, 2 stern, 22); FuMO 29 or FuMO 61 radar, GHG hydrophone.

German submarine of Type IXC, transferred at St-Nazaire in May 1945 under reparations.

FRANCE

Escort and patrol ships

Ex-British LA COMBATTANTE escort destroyer

La Combattante (ex-Haldon) (Fairfield, Govan, UK, 1.1941/27.4.1942/12.1942 - sunk 23.2.1945)

La Combattante 1943

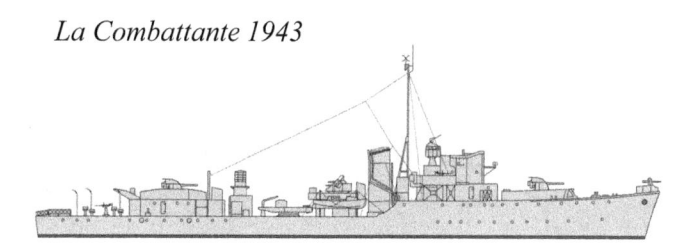

La Combattante 1943

1050/1490t, 85.3x9.6x3.7m, 2gst/2b, 19000hp, 27kts, 328t oil, 2100(20)nm, 168p; 2 x 2 – 102/45 QF Mk XVI, (1 x 4 + 1 x 1) – 40/39 pompom, 3 x 1 – 20/70 Oerlikon, 1 x 2 – 533 TT, 4 DCT, 2 DCR (70); Type 271, Type 285, Type 286 radars, Type 128 sonar.

British escort destroyer *Haldon* of 'Hunt 3' type, transferred to FNFL 15.12.1942. Transfer of two more ships of this class was assumed.

1943-1944, presumably: - Type 271, Type 286 radars; + Type 272, Type 291 radars.

La Combattante was lost after underwater explosion in Humber mouth. The reason considers mining, though sinking of the ship by German midget submarine *KU330* may been.

Ex-US SÉNÉGALAIS class destroyer escorts

Algérien (ex-Cronin) (Dravo, Wilmington, USA, 5.1943/27.11.1943/(1.1944)/1.1944 - returned 5.1964); **Sénégalais** (ex-Corbesier) (Dravo, Wilmington, USA, 4.1943/11.11.1943/(12.1943)/1.1944 - returned 5.1964); **Somali** (Dravo, Wilmington, USA, 10.1943/12.2.1944/4.1944 - experimental vessel 1956); **Hova** (Dravo, Wilmington, USA, 9.1943/22.1.1944/3.1944 - stricken 5.1964); **Marocain** (Dravo, Wilmington, USA, 9.1943/1.1.1944/2.1944 - stricken 1960); **Tunisien** (ex-Crosley) (Dravo, Wilmington, USA, 6.1943/17.12.1943/(2.1944)/2.1944 - stricken 1960)

Sénégalais 1944

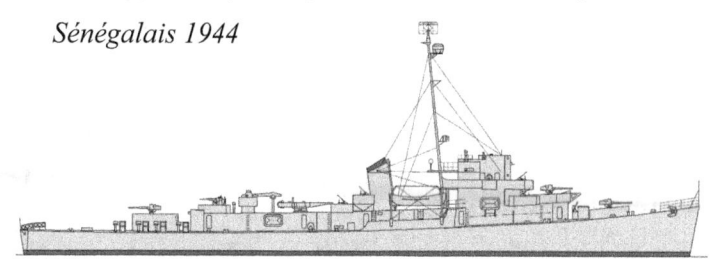

Sénégalais 1944

1253/1602t, 93.3x11.2x3.2m, 2em/4dg, 6000hp, 21kts, 320t diesel oil, 11500(11)nm, 186p; 3 x 1 – 76/50 Mk 20/21, 3 x 1 – 40/56 Bofors, 10 x 1 – 20/70 Oerlikon, 1 x 24 Hedgehog ASWRL, 8 DCT, 2 DCR (120); SC, SF radars, QGA sonar.

US ships of DET class transferred to France under lend-lease still before commission. Formally transferred simultaneously with commission. Provided by design triple 533mm TT during outfitting was replaced with two 40mm Boforses. 8 more ships were transferred to France in 1950-1952.

Sénégalais 4.5.1944 at coast of Algeria was damaged by torpedo from German submarine *U371* and was under repair till the end of a year.

ALDÉBARAN class 1st class aviso (escort sloop)

Altair (Hamilton, Glasgow, UK, 2.1916/6.7.1916/9.1916 - stricken 1940)

Altair 1920

1250/1470t, 81.5x10.5x4.2m, 1vte/2b, 2800hp, 17.5kts, 260t coal, 2400(12)nm, 103p; 2 x 1 – 139/45 M1893, 2 x 1 – 75/35 M1897, 2 DCT, 1 DCR.

Ships of that class were built in UK under French order, on the base of British *Flower* class design. Successful multi-purpose ships, first French ocean-going escorts.

VILLE D'YS 1st class aviso (escort sloop)

Ville d'Ys (ex-Andromédé, ex-Andromeda) (Swan Hunter, Wallsend, UK, 12.1916/6.1917/8.1917 - stricken 6.1945)

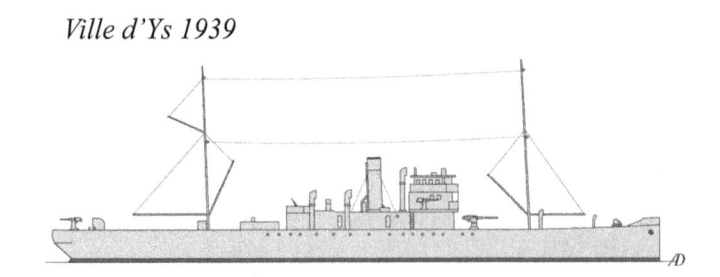

Ville d'Ys 1939

1121/1250t, 83.5x12.0x5.0m, 1vte/2b, 2675hp, 17kts, 270t coal, 2400(10)nm, 103p; 1 x 1 – 100/45 M1917, 3 x 1 – 75/35 M1897, 2 x 1 – 47/40 M1885.

British sloop of *Aubretia* group, purchased during outfitting. *Ville d'Ys* was paid off at Fort-de-France (West Indies) in November 1940.

BOUGAINVILLE class colonial avisos (sloops)

Dumont D'Urville (A C Maritime du Sud Ouest, Bordeaux, 11.1929/21.3.1931/6.1932 - sold 3.1958); **Bougainville** (F C de la Gironde, Bordeaux, 11.1929/21.4.1931/2.1933 - sunk 9.11.1940); **Savorgnan de Brazza** (A C Maritime du Sud Ouest, Bordeaux, 12.1929/18.6.1931/2.1933 - FNFL 1940, sold 3.1957); **D'Entrecasteaux** (A C de Provence, Port-de-Bouc, 1.1930/21.6.1931/5.1933 - damaged 12.1942, never repaired); **Rigault de Genouilly** (F C de la Gironde, Bordeaux, 7.1931/18.9.1932/3.1934 - sunk 4.7.1940); **Amiral Charner** (A C Maritime du Sud Ouest, Bordeaux, 5.1931/1.10.1932/4.1934 - scuttled 10.3.1945); **D'Iberville** (A C Maritime du Sud Ouest, Bordeaux, 7.1931/18.9.1932/3.1934 - scuttled 27.11.1942); **Ville D'Ys**, 4.1940- **La Grandière** (A C de Provence, Port-de-Bouc, 2.1938/20.6.1939/6.1940 - FNFL, sold 11.1959); *Beautemps-Beaupré* (F C de la Gironde, Bordeaux, 5.1938/20.6.1939/ - scuttled incomplete 24.6.1940); *La Pérouse* (F C de la Gironde, Bordeaux, 8.1939// - cancelled 1940)

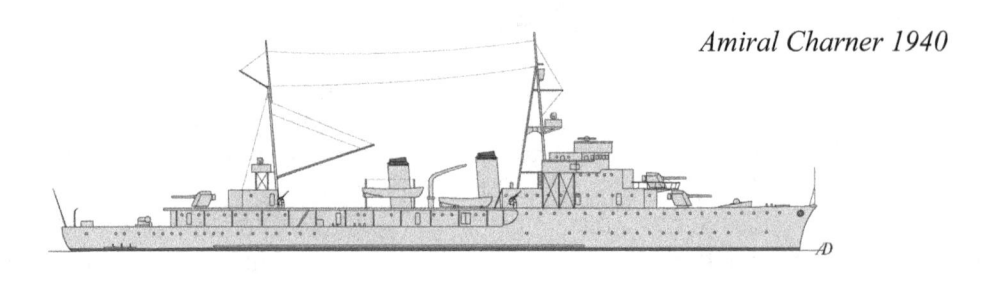

Amiral Charner 1940

1969/2600t, 103.7x12.7x4.5m, 2d, 3200hp, 15.5kts, 297t diesel oil, 9000(10)nm, 183p; 3 x 1 – 139/40 M1927 (completed ships), 3 x 2 – 100/45 M1933 (incomplete ships), 4 x 1 – 37/50 M1925 (completed ships), 2 x 2 – 37/50 M1933 (incomplete ships), 4 x 1 – 20/70 Oerlikon (incomplete ships), 6 x 1 – 8 MG (completed ships), 50 mines, 1 seaplane (GL.832) (completed ships)

Built under 1927 (2 ships), 1928 (2), 1930(3), 1937(2) and 1938(1 ship) Programmes as alternative to cruisers for service in colonies where they should fulfil functions of command ship, flag demonstration, etc. In this regard they were adapted for service in tropics. CT and gun mounts had splinter protection.

Building of *La Pérouse* was cancelled, and *Beautemps-Beaupré*, 84%-available, was scuttled during outfitting before approach of German troops 24.6.1940. On trials ships made from 17.2 (*Dumont D'Urville*) to 18.9 (*Amiral Charner*) kts.

1940, *Savorgnan de Brazza*: - seaplane; + 1 x 2 - 37/50 M1933.
1941, *Dumont D'Urville*: - seaplane; + 4 x 1 - 37/50 M1925, 2 x 1 - 25/60 M1938, 2 x 2 - 13.2 MG, 2 x 1 – 8 MG.
1944, *D'Entrecasteaux*: - 4 x 1 – 8 MG; + 6 x 1 - 13.2 MG. 1944, *Dumont D'Urville*: - 8 x 1 - 37/50, 2 x 1 - 25/60, 2 x 2 - 13.2 MG, 8 x 1 – 8 MG; + 1 x 4 - 40/56 Bofors, 11 x 1 - 20/70 Oerlikon, 4 DCT, 2 DCR (66), SA, SF radars, QJA sonar. 1944, *La Grandière*: - 4 x 1 - 37/50,

Rigault de Genouilly 1938

6 x 1 – 8 MG, seaplane; + 1 x 4 - 40/56 Bofors, 11 x 1 - 20/70 Oerlikon, 4 DCT, 2 DCR (66), SA, SF radars, QJA sonar. 1944, *Savorgnan de Brazza*: - 6 x 1 – 8 MG; + 1 x 2 - 37/50 M1933, 3 x 1 - 25/60 M1938, 2 x 1 - 20/70 Oerlikon, 2 x 2 - 13.2 MG, 4 DCT, 2 DCR (66), SA, SF radars, QJA sonar.

Bougainville, served under Vichy flag, was sunk at Libreville by Gaullist *Savorgnan de Brazza* 9.11.1940. *Rigault de Genouilly* was sunk by British submarine *Pandora* at Oran (Algeria) 4.7.1940 during operation "Catapult". *D'Entrecasteaux* was hard damaged in 1942 during occupancy of Madagascar by British surface ships and never was commissioned again. *Amiral Charner* and *Dumont D'Urville* participated in the French-Thai war and were scuttled 10.3.1945 in Indochina to avoid capture by Japanese.

Ex-British CROIX DE LORRAINE class frigates

L'Aventure (ex-Braid) (Simons, Renfrew, UK, 12.1942/30.11.1943/1.1944 - BU 1962); **L'Escarmouche** (ex-Frome) (Blyth SB, UK, 5.1942/1.6.1943/3.1944 - BU 9.1961); **Tonkinois** (ex-Moyola) (Smiths Dock, South Bank, UK, 2.1942/27.8.1942/(1.1943)/10.1944 - BU 9.1961); **Croix de Lorraine** (ex-Strule, ex-Glenarm) (Robb, Leith, UK, 7.1942/8.3.1943/(7.1943)/9.1944 - BU 9.1961); **La Surprise** (ex-Torridge) (Blyth SB, UK, 10.1942/16.8.1943/4.1944 - to Morocco 1964 (El Maouna)); **La Découverte** (ex-Windrush) (Robb, Leith, UK, 11.1942/18.6.1943/(11.1943)/2.1944 - BU 5.1961)

1420/2130t, 91.8x11.2x3.9m, 2vte/2b, 5500hp, 20kts, 440(*Croix de Lorraine*)-646t oil, 7700(12)nm, 140p; 2 x 1 – 102/40 QF Mk XIX, (2 x 2 + 7 x 1) or 9 x 1 – 20/70 Oerlikon, 1 x 24 Hedgehog ASWRL, 8 DCT, 2 DCR (150); Type 271 or Type 272, Type 286PU or Type 291 or Type 277 radars, Type 144 sonar.

British 'River' class frigates, transferred to France in 1944.

La Surprise 20.6.1944 was damaged by mine at coast of Normandy.

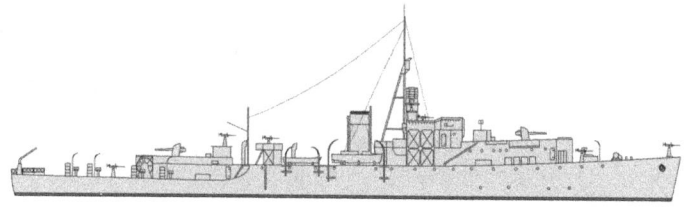

La Surprise 1944

FRIPONNE class 2nd class avisos (ASW gunboats)

Diligente (Arsenal de Brest, 1915/1916/1918 - captured by British 3.7.1940); **Engageante** (Arsenal de Brest, 1916/17.12.1916/1918 - FNFL 11.1942, stricken 1944); **Surveillante** (Arsenal de Brest, 1915/1917/1918 - stricken 1938)

Diligente 1940

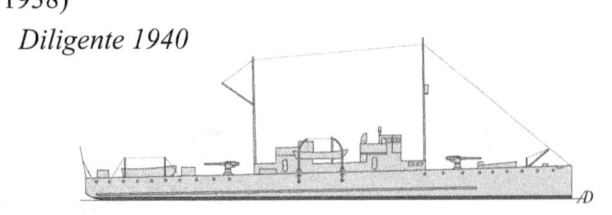

Engageante

315t, 66.4x7.0x2.8m, 2d, 900hp, 14.5kts, 30t diesel oil, 3000(10)nm, 54p; 2 x 1 – 100/45 M1897, 2 DCT.

Differed from each other a little; *Diligente* had straight stem, remaining ships had clipper bow.

Diligente was captured by British 3.7.1940 at Portsmouth and returned after war. *Engageante* came over to the side of Allies in November 1942 and was paid off in 1944.

MARNE class 1st class avisos (sloops)

Aisne (Arsenal de Lorient, 1916/7.1917/1918 - BU 1939); **Marne** (Arsenal de Lorient, 1916/25.11.1916/1917 - scuttled 10.3.1945); **Meuse** (Arsenal de Rochefort, 1916/6.1917/1918 - BU 1938); **Oise** (Arsenal de Brest, 1916/12.10.1916/1917 - BU 1938); **Somme** (Arsenal de Brest, 1916/3.1917/1917 - sold 10.1941); **Yser** (Arsenal de Rochefort, 1916/1.1917/1917 - scuttled 27.11.1942)

Somme 1940

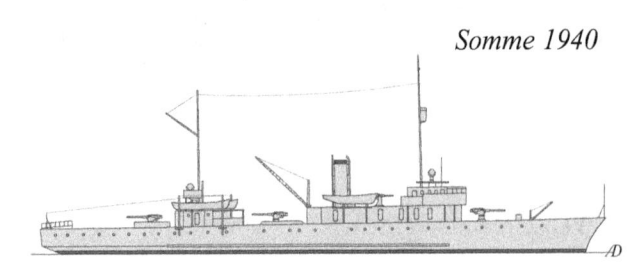

Marne 1919

601(*Marne*)-566t, 78.0x8.9x3.4m, 2gst/2b, 5000(*Marne*)-4000hp 21(*Marne*)-20kts, 143t oil, 4000(11)nm, 113p; 4 x 1 – 100/45 M1917, 1 x 1 – 75/35 (*Somme*), 2 x 1 – 65/50 M1902 or 2 x 1 – 47/50 M1902 (except *Somme*), 1 DCR.

Built under the 1916 Programme. Differed from each other a little, *Marne* and *Aisne* were twin-funneled, remaining ships had one funnel. Besides, *Marne* had more powerful turbines.

Marne participated in the French-Thai war and was scuttled in Indochina 10.3.1945. *Somme* was paid off and broken up 14.10.1941. *Yser* was scuttled at Toulon 27.11.1942, salvaged, served under German flag as *SG37*. She was never commissioned again by French Navy and broken up in 1946.

LURONNE 2nd class aviso (ASW gunboat)

Luronne (Arsenal de Brest, 1916/1917/1917 - BU 4.1941)

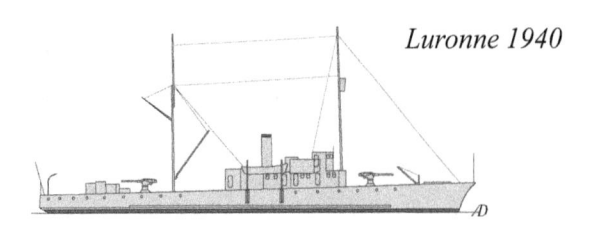

Luronne 1940

266/400t, 60.2x7.2x2.9m, 2d, 630hp, 13.7kts, 30t diesel oil, 3000(10)nm, 54p; 2 x 1 – 100/4 M1897, 2 DCT.

Diesel-engined variant of *Ardent* class.

Luronne was paid off in Morocco in October 1940 and broken up in April 1941.

FRANCE
61

VALLIANTE class 2nd class aviso (ASW gunboat)

Conquérante (Arsenal de Brest, 1916/1917/1917 - captured by British 3.7.1940)

Conquérante

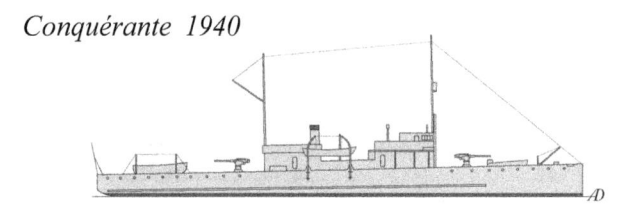

Conquérante 1940

457t, 66.4x7.9x2.8m, 2d, 1800hp, 17kts, 30t diesel oil, 3000(10)nm, 54p; 2 x 1 – 100/45 M1897, 2 DCT.
Development of *Friponne*, differed by twice more powerful machinery and by 0.7m increased hull breadth.
Conquérante was captured by British 3.7.1940 at Falmouth and sunk there by German aircraft 14.4.1941.

AMIENS class 1st class avisos (sloops)

Amiens (F C de la Méditerranée, La Seyne, 1918/5.1919/1920 - captured by British 3.7.1940, FNFL depot ship 7.1940); **Arras** (Arsenal de Brest, 1917/7.1918/1918 - captured by British 3.7.1940, FNFL barrack ship 7.1940); **Bapaume** (Arsenal de Lorient, 1917/8.1918/1920 - BU 1937); **Belfort** (Arsenal de Lorient, 1918/3.1919/1920 - seaplane tender, captured by British 3.7.1940, FNFL accommodation ship 7.1940); **Calais** (F C de la Méditerranée, La Seyne, 1918/11.1919/1920 - sold 11.1946); **Coucy** (Penhoët, St-Nazaire, 1918/6.1919/1920 - captured by British 3.7.1940); **Ypres** (ex-Dunkerque) (Arsenal de Brest, 1917/7.1918/1918 - survey vessel, BU 4.1942); **Épinal** (Penhoët, St-Nazaire, 1918/8.1919/1920 - captured by British 3.7.1940); **Lassigny** (A C de Bretagne, Nantes, 1918/7.1919/1920 - stricken 10.1941); **Les Éparges** (A C de Bretagne, Nantes, 1918/9.1919/1920 - survey vessel, scuttled 27.11.1942); **Nancy** (Arsenal de Cherbourg, 1917/3.1919/1920 - BU 1938); **Reims** (Arsenal de Brest, 1917/7.1918/1918 - BU 1938); **Révigny** (F C de la Gironde, Bordeaux, 1917/9.1920/1921 - BU 1937); **Tahure** (A C de la Loire, St-Nazaire, 1918/3.1918/1920 - sunk 24.9.1944); **Vauquois** (A C de la Loire, St-Nazaire, 1918/8.1919/1920 - TS, sunk 18.6.1940); **Laffaux** (ex-Verdun) (Arsenal de Brest, 1917/11.1918/1920 - BU 1938)

850t, 74.9x8.7x3.2m, 2gst/2b, 5000hp, 20kts, 200t oil, 3000(11)nm, 103p; 2 x 1 – 139/55 M1910, 1 x 1 – 75/35 M1897, 4 x 1 – 8 MG, 2 DCT (20), 1 seaplane (*Belfort*)
Fast turbine-engined sloops with merchant vessel outline profile. On trials exceeded 22kts speed.
Late 1930s, *Épinal*: - 2 x 1 - 139/55; + 2 x 1 - 145/45 M1910.
1940, *Amiens*: + 1 x 2 - 37/48 M1935.
Arras, *Épinal* and *Amiens* 3.7.1940 were captured by British at Portsmouth. *Arras* was transferred to FNFL, used as barrack ship and a source of spares, she was returned after war and BU in 1946. *Belfort* and *Coucy* were captured by British 3.7.1940 at Plymouth and were returned postwar. *Lassigny* was paid off 31.10.1940 in Morocco. *Les Éparges* was scuttled at Toulon 27.11.1942, salvaged by Germans and served in the Kriegsmarine as minesweeper *M6060*. *Tahure* participated in French-Thai war in January 1941 and was sunk by US submarine *Flasher* 24.9.1944 (under some sources 29.4.1944). *Vauquois* was mined 18.6.1940.

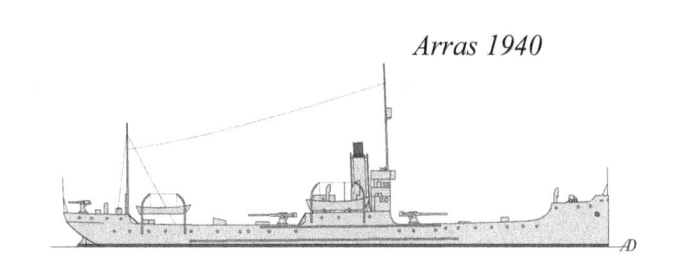

Arras 1940

Ypres 1920

Coucy 1933

AILETTE 1st class aviso (sloop)

Ailette (Arsenal de Brest, 1917/3.1918/1918 - sold 10.1941)

Ailette 1939

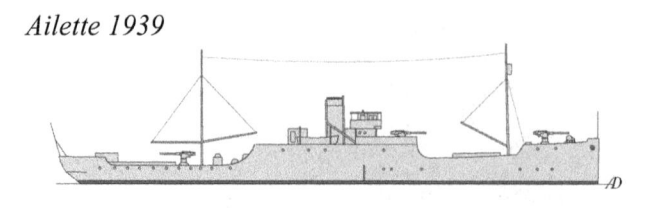

Ailette 1924

492t, 70.0x8.3x3.1m, 2gst/2b, 4000hp, 20kts, 143t oil, 4000(11)nm, 107p; 4 x 1 – 100/45 M1917, 1 x 1 – 75/35 M1897.

Built under the 1917 Programme. Intended for service as decoy ship, therefore had an outline profile of merchant vessel and artillery masked by folding shields.

Ailette before WWII used for fishery protection and paid off 30.10.1941 in Morocco.

SCARPE class 1st class avisos (sloops)

Ancre (Arsenal de Lorient, 1917/4.1918/1918 - stricken 1940); **Scarpe** (Arsenal de Lorient, 1917/31.10.1917/1918 - stricken 1938); **Suippe** (Arsenal de Brest, 1917/4.1918/1918 - captured by British 3.7.1940)

Ancre 1940

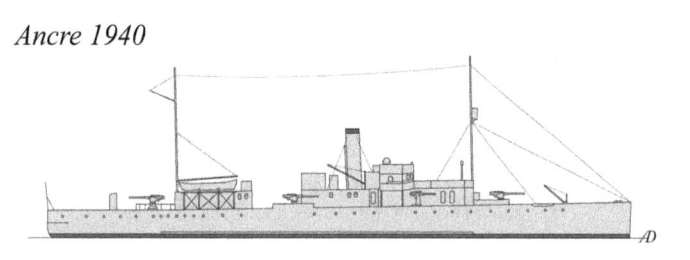

Scarpe 1930

604t, 76.2x8.7x3.3m, 2gst/2b, 5000hp, 20kts, 143t oil, 4000(11)nm, 107p; 4 x 1 – 100/45 M1917, 1 x 1 – 75/35 M1897, 2 DCT.

Flush-decked turbine driven sloops, built under the 1917 Programme. *Scarpe* had clipper bow, remaining two ships had straight stems.

Suippe was captured by British in July 1940 at Falmouth; 4.4.1942 she was sunk there by German aircraft, later salvaged but never commissioned again.

QUENTIN ROOSEVELT 2nd class aviso (sloop)

Quentin Roosevelt (ex-Flamant) (Arsenal de Rochefort, 1913/12.1916/4.1918 - captured by British 3.7.1940, returned 1945, stricken 1947)

Quentin Roosevelt 1939

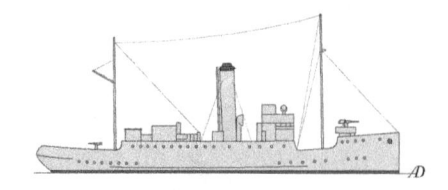

Quentin Roosevelt in the wartime

FRANCE 63

585t, 50.0x8.4x58m, 1vte/2b, 1200hp, 14.5kts, 105t coal, 1200(10)nm, 53p; 1 x 1 – 75/35 M1897, 1 x 1 – 47/50 M1902.

Laid down as fishery protection vessel, in 1914 building was suspended. Ship was commissioned as sloop.

Quentin Roosevelt was captured by British 3.7.1940, used for training and returned after WWII.

DUBORDIEU class 2nd class avisos (sloops)

Du Chaffault (Arsenal de Lorient, 1917/9.1918/1918 - stricken 1938); **Du Couëdic** (Arsenal de Lorient, 1918/7.1919/1920 - stricken 1939); **Dubourdieu** (Arsenal de Lorient, 1917/4.1918/1918 - sunk 8.11.1942); **Enseigne Henry** (ex-Dumont D'Urville) (Arsenal de Lorient, 1917/6.11.1918/1919 – scuttled 18.6.1940)

Dubordieu 1921

Dubordieu 1940

453t, 64.9x8.2x3.1m, 2gst/2b, 2000hp, 16.5kts, 140t oil, 2000(15)nm, 74p; 1 x 1 – 139/45 M1893, 1 x 1 – 100/45 M1917, 2 DCT.

Smaller variant of *Amiens* class.

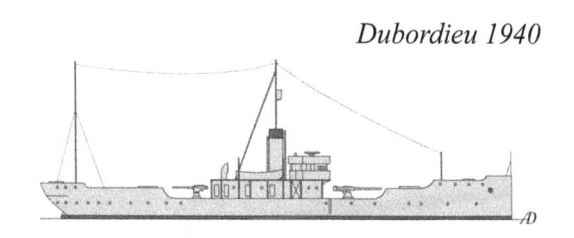

Dubourdieu was paid off at Casablanca 28.10.1940 and sunk 8.11.1942 during Allied landing in the North Africa. *Enseigne Henry* was scuttled at Lorient 18.6.1940, salvaged by Germans and sold for scrap 25.6.1941.

ÉLAN class aviso-minesweepers (sloops)

Élan (Arsenal de Lorient, 8.1936/27.7.1938/1939 - interned in Turkey 6.1941-12.1944, sold 3.1958); **Commandant Bory** (A C de France, Dunkerque, 11.1936/26.1.1939/9.1939 - FNFL 11.1942, sold 2.1953); **Commandant Delage** (A C de France, Dunkerque, 11.1936/25.2.1939/12.1939 - FNFL 11.1942, sold 10.1960); **Commandant Duboc** (A C Dubigeon, Nantes, 12.1936/16.1.1939/8.1939 - captured by British 3.7.1940, FNFL 7.1940, sold 7.1963); **Commandant Rivière** (A C de Provence, Port-de-Bouc, 11.1936/16.2.1939/9.1939 - captured by Germany 8.12.1942 (Italian FR52)); **La Capricieuse** (A C Dubigeon, Nantes, 1.1938/19.4.1939/2.1940 - captured by British 3.7.1940, returned 1945, BU 9.1964); **La Moqueuse** (Arsenal de Lorient, 9.1938/25.1.1940/4.1940- captured by British 3.7.1940, FNFL 7.1940, BU 10.1965); **Commandant Dominié** (ex-La Rieuse) (A C Dubigeon, Nantes, 2.1938/2.5.1939/4.1940 - captured by British 3.7.1940, FNFL 7.1940, BU 10.1960); **L'Impétueuse** (A C de France, Dunkerque, 4.1938/17.8.1939/5.1940 - scuttled 27.11.1942 (later Italian FR54)); **La Curieuse** (Arsenal de Lorient, 8.1938/11.11.1939/1940 - scuttled 27.11.1942 (later Italian FR55)); **La Batalleuse** (A C de Provence, Port-de-Bouc, 12.1937/22.8.1939/3.1940 - captured by Germany 8.12.1942 (Italian FR51)); **La Boudeuse** (A C de France, Dunkerque, 3.1938/9.1939/1940 - FNFL 11.1942, sold 4.1958); **La Gracieuse** (A C de Provence, Port-de-Bouc, 2.1938/30.11.1939/1940 - FNFL 11.1942, sold 9.1958)

630/895t, 78.3x8.7x3.3m, 2d, 4000hp, 20kts, 100t diesel oil, 9000(14)nm, 106p; 1 x 1 – 100/45 M1893 or M1932 or 1 x 2 – 90/50 M1926, (1 x 4 + 2 x 2) – 13.2 MG, 2 DCT, 1 DCR (40).

Built under 1934 (1 ship), 1936 (4) and 1937 (8) Programmes. *La Trompeuse* was cancelled. Under the design they should had minesweeping equipment. Really no one ship received it, they all were equipped instead with 2 DCTs and 1 DCR. May be, some ships under British and FNFL control were rearmed with

Commandant Bory 1939

La Capricieuse 1940

La Capricieuse 1945

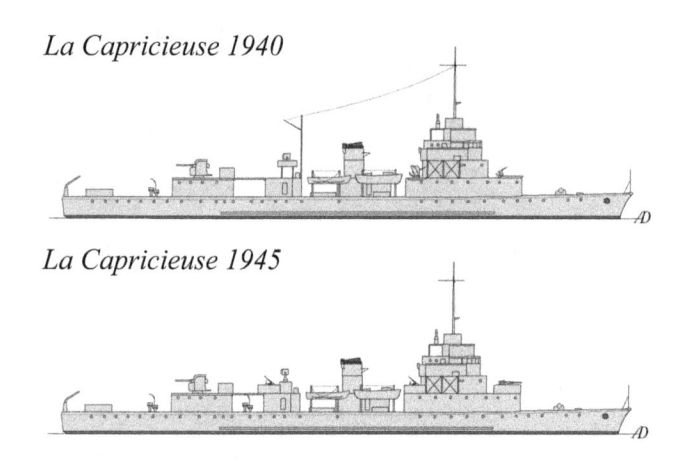

British 102mm guns and single pompoms.
1941-1942, *Commandant Dominié* was rearmed with 1 x 2 - 102/45 QF Mk XVI, 1 x 1 - 40/39 pompom, 2 x 2 - 13.2 MG, (4 x 2 + 2 x 1) - 12.7 MG, 2 DCT, 1 DCR (40), sonar. 1941-1942, *Commandant Duboc* was rearmed with 1 x 2 - 102/45 QF Mk XVI, 1 x 1 - 40/39 pompom, 1 x 1 - 25/60 M1938, 2 x 1 - 20/70 Oerlikon, 4 x 2 - 13.2 MG, 2 DCT, 1 DCR (40), sonar. 1941-1942, *La Moqueuse* was rearmed with 1 x 2 - 102/45 QF Mk XVI, 1 x 1 - 76/40 12pdr 12cwt QF, 1 x 1 - 40/39 pompom, 3 x 2 - 13.2 MG, 2 DCT, 1 DCR (40), sonar.

Commandant Duboc, Commandant Dominié, La Moqueuuse and *La Capricieuse* 3.7.1940 were captured by British. First three were transferred to FNFL. *Élan* participated in the Syrian campaign of 1941 and then was interned in Turkey till 23.12.1944. *Commandant Rivière* and *La Batailleuse* were captured by Germans at Bizerte 8.12.1942 but never commissioned by them. *Commandant Rivière* was sunk by Allied aircraft. *La Batailleuse* was transferred to Italians and named *FR57*; 9.9.1943 she was scuttled at La Spezia, again salvaged by Germans and ultimately scuttled by them at Genoa. *L'lmpétueuse* and *La Curieuse* were scuttled at Toulon 27.11.1942, both salvaged by Italians, named *FR54* and *FR55* respectively and 4.9.1943 were captured by Germans. Former was scuttled by them at Marseilles, latter served as fast escort *SG25* and in 1944 was scuttled by Germans at Toulon. *Commandant Bory, Commandant Delage, La Boudeuse* and *La Gracieuse* after Allied landing in the North Africa came over to the side of Allies.

CHAMOIS class aviso-minesweepers (sloops)

Commandant de Pimodan (ex-Alfred de Courcy) (A C de La Loire, Nantes, 1939/1941/1947 - BU 1.1966); *Amiral Duperré* (A C de la Loire, Nantes, 1939// - abandoned 6.1940); *Amiral Gourdon* (F C de la Méditerranée, La Seyne, 1939// - abandoned 6.1940); *Amiral Sénès* (A C de Provence, Port-de-Bouc, 8.1939/1942/(3.1944) - completed as German SG21 Bernd von Arnim); **Annamite** (Arsenal de Lorient, 4.1938/17.6.1939/2.1940 - FNFL 11.1942, to Morocco 1961 (El Lahiq)); **Chamois** (Arsenal de Lorient, 11.1936/29.4.1938/1939 - scuttled 27.11.1942 (later German SG21)); **Chevreuil** (Arsenal de Lorient, 6.1937/17.6.1939/9.1939 - captured by British 3.7.940, FNFL 7.1940, to Tunisia 10.1959 (Destour)); *Enseigne Ballande* (A C de Provence, Port-de-Bouc, 8.1939/25.5.1942/ - captured by Germans on the stocks (SG22), scuttled incomplete 20.8.1944); *Enseigne Bisson* (A C de La Loire, Nantes, 1939// - abandoned 6.1940); **Gazelle** (Arsenal de Lorient, 6.1937/17.6.1939/10.1939 - FNFL 11.1942, sold 3.1961); **Bisson** (ex-L'Ambitieuse) (Arsenal de Lorient, 1939/5.3.1946/1947 - BU 1964); *La Furieuse* (F C de la Méditerranée, La Seyne, 1939// - cancelled 1940); *La Généreuse* (Arsenal de Lorient, 1939// - abandoned 6.1940); *L'Heureuse* (Arsenal de Lorient, 1939// - abandoned 6.1940); *La Joyeuse* (A C de Provence, Port-de-Bouc, 1939// - cancelled 1940); *La Maliceuse* (Arsenal de Lorient, 1939// - abandoned 6.1940); *Commandant Ducuing* (ex-La Preneuse) (F C de la Gironde, Bordeaux, 1939/8.6.1948/ - abandoned 1948); *La Rieuse* (F C de la Gironde, Bordeaux, 1939// - abandoned 6.1940); *La Sérieuse* (F C de la Gironde, Bordeaux, 1939// - abandoned 6.1940); **La Surprise** (ex-Bambora) (Arsenal de Lorient, 4.1938/17.6.1939/3.1940 - sunk 8.11.1942); *La Trompeuse* (A C de Provence, Port-de-Bouc, 1939// - cancelled 1940); **Commandant Amyot d'Inville** (ex-La Victorieuse) (A C de la Loire, Nantes, 1939/1941/1947 - BU 1965); *Matelot Leblanc* (A C de Provence, Port-de-Bouc, 8.1939/10.7.1942/(5.1943) - completed as German SG41); *Rageot de la Touche* (A C de Provence, Port-de-Bouc, 8.1939/2.9.1942/(10.1943) - completed as German SG15)

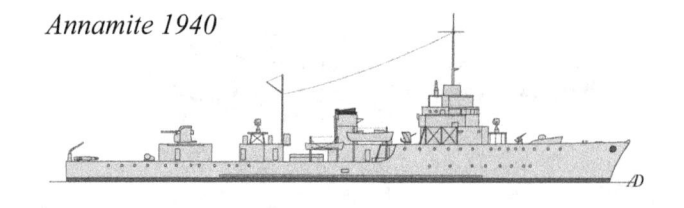

Annamite 1940

647/900t, 78.3x8.7x3.3m, 2d, 4000hp, 20kts, 105t diesel oil, 10000(9)nm, 106p; 1 x 1 – 100/45 M1892 or M1932 or 1 x 2 - 90/50 M1926, (1 x 4 + 2 x 2) – 13.2 MG, 2 DCT, 1 DCR (40). *Copleted postwar:* 2 x 1 – 105/45 SK C/32, 1 x 1 – 40/56 Bofors, 4 x 1 – 20/70 Oerlikon, 4 DCT, 2 DCR

FRANCE

(120), radars, sonar.

1935 (3 ships), 1937 (2) and 1938 (4) Programmes. Building of three ships of the 1938 Programme and 12 of 1939 Programme was cancelled. As a whole design was close to *Élan*, but ships had extended forecastle.

Chamois was scuttled 27.11.1942 at Toulon, salvaged by Germans and commissioned by them as fast escort *SG21*; 23.11.1943 she was sunk by Allied aircraft, salvaged again and ultimately sunk by US destroyers 15.8.1944. *Chevreuil* 3.7.1940 was captured by British at Portsmouth and transferred to FNFL. *La Surprise* was sunk at Oran 8.11.1942 during Allied landing. *Matelot Leblanc* was completed by Germans and commissioned by them as fast escort *SG14*; 24.8.1944 she was sunk at Capri by Allied aircraft. *Rageot de la Touche* was completed by

Chevreuil

Germans and commissioned as fast escort *SG15 (UJ2229)*, she was sunk by British submarine *Universal*. *Amiral Sénès* was captured by Germans, renamed *SG16* and scuttled at Marseilles. *Enseigne Ballande* was captured by Germans, renamed *SG17*, completed but never commissioned and was scuttled.

Auxiliary sloops

P1 Marigot (1932/1939, 4048grt, 104.6(pp)x16.0x6.0m, 15kts, 4 x 1 - 100/45 - paid off 8.1940); **P2 Cyrnos** (1929/1939, 2548grt, 94.4(pp)x12.6x5.2m, 14kts, 5 x 1 - 100/45 - paid off 8.1940); **P3 Sidi Okba** (1930/1939, 2824grt, 100.8(pp) x13.2x5.6m, 15kts, 5 x 1 - 100/45 - paid off 8.1940); **P4 Ville d'Ajaccio** (1929/1939, 2444grt, 85.2(pp)x12.6x5.8m, 16kts, 5 x 1 - 100/45 - paid off 11.1940); **P6 Caraibe** (1932/1939, 4048grt, 104.6(pp)x16.0x6.0m, 15kts, 4 x 1 - 100/45 - paid off 11.1940); **P7 Pascal Paoli** (1932/1939, 3280grt, 96.0(pp)x14.6x5.2m, 18kts, 5 x 1 - 100/45 - paid off 11.1940); **P8 Sampiero Corso** (1936/1939, 3823grt, 105.5(pp)x14.6x5.4m, 16kts, 5 x 1 - 100/45 - paid off 10.1940); **P19 Léoville** (1922/1939, 1049grt, 65.4(pp)x9.3x4.5m, 11.5kts, 4 x 1 - 100/45, 2 x 1 – 37/50, 43 DC - captured by British 7.1940, FNFL 1941, to UK 1945); **P20 Barsac** (1922/1939, 1049grt, 65.8(pp)x9.3x4.5m, 10kts, 4 x 1 - 100/45, 2 x 1 – 37/50, 43 DC - wrecked 7.1.1940); **P21 Cérons** (1923/1939, 1049grt, 65.8(pp)x9.4x4.5m, 10.5kts, 4 x 1 - 100/45, 2 x 1 – 37/50, 43 DC - sunk 12.6.1940); **P22 Sauternes** (1922/1939, 1049grt, 65.8(pp)x9.3x4.5m, 10kts, 4 x 1 - 100/45, 2 x 1 – 37/50, 43 DC - captured by British 3.7.1940); **P23 Pessac** (1907/1939, 878grt, 4 x 1 – 100/45, 2 x 1 – 37/50, 43 DC – captured by British 3.7.1940); **P24 Médoc** (1930/1939, 1166grt, 72.3(pp)x10.4x4.9m, 10kts, 4 x 1 - 100/45, 2 x 1 – 37/50, 43 DC - captured by British 3.7.1940); **P25 Pomerol** (1930/1939, 1167grt, 72.3(pp)x10.4x4.9m, 11kts, 4 x 1 - 100/45, 2 x 1 – 37/50, 43 DC - captured by British 3.7.1940); **P26 Listrac** (1907/1939, 878grt, 4 x 1 – 100/45, 2 x 1 – 37/50, 43 DC – captured by British 3.7.1940)

Former cargo vessels (P1 - 8) and coastal cargo vessels (P19 - 26).

Barsac wrecked 7.1.1940 off Vigo. *Cérons* was sunk by German coastal guns 12.6.1940 off Fecant. *Léoville*, *Sauternes*, *Médoc*, *Pomerol*, *Pessac* and *Listrac* were captured by British 3.7.1940, later former ship was transferred to FNFL.

Auxiliary patrol vessels

More than 500grt capacity

P10 Casoar (1935/1939, 580grt – paid off 1940); **P11 Cap Nord** (1926/1939, 1033grt, 64.3(pp)x10.4x6.0m, 10.5kts, 3 x 1 - 100/45 - captured by Germany 1942 (UJ2207)); **P12 Capricorne** (1921/1939, 741grt, 3 x 1 – 100/45 – paid off 8.1940); **P13 Victoria** (1928/1939, 849grt, 3 x 1 – 100/45 – paid off 12.1940, re-commissioned 1941, scuttled 8.11.1942); **P14 Vaillant** (1921/1939, 916grt, 3 x 1 – 100/45 – captured by British 3.7.1940); **P15 Clairvoyant** (1922/1939, 943grt, 3 x 1 – 100/45 – paid off 10.1940); **P16 Hardi II** (1921/1939, 916grt, 3 x 1 – 100/45 – paid off 10.1940); **P17 Cap Fagnet** (1926/1939, 1017grt, 64.3(pp)x10.4x6.0m, 10.5kts, 3 x 1 - 100/45 - paid off 12.1940); **P18 Terre Neuve** (1921/1939, 780grt, 3 x 1 – 100/45 – captured by British 6.7.1940); **P28 Heureux** (1930/1939, 1116grt,

64.2(pp)x10.4x6.1m, 10kts, 3 x 1 - 100/45, 2 x 1 – 37/50 - paid off 8.1940); **P29 Groënland** (1930/1939, 1178grt, 65.7(pp)x10.6x5.5m, 10kts, 3 x 1 - 100/45, 2 x 1 – 37/50 - captured by British 3.7.1940); **P30 Capitaine Armand** (1920/1939, 584grt, 3 x 1 – 100/45 – paid off early 1941); **P32 Téméraire II** (1926/1939, 965grt, 3 x 1 – 100/45 – paid off 9.1940); **P33 Atlantique** (1920/1939, 659grt, 3 x 1 – 100/45 – captured by British 3.7.1940); **P34 Asie** (1914/1939, 551grt, 3 x 1 – 100/45 – captured by British 3.7.1940); **P36 Patrie** (1920/1939, 753grt, 3 x 1 – 100/45 – captured by British 3.7.1940); **P37 Jutland** (1934/1939, 1160grt, 66.3(pp)x10.9x6.0m,11kts, 3 x 1 - 100/45, 2 x 1 – 37/50, 40 DC - paid off 10.1940); **P38 Mercéditta** (1934/1939, 1160grt, 66.6(pp)x10.5x5.9m, 12kts, 3 x 1 - 100/45, 2 x 1 – 37/50 - paid off 12.1940); **P39 Reine des Flots** (1923/1939, 849grt, 3 x 1 – 100/45 – captured by British 3.7.1940); **P40 Président Houduce** (1930/1939, 1178grt, 65.7(pp)x10.6x5.5m, 10kts, 3 x 1 - 100/45, 2 x 1 – 37/50 - FNFL 1940, paid off 5.1945); **P41 Vikings** (1935/1939, 1150grt, 63.7(pp)x10.5x5.5m, 11kts, 3 x 1 - 100/45, 2 x 1 – 37/50 - captured by British 3.7.1940, FNFL 1941, sunk 17.4.1942); **P42 Minerva** (1937/1939, 1148grt, 66.6(pp)x10.5x5.9m, 12kts, 3 x 1 - 100/45, 2 x 1 – 37/50 - paid off 9.1940); **P43 Sergent Gouarne** (1928/1939, 1146grt, 66.3(pp)x10.1x5.7m, 10.5kts, 3 x 1 - 100/45, 2 x 1 – 37/50, 1 DCT, 2 DCR - sunk 26.3.1943); **P45 Aspirant Brun** (1928/1939, 1131grt, 66.3(pp) x10.1x5.7m, 10.5kts, 3 x 1 - 100/45, 2 x 1 – 37/50, 1 DCT, 2 DCR - mercantile 1944); **P82 Vivagel** (1927/1940, 1096grt, 63.4(pp)x10.3x5.2m, 10kts - conversion cancelled 1940); **P132 La Cancalaise** (1933/1940, 590t, 1 x 1 – 102/40 – sunk 1.5.1940); **P133 La Havraise** (1934/1940, 590t, 1 x 1 – 102/40 – scuttled 27.11.1942); **P134 La Lorientaise** (1933/1940, 590t, 1 x 1 – 102/40 – sunk 21.5.1940); **P135 La Nantaise** (1933/1940, 590t, 1 x 1 – 102/40 – captured by British 3.7.1940); **P136 L'Ajaccienne** (1936/1940, 590t, 1 x 1 – 102/40 – scuttled 9.11.1942, recommissioned 1944, stricken 1956); **P137 La Bônoise** (1934/1940, 590t, 1 x 1 – 102/40 – scuttled 9.11.1942, recommissioned 1944, stricken 1948); **P138 La Toulonnaise** (1934/1940, 590t, 1 x 1 – 102/40 – scuttled 9.11.1942, recommissioned 1944, stricken 1960); **P139 La Sétoise** (1934/1940, 590t, 1 x 1 – 102/40 – scuttled 9.11.1942, recommissioned 1944, stricken 1960).

La Sétoise postwar

100-500grt capacity
Requisitioned: 5 (1939), 15 (1940)
Discarded: 1 (1939), 2 (1940), 1 (1944), 1 (1945)
Lost: 11 (1940)

Merchant vessels (mostly trawlers) converted to patrols.

Vikings was torpedoed by German submarine *U562* 17.4.1942 off Syrian coast, *Sergeant Gouarne* was also torpedoed by German submarine 26.3.1943.

P136 - 139 were scuttled at Oran 9.11.1942, salvaged and re-commissioned in 1944 with following data: 425/466t, 48.8x8.1x3.7m, 1 boiler, 1 VTE, 800hp, 10kts, 1 x 1 - 102/40 Mk IV, 4 x 1 – 13.2 MG, sweeps.

Armed yachts

P98 Alphée (ex-Nimet Allah) (1933/1940, 1060t, 71.3(pp)x9.6x4.0m, 14kts, 1 x 1 - 75/35 - paid off 12.1940); **AD185 Girundia II** (1910/1940, 1200t, 70.4(pp)x9.5m, 14kts, 1 x 1 - 75/35, 2 x 1 - 20/70 - BU 1948); *P140 L'Incomprise II* (ex-Eros) (1926/-, 1109t, 67.0(pp)x9.8x4.5m, 12kts - captured incomplete by Germany 1942 (UJ2216))

Yachts converted to patrols and minesweeper.

'FLOWER' class corvettes

1st group
La Malouine (Smiths Dock, South Bank, UK, 11.1939/21.3.1940/(7.1940) - captured by UK 7.1940 (La Malouine)); *La Bastiaise* (Smiths Dock, South Bank, UK, 11.1939/8.4.1940/ - sunk during trials 22.6.1940); *La Dieppoise* (Smiths Dock, South Bank, UK, 1.1940/21.6.1940/(8.1940) - captured by UK 7.1940 (Fleur de Lys)); *La Paimpolaise* (Smiths Dock, South Bank, UK, 3.1940/4.7.1940/(9.1940) - captured by UK 7.1940 (Nasturtium))

2nd group
Arbalète (Harland & Wolff, Belfast, UK, 1940// - cancelled 1940); *Arc* (Smiths Dock, South Bank, UK, 1940// - cancelled 1940); *Arquebuse* (A C de la St-Nazaire-Penhoët, 1939/16.10.1940/(4.1944) - completed as German PA1); *Carabine* (Smiths Dock, South Bank, UK, 1940// - cancelled 1940); *Dague* (Harland & Wolff, Belfast, UK, 1940// - cancelled 1940); *Flèche* (Harland & Wolff, Belfast, UK, 1940// - cancelled 1940); *Fronde* (Smiths Dock, South Bank, UK, 1940// - cancelled 1940); *Glaive* (Smiths Dock, South Bank, UK, 1940// - cancelled 1940); *Hallebarde* (A C de la St-Nazaire-Penhoët, 1939/27.11.1940/(11.1943) - completed as German PA2); *Javeline* (A C de France, Dunkerque, 1940// - cancelled 1940); *Lance* (Harland & Wolff, Belfast, UK, 1940// - cancelled 1940); *Mousquet* (Harland & Wolff, Belfast, UK, 1940// - cancelled 1940); *Peruisane* (Smiths Dock, South Bank, UK, 1940// - cancelled 1940); *Pique* (Smiths Dock, South Bank, UK, 1940// - cancelled 1940); *Pistolet* (Smiths Dock, South Bank, UK, 1940// - cancelled 1940); *Poignard* (A C de la St-Nazaire-Penhoët, 1939/1941/ - captured by Germany on the stocks (PA4), scuttled incomplete 8.1944); *Sabre* (A C de la St-Nazaire-Penhoët, 1939/29.11.1940/(11.1943) - completed as German PA3); *Tromblon* (A C de France, Dunkerque, 1940// - cancelled 1940)

3rd group
Aconit (ex-Aconite) (Ailsa, Troon, UK, 3.1940/31.3.1941/7.1941 - to UK 4.1947); **Alysse** (ex-Alyssum) (George Brown, Greenock, UK, 6.1940/3.3.1941/(6.1941)/6.1941 - sunk 10.2.1942); **Commandant Drogou** (ex-Chrysanthemum) (Harland & Wolff, Belfast, UK, 12.1940/11.4.1941/1.1942 - to UK 5.1947); **Commandant Détroyat** (ex-Coriander) (Hall Russell, Aberdeen, UK, 1940/9.6.1941/7.1941 - to UK 1947 (Coriander)); **Lobélia** (ex-Lobelia) (Hall, Aberdeen, UK, 6.1940/15.2.1941/7.1941 - to UK 4.1947); **Commandant d'Estienne d'Orves** (ex-Lotus) (Hill, Bristol, UK, 5.1941/17.1.1942/5.1942 - to UK 5.1947); **Mimosa** (ex-Mimosa) (Hill, Bristol, UK, 4.1940/18.1.1941/5.1941 - sunk 9.6.1942); **Renoncule** (ex-Ranonculus) (Simons, Renfrew, UK, 1940/25.6.1941/7.1941 - to UK 1947); **Roselys** (ex-Sundew) (Lewis, Aberdeen, UK, 1940/28.5.1941/9.1941 - to UK 1947)

Lobélia 1942

Aconit 1943

925/1170t, 62.5x10.1x4.1m, 1vte/2b, 2750hp, 16.5kts, 230t oil, 3500(12)nm, 85-109p; *Built for France:* 1 x 1 – 100/45 M1932, 2 x 2 – 13.2 MG, 2 DCR (12); sonar. *Ex-RN ships:* 1 x 1 – 102/45 BL Mk IX, 1 x 1 – 40/39 pompom, 2 x 2 – 7.7 MG, 2 DCT, 2 DCR (40); Type 271 radar, Type 128 sonar.

4 ships of 1st group were built specially for France and should had French armament. After capitulation of France *La Malouine, La Dieppoise* and *La Paimpolaise* 1.7.1940 were confiscated by British Government and commissioned by the RN as *La Malouine, Fleur de Lys* and *Nasturtium*. Fourth ship, *La Bastiaise*, was lost on a mine 22.6.1940 during sea trials, formally being still the property of the builder.

18 more ships for French Navy were ordered in 1939 and 1940 to French and British builders. Any of them did not entered service under French flag.

9 ships of 2nd group were transferred to FNFL from RN in 1941-1942

By 1945, *Lobélia*: - 2 x 2 - 7.7 MG; + 4 x 1 - 20/70 Oerlikon, 2 DCT (72 DC at all), Type 271 radar, Type

128 sonar

By 1945, *Aconit, Commandant Drogou, Cmmandant Détroyat, Commandant d'Estienne d'Orves, Mimosa, Renoncule, Roselys*: - 2 x 2 - 7.7 MG; + 2 x 1 - 57/40 Hotchkiss, 2 x 1 - 20/70 Oerlikon, 2 DCT (72 DC at all).

Two ships became victims of German submarines: *Alysse* 8.2.1942 was damaged by *U654* and sank in two days, *Mimosa* 9.6.1942 was sunk by *U124*.

L'EVEILLÉ class coastal patrols

Sabre (ex-PC1248) (Nashville Bridge, USA, 6.1943/18.8.1943/1.1944 - BU 11.1959); **Cimeterre** (ex-PC1250) (Nashville Bridge, USA, 8.1943/18.12.1943/3.1944 - BU 7.1963); **Pique** (ex-PC1249) (Nashville Bridge, USA, 8.1943/6.11.1943/2.1944-BU 7.1959); **Dague** (ex-PC1561) (Leatham D. Smith SB, Sturgeon Bay, USA, 1943/1944/5.1944 - BU 5.1964); **Coutelas** (ex-PC1560) (Leatham D. Smith SB, Sturgeon Bay, USA, 11.1943/3.2.1944/4.1944 - BU 7.1963); **Javelot** (ex-PC1562) (Leatham D. Smith SB, Sturgeon Bay, USA, 1.1944/4.3.1944/6.1944 - BU 5.1951); **L'Eveillé** (ex-PC471) (Defoe, Bay City, USA, 4.1941/15.9.1941/(11.1941)/6.1944 - BU 12.1959); **L'Indiscret** (ex-PC474) (Defoe, Bay City, USA, 8.1941/15.9.1941/(2.1942)/6.1944 - BU 1.1960); **Le Résolu** (ex-PC475) (Defoe, Bay City, USA, 9.1941/16.12.1941/(12.1941)/6.1944 - stricken 1.1951); **L'Effronté** (ex-PC481) (Defoe, Bay City, USA, 2.1942/31.3.1942/(4.1942)/6.1944 - BU 5.1953); **Le Rusé** (ex-PC472) (Defoe, Bay City, USA, 7.1941/14.11.1941/(12.1941)/6.1944 - BU 1959); **L'Ardent** (ex-PC473) (Defoe, Bay City, USA, 8.1941/19.11.1941/(12.1941)/7.1944 - collision 31.1.1945); **L'Emorté** (ex-PC480) (Defoe, Bay City, USA, 1941/25.10.1941/(4.1942)/7.1944 - BU 7.1959); **L'Ehjoué** (ex-PC482) (Defoe, Bay City, USA, 2.1942/9.4.1942/(4.1942)/7.1944 - sunk 9.1.1945); **Le Volontaire** (ex-PC543) (Defoe, Bay City, USA, 3.1942/5.5.1942/(5.1942)/6.1944 - BU 9.1964); **Le Vigilant** (ex-PC550) (Leatham D. Smith SB, Sturgeon Bay, USA, 6.1941/8.3.1942/(4.1942)/6.1944 - BU 1.1959); **L'Attentif** (ex-PC562) (Jeffersonville, USA, 2.1942/4.6.1942/(8.1942)/6.1944 - BU 2.1953); **Hussard** (ex-PC1235) (Sullivan, Brooklyn, USA, 1942/1943/(1943)/10.1944 - BU 10.1965); **Légionnaire** (ex-PC1226) (Leatham D. Smith SB, Sturgeon Bay, USA, 7.1942/7.9.1942/(1.1943)/11.1944 - BU 7.1958); **Dragon** (ex-PC557) (Luders Marine, Stamford, USA, 10.1941/2.8.1942/(10.1942)/10.1944 - BU 1.1959); **Goumier** (ex-PC545) (Defoe, Bay City, USA, 3.1942/8.5.1942/(6.1942)/10.1944 - to Morocco 1965 (Agadir)); **Carabinier** (ex-PC556) (Luders Marine, Stamford, USA, 10.1941/23.6.1942/(9.1942)/10.1944 - BU 7.1958); **Fantassin** (ex-PC621) (Nashville Bridge, USA, 3.1942/22.5.1942/(12.1942)/10.1944 - BU 3.1961); **Grenadier** (ex-PC625) (Jeffersonville, USA, 5.1942/22.7.1942/(9.1942)/10.1944 - BU 1.1958); **Le Tirailleur** (ex-PC542) (Defoe, Bay City, USA, 2.1942/20.4.1942/(5.1942)/9.1944 - BU 1.1958); **Voltigeur** (ex-PC559) (Jeffersonville, USA, 10.1941/2.1.1942/(5.1942)/10.1944 - BU 3.1970); **Lancier** (ex-PC1227) (Leatham D. Smith SB, Sturgeon Bay, USA, 1942/17.10.1942/(1943)/11.1944 - BU 8.1960); **Franc-Tireur** (ex-PC546) (Defoe, Bay City, USA, 4.1942/15.5.1942/(7.1942)/10.1944 - BU 2.1953); **Mameluck** (ex-PC551) (Leatham D. Smith SB, Sturgeon Bay, USA, 7.1941/12.4.1942/(5.1942)/10.1944 - BU 1.1958); **Lansquenet** (ex-PC626) (Jeffersonville, USA, 6.1942/18.8.1942/(10.1942)/11.1944 - BU 9.1958); **Cavalier** (ex-PC627) (Jeffersonville, USA, 6.1942/7.9.1942/(11.1942)/10.1944 - BU 6.1951); **Spahi** (ex-PC591) (Leatham D. Smith SB, Sturgeon Bay, USA, 5.1942/2.8.1942/(10.1942)/10.1944 - BU 12.1959)

Sabre 1944

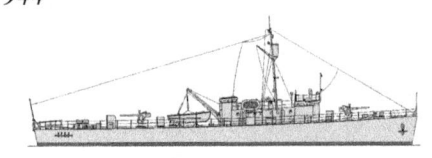

325/430t, 52.9x7.1x2.4m, 2d, 2880hp, 20kts, 49t diesel oil, 3000(12)nm, 65p; 1 x 1 – 76/50 Mk 20/21, 1 x 1 – 40/56 Bofors, 5 x 1 – 20/70 Oerlikon, 2 x 4 Mousetrap ASWRL, 2 DCT, 2 DCR (24); SF or SO or SU radar, QHA sonar.

US-built 173ft PC-type patrols, transferred to France under lend-lease in 1944. 11 more ships were transferred from USA in 1949-1951.

L'Ardent was lost at Casablanca as result of collision 31.1.1945. *L'Enjoué* was sunk by German submarine *U870* 9.1.1945.

FRANCE

LOUP class patrol tugs

Loup (F C de la Méditerranée, La Seyne, 1917 - scuttled 27.11.1942); **Marcassin** (F C de la Méditerranée, La Seyne, 1917 - scuttled 27.11.1942); **Sanglier** (F C de la Méditerranée, La Seyne, 1917 - stricken 1940)

285t, 1vte/1b, 600hp, 10kts; 1 x 1 – 75/35 M1897. Patrol tugs.
Loup and *Marcassin* were scuttled at Toulon 27.11.1942, latter was salvaged by Germans 6.10.1943 but 5.7.1944 sunk again by Allied aircraft.

HIPPOPOTAME class patrol tugs

Hippopotame (Penhoët, St-Nazaire, 1918 - stricken 1952); **Mammouth** (Ch de Normandie, Rouen, 1917 - captured by British 3.7.1940); **Mastodonte** (Ch de Normandie, Rouen, 1919 - captured by British 3.7.1940); **Rhinocéros** (Penhoët, St-Nazaire, 1918 - captured by Germans 8.12.1942)

970t, 1vte/2b, 1800hp, 12kts; 2 x 1 – 75/35 M1897. Patrol tugs.
Mammouth and *Mastodonte* were captured by British 3.7.1940, returned in 1945 and used as tugs. *Rhinocéros* was captured by Germans 8.12.1942 at Bizerte and bombed by Allied aircraft 25.3.1943 at Sousse.

AUROCHS class patrol tugs

Aurochs (A C de Bretagne, Nantes, 1918 - captured by Germans 6.1940, returned 1945, stricken 1949); **Élan**, 1940- **Élan II** (A C de Bretagne, Nantes, 1919 - captured by British 3.7.1940); **Renne** (A C de Bretagne, Nantes, 1918 - captured by Germans 8.12.1942); **Zébu** (A C de Bretagne, Nantes, 1917 - foundered 12.6.1940)

290t, 1vte/1b, 650hp, 10kts; 1 x 1 – 90/24 M1891, 1 x 1 – 47/40 M1885.
Tugs used as patrols.
Élan II was captured by British 3.7.1940, used as barrage balloon vessel and later as target tug, she was returned in 1945 and scrapped. *Renne* was captured by Germans at Bizerte 8.12.1942 and bombed by Allied aircraft 7.12.1943. *Zébu* foundered 12.6.1940 off Le Havre. *Aurochs* was captured by Germans in June 1940 and returned in 1945.

CLAMEUR class patrol tugs

Clameur (SPCN, La Ciotat, 1918 - stricken 1940); **Fracas** (SPCN, La Ciotat, 1917 - minesweeper 1939, scuttled 5.1943); **Tumulte** (F C de la Gironde, Bordeaux, 1918 - sunk 21.5.1940); **Vacarme** (SPCN, La Ciotat, 1918 - foundered 6.8.1940)

370t, 1vte/2b, 720hp, 12kts; 1 x 1 – 90/24 M1891.
Tugs used as patrols.
1939, *Facas*: + sweeps.
Tumulte was bombed by German aircraft 21.5.1940 at Dunkirk. *Vacarme* foundered 6.8.1942.

ATHLETE class patrol tugs

Athlete (Arsenal de Brest, 1917 - scuttled 18.6.1940); **Lutteur** (Arsenal de Brest, 1919 - scuttled 18.6.1940)

585t, 2vte/1b, 500hp, 12kts; 2 x 1 – 120/40 QF Mk IV. Patrol tugs.
Lutteur and *Athlete* were scuttled at Brest 18.6.1940, former was salvaged by Germans but later lost in unknown circumstances.

NAVARIN class patrol vessels

Lutzen (Canadian Car Co, Fort William, Canada, 6.1918/31.8.1918/11.1918 - wrecked 3.2.1939); **Malakoff** (Canadian Car Co, Fort William, Canada, 9.1918/1.10.1918/11.1918 - sold 1951)

640t, 1vte, 500hp, 11kts, 31p; 1 x 1 – 100/45 M1893.   Patrol trawlers, suffered from low stability.

MAUVIETTE class patrol vessel

Passereau II (F C de la Méditerranée, La Seyne, 1918 - stricken 1946)

420/460t, 43.5x7.3x4.2m, 1vte/1b, 10kts, 120t coal; 1 x 1 – 90/24 M1891, 1 x 1 – 47/40 M1885, sweeps.   Patrol/minesweeping trawler.

PLUVIER class patrol tugs

Canard (A C de la Loire, St-Nazaire, 1918/(1939) - minesweeper, scuttled 13.11.1942); **Coq** (A C de la Loire, St-Nazaire, 1918/(1939) – minesweeper, discarded 1945); **Faisan** (A C de la Loire, St-Nazaire, 1918 - captured by British 3.7.1940, returned 1945, discarded 1945); **Gelinotte** (A C de la Loire, St-Nazaire, 1918 - stricken 1951); **Heron II** (A C de la Loire, Nantes, 1918 - scuttled 27.11.1942); **Paon** (A C de la Loire, St-Nazaire, 1918 - captured by Germans 11.1942 (M7601)); **Pigeon** (A C de la Loire, Nantes, 1918 - minesweeper 1939, scuttled 9.11.1942); **Pingouin II** (A C de la Loire, Nantes, 1918 - captured by British 3.7.1940, returned 1945, discarded 1949); **Pintade** (A C de la Loire, Nantes, 1918 - captured by British 3.7.1940, returned 1945, discarded 1945); **Ramier** (A C de la Loire, St-Nazaire, 1918 - captured by British 3.7.1940, returned 1945, discarded 1949); **Tourterelle** (A C de la Loire, Nantes, 1918 - scuttled 9.11.1942, returned 1945, condemned 1956)

680-780t, 1vte, 750hp, 11kts.
Tugs used as patrols.
1939, *Canard, Coq, Pigeon*: + sweeps.

Pingouin II, Pintade, Faisan and *Ramier* were captured by British 3.7.1940 and returned after war. *Tourterelle* was scuttled at Oran 9.11.1942, salvaged by Germans in 1943, returned in 1945. *Heron II* was scuttled 27.11.1942 at Toulon, salvaged in 1946 and discarded in 1949. *Paon* was captured by Germans in November 1942 at Toulon and served under German flag as minesweeper *M7601*, she sank as result of internal explosion 2.10.1944 at La Spezia.

CRABE class patrol tugs

Calmar (Arsenal de Brest, 1920 - captured by Germans 12.1942 (GL4)); **Cèdre** (Arsenal de Lorient, 1918 - stricken 1945); **Chêne** (Arsenal de Lorient, 1918 - scuttled 8.11.1942); **Crabe** (Arsenal de Brest, 1918 - captured by British 7.1940); **Erable** (Arsenal de Lorient, 1918 - stricken 1945); **Frêne** (Arsenal de Lorient, 1919 - captured by British 7.1940); **Hêtre** (Arsenal de Lorient, 1919 - stricken 1946); **Homard** (Arsenal de Brest, 1920 - minesweeper 1939, captured by Germans 12.1942 (GL2)); **Orme** (Arsenal de Lorient, 1918 - scuttled 21.5.1940); **Peuplier** (Arsenal de Lorient, 1919 - captured by British 7.1940); **Platane** (Arsenal de Lorient, 1919 - stricken ~1946); **Tourteau** (Arsenal de Brest, 1918 - minesweeper 1939, captured by British 7.1940)

360-370t, 1vte/1b, 400hp, 9-10kts; 1 x 1 – 90/24 M1891.
Tugs served as patrols.
1939, *Homard, Tourteau*: + sweeps

Crabe, Frêne, Peuplier and *Tourteau* were captured by British in July 1940, used as gate vessels, and returned in 1945 (except *Peuplier* bombed at Plymouth 30.4.1941). *Homard* was captured by Germans in November 1942 and sunk by Allied aircraft 2.10.1944 at La Spezia. *Calmar* was captured by Germans in November 1942 and sunk by Allied aircraft 5.7.1944 at Toulon. *Erable* was captured by Germans in November 1942 at Toulon, served under German flag as minesweeper *M6024* and sunk 11.3.1944 at Toulon by Allied aircraft. *Orme* was scuttled 21.5.1940 at Boulogne, salvaged by Germans, renamed *FH02* and sunk 2.8.1944 by Allied aircraft at Le Havre. *Chêne* was scuttled at Oran 8.11.1942.

FRANCE

Auxiliary harbor patrol craft

100-500grt capacity
Requisitioned: 5 (1939)
Discarded: 3 (1940)
Lost: 1 (1940), 1 (1941)

Small merchant vessels converted for patrol and guard service. Many smaller vessels were also converted and received VP numeration.

AMIRAL MOUCHEZ armed survey vessel

Amiral Mouchez (Arsenal de Cherbourg, 1.1935/3.8.1936/1937 - FNFL 7.1940, BU 8.1965)

781/970t, 62.0x10.3x3.4m, 1d, 800hp, 12kts, 2500(10) nm, 81p; 2 x 1 – 100/45 M1932.

Amiral Mouchez 1945

Heavy armed survey vessel intended also for patrol service in the wartime. After war she received patrol (P) designation.
1942-1943: + 4 x 1 - 20/70 Oerlikon, 2 x 1 - 13.2 MG, 4 DCT, 2 DCR (32), radar.

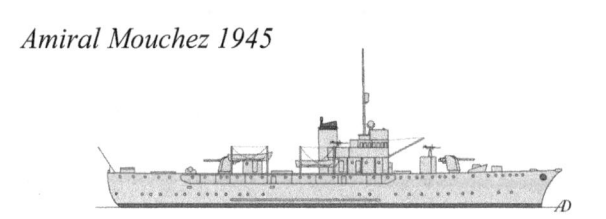

Riverine and coastal forces

DOUDART DE LA GRÉE river gunboat

A C de Bretagne, Nantes: Doudart de la Grée (1909)
Discarding: Doudart de la Grée (1941)

183t, 54.4x6.7x1.0m, 2vte/2b, 900hp, 14kts, 45t coal, 66p; 1 x 1 – 75/35 M1897, 2 x 1 – 37/20 M1885, 4 x 1 – 8 MG.
Designed for service on Yangtze, ordered in 1908.
Doudart de la Grée was laid up at Shanghai in 1939 and scrapped in 1941.

Doudart de la Grée 1920

C101 class river gunboats, former submarine chasers

A C Dubigeon, Nantes: Commandant Bourdais (ex-Ch111, ex-C111), Avalanche (ex-Ch112, ex-C112)
Losses: Commandant Bourdais, Avalanche (1945)

130/150t, 43.4x5.2x2.4m, 2vte/2b, 1300hp, 16.5kts, 32t coal, 31p; 1 x 1 – 75/35 M1897, 1 x 1 – 8 MG.
VTE-engined submarine chasers, designed and built in France in the end of the First World War. Two chasers, *Ch111* and *Ch112*, were converted to river gunboats for service in Indochina.
Both gunboats were destroyed 9.3.1945: *Commandant Bourdais* was scuttled, and *Avalanche* was sunk by gunfire of aviso *Amiral Charner*.

BALNY river gunboat

Balny (A C de Bretagne, Nantes, 1908/6.1914/1920 - laid up 1940, BU 1944)

Balny

201/226t, 54.4x6.7x1.0m, 2vte/2b, 900hp, 14kts, 27t coal, 59p; 2 x 1 – 75/35 M1897, 2 x 1 – 37/40 M1902, 4 x 1 – 8 MG.

Designed for service on Yangtze. Originally, she should be sister-ship of *Doudart de la Grée* but construction was delayed between 1914 and 1918 and ship was completed under little changed design.

Balny was laid up at Chungking in 1940 and scrapped in 1944.

VIGILANTE class river gunboats

Argus (Arsenal de Toulon, 1922/1923 - laid up 1940, BU 1941); **Vigilante** (Arsenal de Toulon, 1922/1923 - scuttled 9.3.1945)

Vigilante 1924

178/218t, 51.8x7.7x1.2m, 2vte/2b, 600hp, 12kts, 42p; 2 x 1 – 75/35 M1897, 2 x 1 – 37/40 M1902, 4 x 1 – 8 MG.

Small gunboats for Chinese rivers.

Argus was laid up at Haiphong in 1940 and scrapped next year. *Vigilante* was scuttled at Haiphong 9.3.1945 to avoid capture by Japanese.

FRANCIS GARNIER river gunboat

Francis Garnier (CNF, Caen, 1926/12.1927/1931 - scuttled 9.3.1945)

Francis Garnier 1940

Francis Garnier 1930

639t, 62.5(pp)x10.3x2.2m, 2vte/2b, 3200hp, 15kts, 100t oil, 103p; 2 x 1 – 100/45 M1917, 1 x 1 – 75/50 M1924, 2 x 1 – 37/50 M1925, 4 x 1 – 8 MG.

Largest gunboat for Chinese rivers ever built.

Francis Garnier was scuttled at Kratie (Mekong) 9.3.1945 to avoid capture by Japanese.

FRANCE

MYTHO class small river gunboats

Arsenal de Saigon, French Indochina: Mytho (1933), Tourane (1936)
Losses: Mytho, Tourane (1945)

95t, 35.0(pp)x5.4x0.9m, 2d, 250hp, 10kts, 500(10)nm; 1 x 1 – 75/35 M1897, 1 x 1 – 47/40 M1885, 2 x 1 – 8 MG, 1 x 1 mortar.
Small river gunboats for Chinese waters, did not had battle value.
Mytho was captured by IJN 9.3.1945 on Mekong and sunk by sloop *Amiral Charner* later that day, *Tourane* was scuttled 9.3.1945 on river Donai to avoid capture by Japanese.

Mytho 1934

VTB1 class motor torpedo boats

Thornycroft, Hampton, UK: VTB1 (1928)
A C de la Loire, Nantes: VTB2 – 7 (1928-1929)
Discarding: VTB4 – 7 (late 1930s)
Losses: VTB1 – 3 (1940)

11t, 18.3x3.4x0.9m, 2pe, 900hp, 40kts, 5p; 1 x 1 – 8 MG, 2 – 400 TC.
Presumably standard Thornycroft "CMB-55" type (m. b. nearly improved).

VTB7 1930

By the outbreak of war three boats were still used for training, all were captured by British 3.7.1940.

VTB8 class motor torpedo boats

A C de la Loire, Nantes: VTB8, 9 (1935)
Losses: VTB8 (1939)
Discarding: VTB9 (1944)

21/28t, 18.9x4.9x1.2m, 2pe, 2200hp, 46kts; 2 x 1 – 7.5 MG, 2 – 400 TT, 6 DC.
First French-origin MTBs.

VTB10 motor torpedo boat

A C de la Loire, Nantes: VTB10 (1936)
Discarding: VTB10 (1939)

21/28t, 20.0x4.0x1.2m, 2pe, 2600hp, 45kts; 2 x 1 – 7.5 MG, 2 – 400 TT, 6 DC.
Nearly sister-boat of previous pair with experimental machinery. Because of problems with engines *VTB10* never served actively.

VTB11 class motor torpedo boats

A C de la Loire, Nantes: VTB11, 12 (1939), VTB13 (incomplete), VTB14 (completed 1945 as auxiliary)
Transfers: UK – VTB11, 12 (1940)

28t, 20.0x4.0x1.2m, 2pe, 2200hp, 45kts, 330(45)nm; 1 x 1 – 12.7 MG (*VTB13, 14*), 1 x 2 – 7.5 MG (*VTB11, 12*), 2 – 400 TT, 1 DCR (6).

VTB13 was completed in 1941 with British guns. *VTB14* was incomplete till the end of war.
Partially completed *VTB11* and *VTB12* in June 1940 escaped to Britain and were commissioned by RN as *MGB98* and *MGB99*.

VTB23 class motor torpedo boats

British Power Boat, Hythe, UK: VTB23 – 27 (1940), VTB28 – 40 (captured incomplete by UK 1940)
Losses: VTB23 - 27 (1940)

34/38t, 21.3x6.1x1.2m, 3pe, 3300hp, 43kts, 11t petrol, 11p; 1 x 2 – 13.2 MG, 4 – 400 TT, 2 DCR (10).

VTB23-40 were ordered in Britain under British Power Boat design.
All completed and incomplete boats were captured by British 3.7.1940 and served under British flag as *MGB50-67*.

Ex-British MTB90 class motor torpedo boats

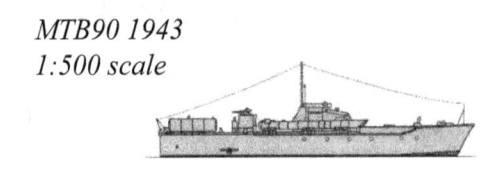

MTB90 1943
1:500 scale

Harland & Wolff, Belfast, UK: MTB90, 91 (1942/1943), MTB92 (1943/1943)
Berthon, UK: MTB94 (1942/1943)
Morgan Gyles, Teignmouth, UK: MTB96 (1942/1943)
Vosper, Portsmouth, UK: MTB98 (1942/1943)
McLean, Renfrew, UK: MTB227 (1942/1943)
Camper & Nicholson, Gosport, UK: MTB239 (1942/1943)

39/47t, 22.1x5.8x1.3m, 3pe, 3750hp, 38kts, 9t petrol, 1800(18)nm, 12-13p; 1 x 2 – 12.7 MG, 2 x 2 – 7.7 MG, 2 – 533 TT, 4 or 2 (*MTB227, 239*) DC; Type 286U or Type 286PU radar.
British-built ex-RN Vosper-type MTBs. Returned to UK in 1946.

VLT1 class motor torpedo boats

C N de Meulan: VLT1 (ex-FL.F307), VLT2 (ex-FL.F305), V120 (ex-FL.F301) (1945), V121 (ex-FK.F302) (1946)

75/94t, 30.4x5.9x1.8m, 4pe+1pe(3), 4400+1800=6200hp, 50kts, 10t petrol, 1000(15)nm, 18p; *VLT1, 2:* 2 x 1 – 40/56 FlaK 28, 1 x 2 – 20/65 C/38, 2 – 550 TT (4); *V120, 121:* 2 x 3 – 15 MG.
Ex-German Lüftwaffe rescue boats, completed after war by French as MTBs. Planned V122-125 *(ex-FL.F303, 304, 306* and *308)* were never completed.

Ex-US C1 class submarine chasers

Ch25 1940

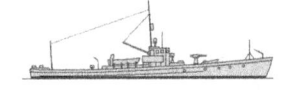

Wheeler, Brooklyn, USA: Ch25 (ex-C25, ex-SC160) (1917)
Matthews Boat, Port Clinton, USA: Ch26 (ex-C26, ex-SC172, 9.1939- VP108, 1942- V88) (1917), VP107

FRANCE

Colonel Casse (ex-C31, ex-SC173), Ch81 (ex-C81, ex-SC386), Ch91 (ex-C91, ex-SC389) (1918)
ELCO, Bayonne, USA: Ch51 (ex-C51, ex-SC364) (1918)
College Point Boat, USA: Ch56 (ex-C56, ex-SC358) (1918)
Hiltebrant, Kingston, USA: Ch58 (ex-C58, ex-SC372) (1918)
Kyle & Purdy, City Is, USA: Ch74 (ex-C74, ex-SC376) (1918)
Gibbs Gas Engine, Jacksonville, USA: Ch95 (ex-C95, ex-SC368) (1918)
New York Yacht, Morris Heights, USA: Ch98 (ex-C98, ex-SC401) (1918)
Losses: Ch91 (1937), Ch98 (1940), Ch25, V88, Ch81 (1942)
Discarding: Ch51, 56, 58, 74, 95 (1939)

C60 1920

75/85t, 33.5x4.7x2.3m, 3pe, 660hp, 16.5kts, 7t petrol, 1000(12)nm, 27p; 1 x 1 – 75/35 M1897, 2 x 1 – 8 MG, 1 DCT; hydrophone.
Sister-boats of USN 110ft SCs built in 1917-1919.
Ch25 was scuttled at Toulon 27.11.1942. *Ch81* was 8.121942 captured by Germans at Bizerte and scuttled 6.5.1943. *Ch98* was captured by British 3.7.1940.

C101 class submarine chasers

Augustin-Normand, Le Havre: Ch106 (ex-C106) (1919)
A C de la Loire, Nantes: Ch107 (ex-C107) (1919)
A C Dubigeon, Nantes: Ch115 (ex-C115) (1920)
Losses: Ch106, 107 (1940)
Discarding: Ch115 (1938)

130/150t, 43.4x5.2x2.4m, 2vte/2b, 1300hp, 16.5kts, 32t coal, 31p; 1 x 1 – 75/35 M1897, 1 x 1 – 8 MG, 1 DCT (8), 1 Pinocchio towed AS torpedo.
VTE-engined submarine chasers, designed and built in France in the end of the First World War.

C105 1930

Ch106 was captured by British 3.7.1940. *Ch107* was lost in Loire mouth 12.4.1940.

CH1 class submarine chasers

A C de Bretagne, Nantes: Ch1 – 4 (1934)
Losses: Ch1, 4 (1942)
Discarding: Ch2 (1945)

148/180t, 48.1x5.5x1.9m, 2d, 2400hp, 20kts, 41p; 1 x 1 – 75/35 M1897, 2 x 1 – 8 MG, 1 DCR, sweeps.
First French inter-war submarine chasers.
By 1940, all: ASW armament consisted of 4 DCT, 1 DCR (10).
Ch1 and *Ch4* were scuttled at Toulon 27.11.1942, both were salvaged by Germans. *Ch1* was sunk by Allied aircraft 6.8.1944, *Ch4* served under German flag as *UJ6077* and was sunk by Allied aircraft 5.7.1944.

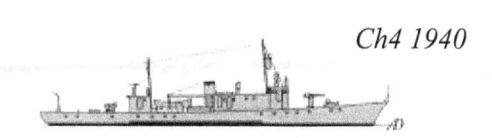

Ch4 1940

Ch3 1936

CH5 class submarine chasers

A C de France, Dunkerque: Ch5 (1943- Carentan), Ch6, 7, Ch8 (1942- Rennes) (1940)
F C de la Méditerranée, Le Havre: Ch9, Ch10 (1942- Bayonne), Ch11 (1941- Boulogne), Ch12 (1941- Bénodet) (1940), Ch19, 21 (1946), Ch17, 18 (completed for Germany), Ch20 (incomplete)
A C de la Seine-Maritime, Le Trait: Ch13 (1942- Calais), Ch14 (1942- Diélette), Ch15 (1941- Paimpol) (1940), Ch16 (incomplete)
From UK: Boulogne (ex-Ch11), Bénodet (ex-Ch12), Diélette (ex-Ch14), Paimpol (ex-Ch15) (1940/1941), Rennes (ex-Ch8), Bayonne (ex-Ch10), Calais (ex-Ch13) (1940/1942), Carentan (ex-Ch5) (1940/1943)
Losses: Ch5 - 15 (1940), Rennes (1942), Carentan (1943)

107/137t, 37.1x5.7x2.0m, 2d, 1130hp, 15.5kts, 5.5t diesel oil, 1200(8)nm, 23p; 1 x 1 – 75/35 M1897, 2 x 1 – 8 MG, 4 DCT, 1 DCR (10), sweeps.

Close to the previous class. Incomplete *Ch16* was scuttled at Lorient 18.6.1940. Incomplete *Ch17-21* received German names *RA6, 7, 1, 2* and *8*, respectively.
1942, FNFL ships: - 2 x 1 – 8 MG; + 1 x 1 - 40/39 pompom, 1 x 2 - 12.7 MG, 2 x 2 - 7.7 MG (20 DC at all).
Ch9 21.5.1940 off Dunkirk was damaged by German aircraft and ran aground. *Ch5, 8, 10-13* and *15* were captured by British 3.7.1940. All were subsequently transferred to FNFL – *Boulogne (ex-Ch11), Bénodet (ex-Ch12), Diélette (ex-Ch14)* and *Paimpol (ex-Ch15)* in 1941, *Rennes (ex-Ch8), Bayonne (ex-Ch10)* and *Calais (ex-Ch13)* in 1942 and *Carentan (ex-Ch5)* in 1943. *Ch5* was lost 21.12.1943 in La Manche during a storm. *Ch6* and *Ch7* were sunk 11.11.1940 in La Manche by German torpedo boats. According to some information, they were crewed by Polish seamen. *Ch8* was sunk 13.7.1942 by German aircraft in La Manche. *Ch11* and *Ch15* served since 19.7.1940 till 6.2.1941 under Polish flag.

CH41 class submarine chasers

Ch de Normandie, Fécamp: Ch41 (1940- Audierne), Ch42 (1942- Larmor), Ch43 (1940- Lavandou) (1940), Ch44 – 48 (completed for Germany)
From UK: Audierne (ex-Ch41), Larmor (ex-Ch42), Lavandou (ex-Ch43) (1940/1940)
Losses: Ch41 – 43 (1940)

126/160t, 37.4x5.5x2.4m, 2d, 1130hp, 15.5kts, 6.5t diesel oil, 1100(13)nm, 23p; 1 x 1 – 75/35 M1897, 2 x 1 – 8 MG, 4 DCT, 1 DCR (10).
Wooden hull. *Ch44, 45* and *46* were completed by Germans as *RA4, 3* and *5*, respectively. *Ch47* and *48* were broken up by Germans on slipways.
1942, FNFL ships: + 1 x 1 - 40/39 pompom.
Ch41, 42 and *43* were captured by British 3.7.1940 and later transferred to FNFL.

Ex-US CH5 class submarine chasers

Ch5 1944

Calderwood, Manchester, USA: Ch5 (ex-SC1359), Ch107 (ex-SC693) (1943/1944), Ch131 (ex-SC692) (1942/1944)
Simms Bros, Dorchester, USA: Ch6 (ex-SC1331), Ch146 (ex-SC979) (1943/1944), Ch94 (ex-SC977), Ch145 (ex-SC978) (1942/1944)
Thomas Knutson, Halesite, USA: Ch51 (ex-SC1336), Ch52 (ex-SC1335), Ch71 (ex-SC1337) (1943/1943)
Rice Bros, E. Boothbay, USA: Ch61 (ex-SC1345), Ch62 (ex-SC1344) (1943/1943), Ch72 (ex-SC1346), Ch126 (ex-SC1044) (1943/1944) (1943/1944), Ch112 (ex-SC503, ex-PC503), Ch125 (ex-SC1043) (1942/1944)
Elizabeth City, USA: Ch81 (ex-SC516, ex-PC516), Ch82 (ex-SC517, ex-PC517), Ch93 (ex-SC639, ex-PC639), Ch116 (ex-SC638, ex-PC638), Ch121 (ex-SC515, ex-PC515) (1942/1944)
Vineyard, Milford, USA: Ch83 (ex-SC519, ex-PC519) (1942/1944)
Mathis Yacht, Camden, USA: Ch84 (ex-SC529, ex-PC529), Ch85 (ex-SC507, ex-PC507), Ch95 (ex-SC508, ex-PC509), Ch101 (ex-SC524, ex-PC524), Ch102 (ex-SC525, ex-PC525), Ch114 (ex-SC526, ex-PC526) (1942/1944)
Delaware Bay, Leesburg, USA: Ch91 (ex-SC649, ex-PC649) (1942/1944)

Daytona Beach, USA: Ch92 (ex-SC697), Ch133 (ex-SC695) (1942/1944)
Westergard, Rockport, USA: Ch96 (ex-SC497, ex-PC497), Ch115 (ex-SC530, ex-PC530), Ch135 (ex-SC651, ex-PC651), Ch142 (ex-SC498, ex-PC498), Ch144 (ex-SC655, ex-PC655) (1942/1944)
Luders Marine, Stamford, USA: Ch103 (ex-SC532, ex-PC532), Ch104 (ex-SC533, ex-PC533), Ch113 (ex-SC506, ex-PC506), Ch122 (ex-SC534, ex-PC534), Ch143 (ex-SC535, ex-PC535) (1942/1944)
W. A. Robinson, Ipswich, USA: Ch105 (ex-SC676, ex-PC676) (1942/1944)
Annapolis Yacht, USA: Ch106 (ex-SC690), Ch111 (ex-SC522, ex-PC522), Ch132 (ex-SC691) (1942/1944)
Donovan, Burlington, USA: Ch123 (ex-SC1029), Ch136 (ex-SC1030) (1942/1944)
Seabrook Yacht, USA: Ch124 (ex-SC771) (1943/1944), Ch141 (ex-SC770) (1942/1944)
Weaver, Orange, USA: Ch134 (ex-SC666) (1942/1944)
Losses: Ch116 (1945)

110/138t, 33.8x5.2x1.9m, 2d, 1000 or 2400hp, 16 or 21kts, 18t diesel oil, 1500(12)nm, 27p; 1 x 1 – 40/56 Bofors, 3 x 1 – 20/70 Oerlikon, 2 x 4 Mousetrap ASWRL, 2 DCT, 2 DCR (34); SF or SU or SO or SCR-517A or SW-1C radar, QC sonar.
US-built 110ft submarine chasers, transferred to France under lend-lease in 1943-1944. 7 more boats were transferred in 1951.
Ch116 was lost on a mine 21.8.1945.

Ex-British 'Fairmile B' type motor launches

H. J. Percival, Horning, UK: Ved.101 St-Ronan (ex-ML244) (1941/1943)
Boat Construction Co., Falmouth, UK: Ved.102 St-Yves (ex-ML271) (1941/1943)
King, Burnham, UK: Ved.103 St-Guénolé (ex-ML266), Ved.104 St-Alain (ex-ML302) (1941/1943)
Curtis, Looe, UK: ML123 (1941/1942)
Leo Robertson, Tewkesbury: ML182 (1941/1942)
Jas Taylor, Chertsey, UK: ML205 (1941/1942)
Sheerness DYd, UK: ML245, 246 (1941/1942)
J. W. & A. Upham, Brixham, UK: ML247 (1941/1942)
Solent SYd, Sarisbury Green, UK: ML267 (1941/1942)
Dorset Yacht, Hamworthy, UK: ML268 (1941/1942)
William Weatherhead, Cockenzie, UK: ML269 (1941/1942)
Jas Miller, St. Monace, UK: ML303 (1941/1942)
Taylor, Toronto, Canada: V111 Galantry (ex-ML052) (1941/1943)
Mac Craft, Sarnia, Canada: V112 Langdale (ex-ML062), V113 Colombier (ex-ML063) (1942/1943)

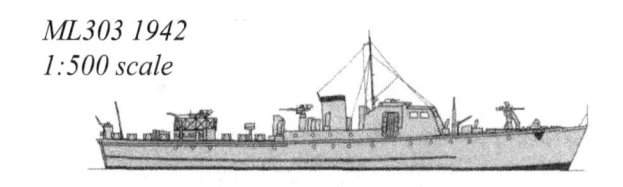

ML303 1942
1:500 scale

Losses: ML267, 268 (1942)
Transfers: UK – ML123, 182, 205, 245 – 247, 267 – 269, 303 (1942); Canada – V112 Langdale (1945)

76/86t, 34.8x5.6x1.5m, 2pe, 1200hp, 18kts, 9t petrol, 16p; 1 x 1 – 47/40 Hotchkiss, 1 x 1 – 20 Oerlikon, 2 x 2 – 7.7 MG, 1 DCR (12), Type 286PU radar (since 1942-1943), Type 134 sonar.
Ex-British and Canadian MLs of 'Fairmile B' type.
1943-1944, most survived: - Type 286PU radar; + Type 291U or Type 293 radar.
ML267 and *ML268* were lost during St-Nazaire raid 28.3.1942.

Ex-British 'HDML' type motor launches

Newman, Hamworthy, UK: VP1 (ex-ML1249), VP10 (ex-ML1250), VP12 (ex-ML1225) (1942/1943)
Leo Robinson, Lowestoft, UK: VP2 (ex-ML1138), VP16 (ex-ML1139) (1942/1943), VP41 Aventure (ex-ML1425) (1945/1945)
Anderson, Ridgen & Perkins, Whitstable, UK: VP3 (ex-ML1233) (1942-1943)

VP15 1943
1:500 scale

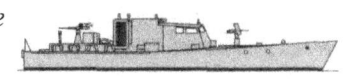

Berthon Boat, Lymington, UK: VP4 (ex-ML1240) (1942/1943)
Walker, Colombo, Ceylon: VP5 (ex-ML1166) (1943/1943), VP32 Baalbeck (ex-ML1164) (1942/1943)
Sittingbourne SB, UK: VP6 (ex-ML1228) (1943/1943), VP21 (ex-ML1072) (1941/1943)
Thornycroft, Hampton, UK: VP7 (ex-ML1133), VP8 (ex-ML1132), VP14 (ex-ML1136) (1942/1943)
Berthon Boat, Lymington, UK: VP9 (ex-ML1127) (1942/1943)
Blackmore, Bideford, UK: VP11 (ex-ML1152), VP23 (ex-ML1231) (1942/1943), VP42 Revanche (ex-ML1457) (1944/1945)
Woods, Potter Heigham, UK: VP13 (ex-ML1142), VP15 (ex-ML1144), VP31 Pal,yre (ex-ML1143) (1942/1943)
Bolson, Poole, UK: VP22 (ex-ML1141) (1942/1943)

44-46/52-54t, 22.0x4.8x1.4m, 2d, 260-300hp, 11-11.8kts, 6t diesel oil, 10p; 2 x 1 – 20/70 Oerlikon, 2 x 2 – 7.7 MG, 8 DC; Type 291U radar (some), Type 134 sonar.
British-built HDML-type wooden-hulled motor launches. 7 boats were additionally transferred in 1946-1955.

VP51 class motor launches

USA: VP51, 52, 61 – 63 (1943)

48(std)t, 15.9x4.4x1.6m, 2pe, 250hp, 12kts, 10p; 1 x 1 – 7.6 MG.
US-built MLs for Tahiti.

Mine warfare ships

Ex-Russian icebreakers converted to minelayers

Castor (ex-Koz'ma Minin) (1916/1929, 4576t, 75.2(pp)x17.3x6.4m, 14kts, 4 x 1 - 100/45, 2 x 1 – 37/50, 268 mines - paid off 1940); **Pollux** (ex-Ilya Muromets) (1917/1929, 2463t, 64.2(pp)x15.5x6.0m, 14kts, 4 x 1 - 100/45, 2 x 1 - 37, 236 mines - captured by British 3.7.1940)

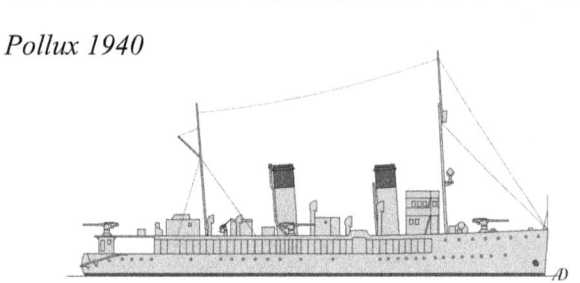

Castor 1930

Pollux 1930

Pollux 1940

Ex-Russian icebreakers, escaped from Russia to Bizerte under Wrangel command in 1922 and transferred to French Navy as payment for basing of White Russian squadron. Both were converted to minelayers in 1928-1929.
Castor was paid off at Bizerte after armistice, captured by Germans 8.12.1942 and scuttled there 6.5.1943. *Pollux* was captured by British 3.7.1940, served as TS and returned after war.

FRANCE

Auxiliary minelayers

Indéfatigable (1899/1939, 1142grt – captured by British 3.7.1940); **Samson** (1907/1939, 660grt – sunk 29.5.1940)

Tugs converted for service as minelayers.

LE GLADIATEUR netlayer

Le Gladiateur (Arsenal de Lorient, 1932/10.4.1933/1935 - scuttled 27.11.1942 (later German SG18))

1858/2293t, 113.0x12.7x3.5m, 2gst/2b, 6000hp, 18kts, 399t oil, 132p; 4 x 1 – 90/50 M1926, 6 x 1 – 8 MG, nets.
Unique purpose-built "offensive" netlayer of French Navy, analogue of British *Protector*.
Le Gladiateur was scuttled 27.11.1942 at Toulon by own crew to avoid capture. 30.3.1943 ship was salvaged by Italians but later captured by Germans and commissioned them in January 1944 as *SG18*. She was bombed and sunk by Allied aircraft 4.2.1944.

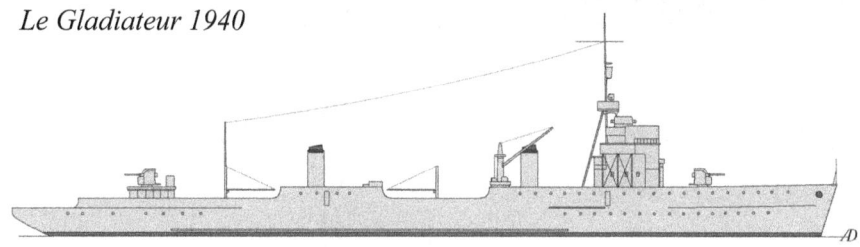

Le Gladiateur 1935

Le Gladiateur 1940

AVENTURIER class fast minesweepers

Aventurier (ex-Mendoza) (Dyle et Bacalan, Bordeaux, 1910/18.2.1911/9.1914 - stricken 1938); **Intrépide** (ex-Salta) (A C de Bretagne, Nantes, 1910/25.9.1911/11.1914 - stricken 1937)

915/1180t, 88.5x8.8x3.1m, 2st/5b, 12000hp, 26kts, 280t oil, 3000(15)nm, 140p; 3 x 1 – 100/45 M1893, 1 x 1 – 47/50 M1902, sweeps.
Former destroyers ordered in 1910 by Argentinean Navy but requisitioned by France 9.8.1914 when the World War One begun. In 1926 they were converted to fast minesweepers.

Intrépide 1928

ARDENT class 2nd class avisos - minesweepers

Audacieuse (A C de Provence, Port-de-Bouc, 1916/1917/1917 - BU 1.1940); **Batailleuse** (A C de Provence, Port-de-Bouc, 1916/1917/1917 - sunk as target 1938); **Dédaigneuse** (F C de la Gironde, Bordeaux, 1916/1916/1917 - scuttled 27.11.1942); **Étourdi** (Arsenal de Lorient, 1916/21.3.1916/1917 - scuttled 19.6.1940); **Gracieuse** (Arsenal de Lorient, 1916/1916/1916 - stricken 1938); **Impétueuse** (F C de la Gironde, Bordeaux, 1916/1917/1917 - stricken 1938); **Malicieuse** (A C de Provence, Port-de-Bouc, 1916/1916/1916 - stricken 1939); **Tapageuse** (A C de Provence, Port-de-Bouc, 1916/1917/1917 - FNFL 11.1942, BU 1944)

Gracieuse 1921

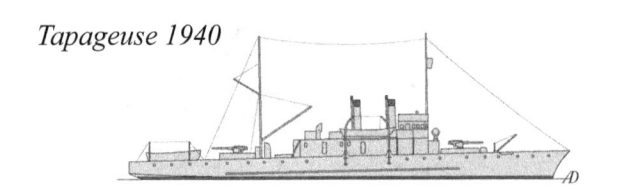

Tapageuse 1940

266/400(*Étourdi*)-310/410t, 60.2x7.2x2.9m, 1vte/2b(*Étourdi*) or 2vte/2b, 1200-1500(*Étourdi*) or 1200-2200hp, 14-17kts, 85t coal, 2000(10)nm, 55-60p; 2 x 1 – 145/45 M1910 (*Étourdi*), 2 x 1 – 100/45 (except *Étourdi*), 2 DCT, sweeps.

These ships were officially classified as "anti-submarine gunboats". Partly they were equipped with steam engines removed from old torpedo boats, therefore significantly differed from each other by machinery power and speed. Converted to minesweepers in 1920s.

Étourdi was scuttled at Brest 18.6.1940, year later salvaged by Germans and broken up. *Dédaigneuse* was scuttled at Toulon 27.11.1942, salvaged by Italians and named *FR56*; 9.9.1943 she was captured by Germans and served as minesweeper *M6020*, her ultimate fate is unknown.

GRANIT class minesweepers

Granit (A C de la Loire, Nantes, 1918/1918 - scuttled 27.11.1942); **Mica** (A C de la Loire, St-Nazaire, 1918/1918 - condemned 1938)

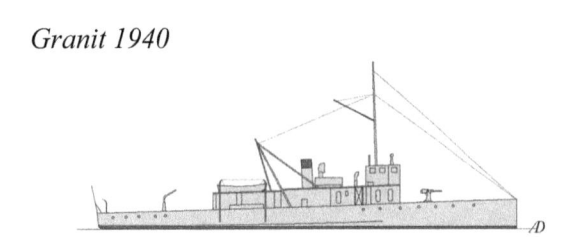

Granit 1940

Granit 1920

360t, 57.6x7.9x2.3m, 1vte/1b, 600hp, 12.5kts, 63p; 1 or 2 x 1 – 65/50 M1902, sweeps.
Purpose-built minesweepers, laid down under 1917 Programme, officially rated as 2nd class avisos.
Granit was scuttled 27.11.1942 at Toulon, later salvaged and commissioned by Germans as *SG26*.

ALBÂTRE class minesweepers

Meulière (A C de la Loire, St-Nazaire, 1919/1919 - stranded 24.5.1941); **Quartz** (A C de la Loire, Nantes, 1919/1919 - unlisted 1939)

Meulière 1936

380t, 57.6x7.9x2.3m, 1vte/1b, 500hp, 10.5kts, 63p; 1 x 1 – 65/50 M1902, sweeps.
2nd series of *Granit* class avisos with boilers of older construction, built under 1917 Programme.
Meulière stranded 24.5.1941 and lost at Corsica.

Ex-German LA NYMPHE II minesweeper

AD204 La Nymphe II (ex-M42) (Vulcan, Bremen, Germany, 1915/11.8.1916/(9.1916)/1939 - captured by Germany 1940 (M42))

480/507t, 58.4x7.3x2.3m, 2vte/2b, 1800hp, 16.5kts, 115t coal, 2000(14)nm; 2 x 1 – 105/42 Tbts C/16, 30 mines, sweeps.

Former German minesweeper *M42* of Type 1915 was sold mercantile in 1920 but requisitioned by the French navy in 1939.

AD204 was captured by Germans in 1940 and served in the Kriegsmarine as minesweeper (later minelayer) *M42*, renamed *Nymphe* in 1944.

Ex-US D201 class coastal minesweepers

D201 (ex-YMS23), 1944- **D351** (Greenport Basin, USA, 7.1941/13.12.1941/(5.1942)/10.1944 - stricken 12.1963); **D202** (ex-YMS77) (Stadium, Cleveland, USA, 5.1941/11.10.1941/(5.1942)/3.1944 - sunk 25.10.1944); **D211** (ex-YMS26), 1944- **D352** (Greenport Basin, USA, 12.1941/28.2.1942/(6.1942)/3.1944 - stricken 6.1962); **D212** (ex-YMS31), 1944- **D353** (Greenport Basin, USA, 3.1942/23.5.1942/(8.1942)/3.1944 - stricken 6.1962); **D271** (ex-BYMS2207, ex-BYMS207, ex-YMS207), 1944- **D354** (Robert Jacob, New York, USA, 4.1942/1.8.1942/(1.1943)/3.1944 - stricken 11.1961); **D272** (ex-BYMS2208, ex-BYMS208, ex-YMS208), 1944- **D355** (Robert Jacob, New York, USA, 4.1942/8.8.1942/(2.1943)/3.1944 - stricken 11.1961); **D273** (ex-YMS227), 1944- **D356** (Frank L. Sample, Boothbay Harbor, USA, 4.1942/7.9.1942/(3.1943)/3.1944 - stricken 11.1961); **D301** (ex-YMS169) (Dachel-Carter, Benton Harbor, USA, 9.1942/24.4.1943/(6.1943)/8.1944 - stricken 3.1961); **D311** (ex-YMS34) (Hiltebrant, Kingston, USA, 5.1941/21.10.1941/(6.1942)/10.1944 - stricken 5.1964); **D312** (ex-YMS63) (Gibbs Gas Engine, Jacksonville, USA, 11.1941/6.3.1942/(6.1942)/10.1944 - stricken 1961); **D313** (ex-YMS58) (Gibbs Gas Engine, Jacksonville, USA, 6.1941/22.12.1941/(4.1942)/10.1944 - stricken 11.1959); **D314** (ex-BYMS2226, ex-BYMS226, ex-YMS226) (Frank L. Sample, Boothbay Harbor, USA, 3.1942/31.8.1942/(1.1943)/10.1944 - stricken 2.1969); **D315** (ex-YMS28) (Greenport Basin, USA, 1.1942/31.3.1942/(7.1942)/10.1944 - to South Vietnam 2.1954 (Hàm Tử)); **D316** (ex-YMS37) (Hiltebrant, Kingston, USA, 10.1941/28.1.1942/(8.1942)/10.1944 - stricken 8.1960); **D317** (ex-YMS13) (Rice Bros, E. Boothbay, USA, 4.1941/2.5.1942/(8.1942)/10.1944 - stricken 12.1963); **D318** (ex-YMS78) (Stadium, Cleveland, USA, 5.1941/11.12.1941/(6.1942)/10.1944 - to South Vietnam 2.1954 (Bạch Đằng)); **D321** (ex-YMS36) (Hiltebrant, Kingston, USA, 10.1941/21.1.1942/(7.1942)/10.1944 - stricken 3.1961); **D322** (ex-YMS16) (Rice Bros, E. Boothbay, USA, 3.1942/7.9.1942/(2.1943)/10.1944 - stricken 2.1955); **D323** (ex-YMS62) (Gibbs Gas Engine, Jacksonville, USA, 11.1941/25.2.1942/(5.1942)/10.1944 - stricken 6.1954); **D324** (ex-YMS43) (Wheeler, Brooklyn, USA, 6.1941/30.3.1942/(5.1942)/10.1944 - stricken 1961); **D325** (ex-YMS82) (Stadium, Cleveland, USA, 10.1941/13.6.1942/(8.1942)/10.1944 - stricken 1.1959); **D326** (ex-YMS83) (Stadium, Cleveland, USA, 10.1941/27.6.1942/(8.1942)/10.1944 - to South Vietnam 2.1954 (Chương Dương)); **D327** (ex-YMS20) (Greenport Basin, USA, 6.1941/1.11.1941/(4.1942)/10.1944 - stricken 8.1960); **D331** (ex-YMS55) (Gibbs Gas Engine, Jacksonville, USA, 5.1941/22.11.1941/(3.1942)/9.1944 - stricken 11.1954); **D332** (ex-YMS18) (Herreshoff, Bristol, USA, 6.1941/8.12.1941/(5.1942)/10.1944 - sunk 28.5.1949); **D333** (ex-YMS27) (Greenport Basin, USA, 12.1941/7.3.1942/(6.1942)/10.1944 - stricken 3.1961); **D334** (ex-YMS3) (Henry B. Nevins, New York, USA, 3.1941/13.4.1942/(4.1942)/10.1944 - stricken 12.1965); **D335** (ex-YMS29) (Greenport Basin, USA, 1.1942/11.4.1942/(7.1942)/10.1944 - stricken 6.1963); **D336** (ex-YMS64) (Gibbs Gas Engine, Jacksonville, USA, 1.1942/25.3.1942/(6.1942)/10.1944 - stricken 11.1964); **D337** (ex-YMS69) (Weaver, Orange, USA, 7.1941/5.3.1942/(8.1942)/9.1944 - to Madagascar 2.1961 (Tanamasoandro)); **D338** (ex-YMS15) (Rice Bros, E. Boothbay, USA, 7.1941/16.7.1942/(12.1942)/10.1944 - sunk 20.6.1949)

270/320t, 41.5x7.5x2.4m, 2d, 800hp, 14kts, 2000(12)nm, 60p; 1 x 1 – 76/50 Mk 20/21, 2 x 1 – 20/70 Oerlikon, 2 DCT, 2 DCR, sweeps (inc. magnetic and acoustic); SF or SO or SU radar.

Ex-USN motor minesweepers of YMS type.

D351 1944

D202 was lost on German mine 25.10.1944.

Ex-British D241 class coastal minesweepers

D241 (ex-MMS21), 1944- **D361** (Herd & McKenzie, Buckie, UK, 1941/(6.1941)/1944 - returned to UK 10.1947); **D242** (ex-MMS184), 1944- **D362** (George Forbes, Peterhead, UK, 7.3.1942/(5.1942)/1944 - returned to UK 10.1947); **D251** (ex-MMS47), 1944- **D363** (J. W. & A. Upham, UK, 14.5.1941/(8.1941)/1944 - returned to UK 10.1947); **D252** (ex-MMS9), 1944- **D364** (P. K. Harris, Appledore, UK, 5.9.1940/(3.1941)/1944 - returned to UK 10.1947 (MMS1509)); **D261** (ex-MMS116), 1944- **D365** (J. S. Doig, Grimsby, UK, 23.8.1941/(12.1941)/1944 - returned to UK 10.1947); **D262** (ex-MMS118), 1944- **D366** (J. S. Doig, Grimsby, UK, 5.2.1942/(6.1942)/1944 - returned to UK 10.1947); **D291** (ex-MMS133), 1944- **D367** (Wilson Noble, Fraserburgh, UK, 6.9.1941/(1.1942)/1944 - returned to UK 10.1947); **D292** (ex-MMS134), 1944- **D368** (Wilson Noble, Fraserburgh, UK, 5.1.1942/(4.1942)/1944 - returned to UK 10.1947)

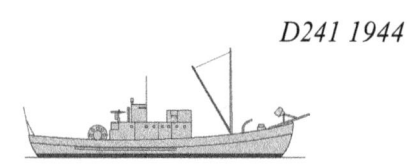

D241 1944

255/295t, 36.4x7.1x2.7m, 1d, 375-500hp, 10-11kts, 24-26t diesel oil, 2500(10-11)nm, 20p; (1 x 1 – 20/70 Oerlikon, 1 x 2 – 12.7 MG) or 2 x 2 – 12.7 MG or 2 x 1 – 20/70 Oerlikon, sweeps (inc. magnetic and acoustic)
Ex-RN 105ft Admiralty motor minesweepers.

Ex-British D341 class coastal minesweepers

D341 (ex-MMS1039) (Wivenhoe Shipyard, Milford Haven, UK, 1943/(9.1944)/1944 - returned to UK 1947); **D342** (ex-MMS1032) (Frank Curtis, Par, UK, 23.3.1943/(8.1943)/1944 - returned to UK 1947); **D343** (ex-MMS1024) (Wilson Noble, Fraserburgh, UK, 6.3.1943/(7.1943)/1944 - returned to UK 1947); **D344** (ex-MMS1040) (Frank Curtis, Par, UK, 29.10.1943/(4.1944)/1944 - returned to UK 1947); **D345** (ex-MMS1033) (Frank Curtis, Par, UK, 21.5.1943/(11.1943)/1944 - returned to UK 1947); **D346** (ex-MMS1036) (Frank Curtis, Totnes, UK, 25.3.1943/(11.1943)/1944 - returned to UK 1947)

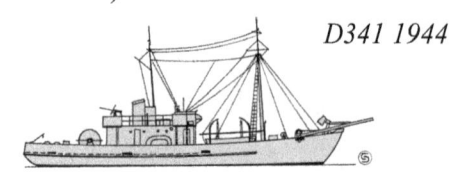

D341 1944

360/430t, 42.7x8.5x3.2m, 1d, 500hp, 10kts, 54t diesel oil, 21p; 2 x 1 or 2 x 2 – 20/70 Oerlikon, sweeps (inc. magnetic and acoustic)
Ex-RN 126ft Admiralty motor minesweepers.

Auxiliary minesweepers

More than 500grt capacity
AD56 La Bretonnière (1907/1939, 628grt – sunk 11.6.1940); **AD205 Lézardrieux** (1922/1940, 933grt – paid off 10.1940); **AD232 Jeanne Schiaffino** (1922/1939, 1220grt, 66.8(pp)x9.9m, 10kts - paid off 10.1940); **AD241 Ville de Bougie** (1907/1939, 1132grt, 77.9(pp)x11.0m, 13.5kts - paid off 10.1940); **AD252 Mascot** (1922/1939, 1256grt, 72.6(pp)x11.0m - paid off 10.1940); **AD261 les Issers** (1920/1940, 726grt – paid off 10.1940); **AD267 St-Joseph** (1908/1940, 905grt – paid off 8.1940); **AD305 Béryl** (1920/1940, 670grt – sunk 21.11.1943); **AD316 Jean Dupuis** (/1940, 682grt – paid off 4.1941); **AD358 Béarnais** (1920/1939, 1162grt - paid off 1945); **AD371 Corsaire** (1920/1939, 1057grt - paid off 8.1939); **AD372 Prado** (1905/1940, 997grt – paid off 10.1940)

100-500grt capacity
Requisitioned: 243 (1939-1940), 3 (1941), 5 (1944)
Lost: 87 (1940), 13 (1941), 15 (1942), 1 (1943), 2 (1944), 2 (1945)

Discarded: 6 (1939), 97 (1940), 10 (1941), 5 (1942), 1 (1943), 1 (1944), 2 (1945)

Merchant and fishery vessels converted to minesweepers.

Tugs converted to minesweepers

100-500grt capacity
Requisitioned: 9 (1939)

Discarded: 2 (1940), 1 (1941), 1 (1945)
Lost: 2 (1940), 3 (1942)

Miscellaneous vessels, intended for combat support

Submarine depot ship

Jules Verne (Arsenal de Lorient, 3.2.1931/1932 – transport 1.1944) – 4347/6340t, 122.0x17.2x6.8m, 2d, 7000hp, 16kts, 286p; 4 x 1 – 90/50, 4 x 1 – 37/50.

Jules Verne 1940

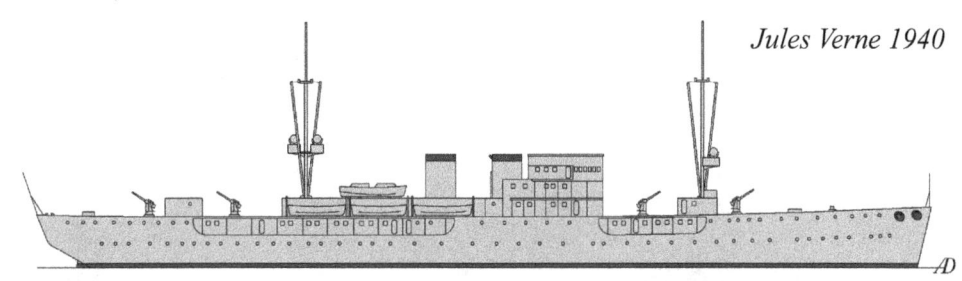

Fleet oilers

La Dordogne (ex-San Isidoro) (Armstrong, Low Walker, UK, 1914/1914 – scuttled 18.6.1940) – 7333/15160t, 161.5x20.4x8.8m, 1vte, 4150hp, 11.7kts, 80p.
La Garonne (1911/1912 – scuttled 27.11.1942) – 3533t, 120.0x15.4x8.3m, 1vte, 2600hp, 11kts, 65p; 2 x 1 – 100/45.
Le Loing (A C de Seine Maritime, Le Trait, 4.4.1927/1928 – damaged 18.6.1940, never repaired) – 3481/9900t, 153.5x15.4x7.6m, 2d, 4100hp, 13.5kts, 70p; 2 x 1 – 100/45, 2 x 1 – 75/50.
Le Mékong (A C de la Loire et Penhoët, St-Nazaire, 31.8.1928/1929 – stricken 11.1959); **Le Niger** (Ch Maritime du Sud Ouest, Bordeaux, 14.3.1930/1930 – sunk 21.5.1940); **Elorn** (Deutsche Werft, Hamburg, Germany, 1930/1931 – stricken 3.1958); **Var** (Deutsche Werft, Hamburg, Germany, 1931/1932 – stricken 2.1960) – 5482/15150t, 139.0x18.8x7.9m, 2d, 4850hp, 13.5kts, 75p; 2 x 1 – 100/45, 2 x 1 – 37/50.
Nivôse (Deutsche Werft, Hamburg, Germany, 1931/1934 – sunk 11.11.1943) – 8500/14160t, 142.3x18.8x8.8m, 1vqe, 3400hp, 11kts; 2 x 1 – 100/45, 2 x 1 – 37/50.
L'Adour (A C de La Ciotat, 9.10.1938/1939 – damaged 6.1941, repaired after war); **Le Lot** (A C de France, Dunkirk, 1939/1939 – sunk 22.6.1943); **Le Tarn** (A C de France, Dunkirk, 1939/1939 – captured 8.12.1942); *La Baïse* (Worms, Le Trait, 1939/1948/(1948)/1957 – stricken 8.1966); **La Mayenne** (Worms, Le Trait, 1939/1949/3.1950 – stricken 5.1964); *La Charente (ex-Ostfriesland)* (Worms, Le Trait, 1939/19.5.1943/(10.1943)/4.1946 – stricken 9.1959) – 4220/7400t, 132.0x16.0x6.2m, 1gst/2b, 5200hp, 15kts; 2 x 1 – 100/45, 2 x 1 – 37/50.
La Saône (A C de France, Dunkirk, 5.1939/26.2.1948/(7.1948)/9.1953 – stricken 1.1980); *La Seine* (A D de France, Dunkirk, 4.1939/7.9.1948/(4.1949)/9.1953 – stricken 1.1982); **Le Liamone** (A C de France, Dunkirk, 3.1940// - abandoned 6.1940); *La Medjerda* (A C de France, Dunkirk, 1.1940// - abandoned 6.1940) – 19900t, 160.1x22.1x10.1m, 2gst/3b, 15800hp, 17kts; 2 x 1 – 100/45, 2 x 1 – 37/50.

La Dordogne was scuttled at Brest 18.6.1940. *La Garonne* was scuttled at Toulon 27.11.1942, salvaged by Germans but scuttled by them again at Toulon 20.6.1944. *Le Loing* was damaged by crew in La Pallice Roads 18.6.1940, captured later by Germans and scuttled by them in 1944. *Le Niger* was bombed at Dunkirk 21.5.1940. *Nivôse* was torpedoed by German aircraft off Tenes 11.11.1943.

L'Adour was torpedoed by British aircraft at Beirut in June 1941, later interned in Turkey and returned to France after war. *Le Lot* was torpedoed by German submarine off Cap Juby 22.6.1943. *Le Tarn* was captured by Germans at Bizerte 8.12.1942, towed by them to Genoa and scuttled 9.9.1943.

Le Mékong 1929

La Charente 1946

Ship-based aircraft

Fighters

Wibault Wib.74 (36, 1929 – 1937)

Wib.74: 10.95x8.55x2.96m, 22.0m², 1043/1535kg, 1 Lorraine 12Eb, 450hp, 243km/h, 600(206)km, 5.75m/s, 7400m, 1p; 2 x 7.7 Vickers.

Wib. 73

Dewoitine D.37 (40, 1937 – 1939)

D.376: 11.80x7.44x3.40m, 17.8m², 1295/1860kg, 1 Gnome-Rhône 14Kfs, 930hp, 405km/h, 900(376)km, 14.9m/s, 11000m, 1p; 2 x 7.7 Vickers (later 2 x 13.2

Seafire (93, 1945 – 1949)

Seafire L.IIIc: 11.23x9.12x3.02m, 22.5m², 2258/3465kg, 1 Rolls-Royce Merlin 55M, 1585hp, 594km/h, 1170km, 27.6m/s, 11125m, 1p; 2 x 20 Hispano, 4 x 7.7 Browning, 227 kg bombs
Seafire F.XV: 11.23x9.12x3.02m, 22.5m², 2267/2911kg, 1 Rolls-Royce Griffon VI, 1850hp, 630km/h, 1024km,

Wib.74 (fighter, 18 built in 1929, serv. 1929-1937, 1 seat, Lorraine 12Eb engine (450 hp), 2 7.7mm MG); **Wib.75** (reconnaissance fighter, 18 built in 1929, serv. 1929-1937, photo camera)

D.373

Hotchkiss), 2 x 7.5 MAC.
D.373 (fighter, 20 built in 1937, serv. 1937-1939, 1 seat, Gnome-Rhône 14Kfs engine, 2 x 7.7 Vickers, 2 x 7.5 MAC); **D.376** (fighter, 20 built in 1937, serv. 1937-1939, folding wing)

27.6m/s, 11125m, 1p; 2 x 20 Hispano, 4 x 7.7 Browning, 227 kg bombs.
Seafire L.IIIc (fighter, 48 delivered in 1945, serv. 1945-1949, Rolls-Royce Merlin 55M engine (1585hp), 594km/h); **Seafire F.XV** (fighter, 45 delivered in 1945, serv. 1945-1949, Rolls-Royce Griffon VI engine (1850hp), 630km/h)

Seafire III

L.N.411

FRANCE

Diving bombers

Loire-Nieuport L.N.40 (48, 1939-1940)

L.N.401: 14.00x9.76m, 2850kg, 1 Hispano-Suiza 12X, 690hp, 320km/h, 1200km, 1p; 1 x 20 Hispano-Suiza, 3 x 7.5 MAC, 225 kg bombs.

Vought V.156F (39, 1939 – 1940)

V.156F: 12.80x10.36x3.12m, 28.3m², 2555/4272kg, 1 Pratt & Whitney R-1535-96, 825hp, 391km/h, 1803(244) km, 5.4m/s, 7195m, 2p; 2 x 7.5 MAC, 454 kg bombs.

L.N.401 (diving bomber, 24 built late 1939-1940, serv. late 1939-late 1940); **L.N.411** (diving bomber, 24 built late 1939-1940, serv. late 1939-late 1940, non-folding wing).

V.156F (SB2U-2 Vindicator) (diving bomber, 39 built in 1939, serv. 1939-1940)

V.156F

SBC-4

SBC Helldiver (44, 1940 – 1943)

SBC-4: 10.36x8.57x3.17m, 29.5m², 2066/3211kg, 1 Wright R-1820-34, 950hp, 377km/h, 950((282)km, 7315m, 2p; 2 x 7.6 Browning, 454 kg bombs.

SBC-4 (diving bomber – reconnaissance plane, 44 delivered in 1940, serv. 1940-1943)

SBD Dauntless (32, 1944 – 1949)

SBD-5: 12.65x10.06x3.94m, 30.2m², 2940/4318kg, 1 Wright R-1820-60, 1200hp, 410km/h, 1244(298)km, 8.6m/s, 7680m, 2p; 2 x 12.7 Browning, 2 x 7.6 Browning, 816 kg bombs (1 726-kg and 2 45-kg).

SBD-5 (US Navy)

PL.7

Torpedo bombers

Levasseur PL.7 (50, 1931-1939)

PL.7: 16.50x11.68x4.86m, 71.0m², 2800/3950kg, 1 Hispano-Suiza 12Lbr, 600hp, 170km/h, 645(1388)km, 2900m, 3p; 2 x 7.5 MAC, 1 torpedo or 450 kg bombs.

PL.7 (torpedo bomber, 50 built 1931-1933, serv. 1931-1939)

Reconnaissance planes

Levasseur PL.10 (60, 1930 – 1940)

PL.10: 14.20x9.75x3.75m, 56.9m², 1810/2800kg, 1 Hispano-Suiza 12Lb, 600hp, 200km/h, 650(130)km, 5400m, 2p; 2 x 7.5 MAC, 60 kg bombs.
PL.101: 14.20x9.75x3.75m, 56.9m², 2020/3150kg, 1 Hispano-Suiza 12Lb, 600hp, 220km/h, 600(130)km, 4500m, 2p; 2 x 7.5 MAC, 60 kg bombs.
PL.10 (reconnaissance plane, 30 built in 1930-1931, serv. 1930-1938); **PL.101** (reconnaissance plane, 30 built in 1933-1934, serv. 1933-3.1940, minor alterations)

PL.10

CAMS.37A

Amphibians

CAMS.37 (103, 1928-1942)

CAMS.37A: 14.50x11.43x4.20m, 59.9m², 2170/3000kg, 1 Lorraine 12Ed, 450hp, 185km/h, 1200(148)km, 3500m, 3p; 4 x 7.7 Vickers, 300 kg bombs.
CAMS.37A (reconnaissance amphibian, 103 built 10.1928-1935, serv. 10.1928-1942)

Seaplanes and flying boats

CAMS.37 (45, 1933 – 1942)

CAMS.37.2: 14.50x11.43x4.20m, 59.9m², 2170/3000kg, 1 Lorraine 12Ed, 450hp, 185km/h, 1200(148)km, 3500m, 3p; 4 x 7.7 Vickers, 300 kg bombs
CAMS.37.2 (reconnaissance flying boat, 45 built 1933-1935, serv. 1933-1942)

CAMS.37.2

G.L.813Hy

Gourdou-Lesseur G.L.81Hy (86, 1931 – 1943)

G.L.810Hy: 16.0x10.49x3.56m, 41.0m², 1670/2290kg, 1 Gnome-Rhône 9Ady, 420hp, 195km/h, 560(150)km, 5800m, 3p; 3 x 7.7 Vickers, 150 kg bombs.
G.L.810Hy (reconnaissance seaplane, 24 built 7.1931-1932, serv. 7.1931-7.1943); **G.L.811Hy** (reconnaissance seaplane, 20 built 1932-1933, serv. 1932-7.1943, folding wing); **G.L.812Hy** (reconnaissance seaplane, 29 built 1933-1934, serv. 1933-7.1943, minor alterations); **G.L.813Hy** (reconnaissance seaplane, 13 built in 1934, serv. 1934-7.1943, minor alterations).

FRANCE

Gourdou-Lesseur G.L.832 (22, 1933 – 1940)

G.L.832Hy: 13.00x8.74x3.48m, 29.5m², 1110/1695kg, 1 Hispano-Suiza 9Qb, 230hp, 196km/h, 590(158)km, 5000m, 2p; 1 x 7.7 Vickers.
G.L.832Hy (reconnaissance seaplane, 22 built 1933-1934, serv. 1933-autumn 1940)

G.L.832Hy

P.L.15

Levasseur P.L.15 (16, 1933 – 1940)

P.L.15: 18.00x12.85x5.10m, 74.5m², 2835/4350kg, 1 Hispano-Suiza 12Nbr, 650hp, 208km/h, 750(181)km, 3.1m/s, 4500m, 3p; 3 x 7.7 Vickers, 1 750-kg torpedo or 450 kg bombs
P.L.15 (torpedo bomber seaplane, 16 built 1933-1934, serv. 1933-8.1940)

Potez 452 (16, 1936 – 1944)

Potez 452: 13.00x10.33x3.26m, 24.3m², 1059/1500kg, 1 Hispano-Suiza 9Qd, 350hp, 217km/h, 500(178)km, 5.3m/s, 6500m, 1-2p; 2 x 7.5 Darne.
Potez 452 (reconnaissance flying boat, 16 built 1936-1937, serv. 1936-9.1944)

Potez 452

Loire 130M

Loire 130 (150, 1936 – 1949)

Loire 130M: 16.00x11.30x3.85m, 40.1m², 2090/3396kg, 1 Hispano-Suiza 12Xirs, 690hp, 226km/h, 1100(172)km, 6000m, 3p + 4 passengers; 2 x 7.5 MAC, 150 kg bombs.
Loire 130M (reconnaissance flying boat, 126 built 8.1936-1941, serv. 8.1936-9.1947); **Loire 130C** (reconnaissance flying boat, 24 built 8.1936-10.1938, serv. 8.1936-12.1949, variant for colonial service, strengthened wing, advanced cooling)

Latécoere Laté 298 (177, 1938 – 1946)

Laté 298A: 15.50x12.56x5.25m, 31.6m², 3060/4795kg, 1 Hispano-Suiza 12Ycrs, 880hp, 290km/h, 2200(245)km, 4.4m/s, 6500m, 3p; 3 x 7.5 Darne, 1 670-kg torpedo or 500 kg bombs or 3 DCs.
Laté 298A (torpedo bomber seaplane, 29 built 12.1938-1939, serv. 12.1938-4.1946, unfolding wing); **Laté 298B** (torpedo bomber seaplane, 42 built 12.1938-1939, serv. 12.1938-4.1946, 4 seats, folding wing); **Laté 298D** (torpedo bomber seaplane, 106 built 1939-6.1940, serv. 1939-4.1946, unfolding wing)

Laté 298

L.N.210

Loire L.N.210 (20, 1939 – 1939)

L.N.210: 11.70x9.51x3.80m, 20.3m², 1440/2100kg, 1 Hispano-Suiza 9Vbs, 980hp, 315km/h, 750(265)km, 8000m, 1p; 4 x 7.5 MAC
L.N.210 (fighter seaplane, 20 built 8-11.1939, serv. 8-11.1939)

Liore-et-Olivier H.43 (20, 1940 – 1940)

H.43: 16.00x11.00x3.85m, 36.0m², 1760/3375kg, 1 Hispano-Suiza 9Vb, 650hp. 222km/h, 850(187)km, 6200m, 3p; 2 x 7.5 MG, 150 kg bombs.
H.43 (reconnaissance seaplane, 20 built 2-5.1940, serv. 2-8.1940)

H.43

Naval weapons

Guns

Machine guns

Caliber, mm	Bore Length, cal	No of bores	Type of mount	Guns used	Year	Ships used on	Max imal elevation angle, °	Shell mass, kg	Initial velocity, m/s	Rate of fire of one bore, rounds per min	Fire range / AA ceiling, km
7.50	80.0	1	MAC	7.5mm MAC Mil	1931	MTB	80	0.009	850	400	0.55 / 0.4
7.50	80.0	1	Darne	7.5mm MAC Mil	1931	MTB	80	0.009	850	400	0.55 / 0.4
7.50	80.0	2	MAC	7.5mm MAC Mil	1931	MTB	80	0.009	850	400	0.55 / 0.4
7.50	80.0	4	MAC	7.5mm MAC Mil	1931	MTB	80	0.009	850	400	0.55 / 0.4
7.62	80.0	1	Browning M1919A4	.3" Browning M1919A4 MG	1943	YP	80	0.010	854	250	0.6 / 0.4

FRANCE

Caliber	Bore Length	No of bores	Type of mount	Guns used	Year	Ships used on	Max elevation	Shell mass	Initial velocity	Rate of fire	Fire range / AA ceiling
7.71	66.0	1	Vickers MG	0.303" Vickers Mk I MG	1940	some	~90	0.011	744	250	0.4 / 0.15
7.71	66.0	2	Vickers MG	0.303" Vickers Mk I MG	1940	MTB	~90	0.011	744	250	0.4 / 0.15
7.71	82.0	1	Bren MG	0.303" Bren Mk I MG	1939	launchers	90	0.011	744	250	
7.71	87.0	1	Lewis MG	0.303" Lewis MG	1914	some	~90	0.011	744	100 - 150	0.4 / 0.15
7.71	87.0	2	Lewis MG	0.303" Lewis MG	1914	some	~90	0.011	744	100 - 150	0.4 / 0.15
8.00	80.0	1	Hotchkiss MG	8mm Hotchkiss Mil		many	90				
8.00	80.0	2	Hotchkiss MG	8mm Hotchkiss Mil		many	90				
8.00	80.0	4	Hotchkiss MG	8mm Hotchkiss Mil		many	90				
12.7	62.2	1	Mk VI	0.5" Vickers Mk III No. 3 MG	1926	Many	~90	0.038	768	150 - 200	0.7 / 0.3
12.7	62.2	2	Mk IV, V, VC	0.5" Vickers Mk III No. 2 MG	1940	Many	~90	0.038	768	150 - 200	0.7 / 0.3
12.7	62.2	4	Mk I, I*, II, II*, III	0.5" Vickers Mk III No. 1 MG	1940	Many	~90	0.038	768	150 - 200	0.7 / 0.3
12.7	90.0	1	Mk 3	0.5" Browning M2 MG	1940	Lend-lease ships, escorts and boats	80	0.049	893	150 - 200	2.4 / 2.4
13.2	76.0	2	M1929	13.2mm Hotchkiss M1929 Mil	1935	many	90	0.052	800	200	7.2 / 4.2
13.2	76.0	4	M1929	13.2mm Hotchkiss M1929 Mil	1935	many	90	0.052	800	200	7.2 / 4.2
13.2	90.0	1	Browning	13.2mm Browning Mil	1940	many	80	0.052	893	150 - 200	2.4 / 2.4

Automatic guns

Caliber, mm	Bore Length, cal	No of bores	Type of mount	Guns used	Year	Ships used on	Max Imal elevation angle, °	Shell mass, kg	Initial velocity, m/s	Rate of fire of one bore, rounds per min	Fire range / AA ceiling, km
20.0	65.0	1	MPLC/30	2cm FlaK 38	1945	ex-German and rearmed ships	85	0.120	875	450 - 500	4.8 / 3.7
20.0	65.0	2	LM44U	2cm FlaK 38	1945	ex-German and rearmed ships	78	0.120	875	450 - 500	4.8 / 3.7
20.0	65.0	4	Vierling L/38	2cm FlaK 38	1945	ex-German and rearmed ships	90	0.120	875	450 - 500	4.8 / 3.7

20.0	70.0	1	Mk I, IA, II, IIA, IIA S/M, IIIA, VRCN, VIIA, VIIA* S/M	20 mm/70 Mk II (Oerlikon)	1941	Many	85	0.123	844	250 - 320	4.7 / 3.0
20.0	70.0	1	Mk VIIIA	20 mm/70 Mk II (Oerlikon)	1942	Littoral combats	20	0.123	844	250 - 320	3.9
20.0	70.0	1	Mk 2	20 mm/70 Oerlikon Mk 2, 3, 4	1942	many	87	0.123	844	450	4.4 / 3.0
20.0	70.0	1	Mk 4	20 mm/70 Oerlikon Mk 2, 3, 4	1942	many	87	0.123	844	450	4.4 / 3.0
20.0	70.0	1	Mk 5	20 mm/70 Oerlikon Mk 2, 3, 4	1942	many	87	0.123	844	450	4.4 / 3.0
20.0	70.0	1	Mk 6	20 mm/70 Oerlikon Mk 2, 3, 4	1942	many	90	0.123	844	450	4.4 / 3.0
20.0	70.0	1	Mk 10	20 mm/70 Oerlikon Mk 2, 3, 4	1943	many	90	0.123	844	450	4.4 / 3.0
20.0	70.0	1	Mk 12	20 mm/70 Oerlikon Mk 2, 3, 4	1943	many	90	0.123	844	450	4.4 / 3.0
20.0	70.0	1	Mk 14	20 mm/70 Oerlikon Mk 2, 3, 4	1943	many	90	0.123	844	450	4.4 / 3.0
20.0	70.0	1	Mk 16	20 mm/70 Oerlikon Mk 2, 3, 4	1943	many	90	0.123	844	450	4.4 / 3.0
20.0	70.0	2	Mk V, VC, IX, XIA, XIIA	20 mm/70 Mk II (Oerlikon)	1945	CVE	85	0.123	844	250 - 320	4.7 / 3.0
20.0	70.0	2	Mk 20	20 mm/70 Oerlikon Mk 2, 3, 4	1944	many	90	0.123	844	450	4.4 / 3.0
20.0	70.0	2	Mk 24	20 mm/70 Oerlikon Mk 2, 3, 4	1944	many	90	0.123	844	450	4.4 / 3.0
25.0	60.0	1	M1938	25mm M1938	1940	many	85	0.250	900	110 - 120	7.5 / 5.5
25.0	60.0	2	M1938	25mm M1938	1940	many	85	0.250	900	110 - 120	7.5 / 5.5
37.0	48.0	2	M1935	37mm M1935	1936	FS	85	0.831	825	165	8.0 / 6.0
37.0	50.0	1	CA/SMCA M1925	37mm M1925	1927	many	80	0.725	850	30 - 42	7.2 / 5.5
37.0	50.0	2	CAD M1933	37mm M1933	1936	many	80	0.725	850	30 - 42	7.2 / 5.5
37.0	50.0	2	CAIL M1933	37mm M1933	1940	many	80	0.725	850	30 - 42	7.2 / 5.5
37.0	56.9	1	FlaK LM43	3.7cm FlaK M/43	1945	ex-German and rearmed ships	90	0.644	820	180	6.5 / 4.8
37.0	56.9	1	FlaK LM44	3.7cm FlaK M/43	1945	ex-German and rearmed ships	90	0.644	820	180	6.5 / 4.8

FRANCE

Caliber, mm	Bore Length, cal	No of bores	Type of mount	Guns used	Year	Ships used on	Max Imal elevation angle, °	Shell mass, kg	Initial velocity, m/s	Rate of fire of one bore, rounds per min	Fire range / AA ceiling, km
37.0	69.2	1	FlaK LM42	3.7cm FlaK M/42	1945	ex-German and rearmed ships	90	0.644	845	180	6.6 / 4.9
37.0	69.2	2	Dopp FlaK LM42	3.7cm FlaK M/42	1945	ex-German and rearmed ships	90	0.644	845	180	6.6 / 4.9
37.0	80.0	1	Ein LC/34	3.7cm SK C/30	1945	ex-German and rearmed ships	80	0.748	1000	30	8.5 / 6.8
37.0	80.0	1	Ubts LC/39	3.7cm SK C/30U	1945	ex-German and rearmed submarines	90	0.748	1000	30	8.5 / 6.8
37.0	80.0	2	Dopp LC/30	3.7cm SK C/30	1945	ex-German and rearmed ships	85	0.748	1000	30	8.5 / 6.8
40.0	39.4	1	Mk VIII	Vickers 2-pdr Mk VIII CLV (pompom)	1940	DD, TB, DE, FS, SC	70	0.910	585	96 - 98	3.5 / 3.0
40.0	39.4	1	Mk XVI	Vickers 2-pdr Mk VIII ALV (pompom)	1940	DD, TB, DE, FS, SC	70	0.910	585	115	3.5 / 3.0
40.0	39.4	4	Mk VII	Vickers 2-pdr Mk VIII CLV (pompom)	1942	DE	80	0.910	585	96 - 98	3.5 / 3.0
40.0	56.3	1	Mk 3	40 mm/56 Bofors Mk 1, 2	1943	BB, CV, CA, CL, DD, DE, FS, PC, SC	90	0.900	881	120	10.1 / 7.0
40.0	56.3	1	FlaK 28	4cm FlaK 28	1945	ex-German TB, MTB	90	0.955	850	120 - 240	8.8 / 6.8
40.0	56.3	2	Mk 1	40 mm/56 Bofors Mk 1, 2	1942	DD, DE	90	0.900	881	120	10.1 / 7.0
40.0	56.3	4	Mk 2	40 mm/56 Bofors Mk 1, 2	1943	BB, CV, CL, DD, SL	90	0.900	881	120	10.1 / 7.0

Light guns

Caliber, mm	Bore Length, cal	No of bores	Type of mount	Guns used	Year	Ships used on	Max Imal elevation angle, °	Shell mass, kg	Initial velocity, m/s	Rate of fire of one bore, rounds per min	Fire range / AA ceiling, km
47.0	40.0	1	M1885	47mm Hotchkiss M1885	1885	Many	25	1.50	574	20	5.9

47.0	40.0	1	Mk V HA	Hotchkiss 3-pdr QF Mk I, II	1943	ex-British ships and craft	70	1.50	574	20	7.2 / ~4.0
47.0	50.0	1	M1902	47mm Hotchkiss M1902	1903	Many	30	1.50	785	25	~7.5
47.0	50.0	1	M1902 AA	47mm Hotchkiss M1902	1915	Many	80	1.50	785	25	~7.5 / 4.5
57.0	40.0	1	Mk I, IV	Hotchkiss 6-pdr / 8cwt QF Mk I, I*, I***, II	1943	FS	25	2.72	538	20	~7.0
65.0	50.0	1	M1888-91	65mm/50 M1888-91	1892	many	25	4.17	715	15	~8.0
65.0	50.0	1	M1902	65mm/50 M1902	1903	many	25	4.17	800	15	~9.0
75.0	34.5	1	M1897	75mm/34.5 M1897	1898	SC, PC, PGR, PS, MS	20	6.18	570	10	~6.0
75.0	34.5	1	M1915	75mm/34.5 M1915	1916	DD, SS	80	6.18	570	10	~7.0 / ~4.5
75.0	34.5	1	M1915-18	75mm/34.5 M1915-18	1919	DD, SS, SL, FS, ML	80	6.18	570	10	~7.0 / ~4.5
75.0	34.5	1	M1925	75mm/34.5 M1925	1926	SS	80	6.18	570	10	~7.0 / ~4.5
75.0	34.5	1	M1928	75mm/34.5 M1928	1929	SS	80	6.18	570	10	~7.0 / ~4.5
75.0	50.0	1	M1922	75mm/50 M1922	1924	BB, CA, CL, DD	90	5.93	850	8 - 15	14.1 / 10.0
75.0	50.0	1	M1924	75mm/50 M1924	1925	CV, CA, DD, PGR	90	5.93	850	8 - 15	14.1 / 10.0
75.0	50.0	1	M1927	75mm/50 M1927	1928	AV, CL, CM, DD	90	5.93	850	8 - 15	14.1 / 10.0
75.0	62.5	1	M1908	75mm/62.5 M1908	1911	BB, ML	20	6.18	860	10	9.1
76.2	40.0	1	HA/LA Mk IX, IX*, IX**	12-pdr / 12cwt QF HA Mk V	1940	DD, FS	70	5.87	681	15	10.7 / 5.8
76.2	45.0	1	CP Mk V	12-pdr / 20cwt QF HA Mk I, I*, IB, IC, I*C, IE, SIE, II, III, IV, IVA	1943	SS	40	7.94	617	12 - 14	11.8
76.2	50.1	1	Mk 11	3"/50 Mk 10	1944	DE, PC, MS	85	5.90	823	15 - 20	13.4 / 9.3
76.2	50.1	1	Mk 20	3"/50 Mk 20	1944	DE, PC, MS	85	5.90	823	15 - 20	13.4 / 9.3
76.2	50.1	1	Mk 22	3"/50 Mk 21	1944	DE, PC, MS	85	5.90	823	15 - 20	13.4 / 9.3
88.0	30.0	1	Ubts.L	8.8cm/30 Ubts L/30	1918	SS	30	9.75	590	12	10.5
88.0	42.4	1	Ubts LC/35	8.8cm/45 SK C/35	1945	ex-German SS	30	9.00	700	15	12.0
88.0	45.0	1	MPLC/13	8.8cm FlaK L/45	1920	ex-German CL	70	10.0	650	15	11.8
90.0	24.0	1	M1891	90mm/24 M1877	1878	PC	20	8.30	490	5	~5.0
90.0	50.0	1	M1926	90mm/50 M1926	1927	CA, CL, FS, NL	80	9.51	850	10	15.4 / 10.6

FRANCE

Caliber, mm	Bore Length, cal	No of bores	Type of mount	Guns used	Year	Ships used on	Max imal elevation angle, °	Shell mass, kg	Initial velocity, m/s	Rate of fire of one bore, rounds per min	Fire range / AA ceiling, km
90.0	50.0	2	M1930	90mm/50 M1930	1931	CA, CL	80	9.51	850	10	15.4 / 10.6
100.0	34.0	1	M1936	100mm/34 M1936	1940	SS	30	14.9	~510	10	~10.0
100.0	45.0	1	M1892	100mm/45 M1892	1893	BC, FS	20	16.0	703	6	~14.0
100.0	45.0	1	M1893	100mm/45 M1893	1894	CL, DD, PG	20	16.0	703	6	~14.0
100.0	45.0	1	M1897	100mm/45 M1897	1898	CA, FS, PC, ML	20	16.0	703	6	~14.0
100.0	45.0	1	M1897 T^e 1917	100mm/45 M1897 T^e 1917	1917	PGT, SS, SL, FS, PGR	20	16.0	703	6	~14.0
100.0	45.0	1	M1917	100mm/45 M1917	1918	PGT, SS, SL, FS, PGR	20	16.0	703	10	~14.0
100.0	45.0	1	M1925	100mm/45 M1925	1929	SS	70	14.5	760	10	15.8 / 9.5
100.0	45.0	1	M1927	100mm/45 M1927	1931	AV	85	15.0	755	10	15.8 / 10.0
100.0	45.0	2	M1930	100mm/45 M1930	1932	BB, CA	80	15.0	755	10	15.8 / 10.0
100.0	45.0	1	M1932	100mm/45 M1932	1936	FS	34	15.0	755	10	15.0
100.0	45.0	2	M1932	100mm/45 M1932	1936	TB, FS	34	15.0	755	10	15.0
100.0	45.0	2	M1933	100mm/45 M1933	1936	CL, TB, SL, FS	90	14.9	760	10	15.8 / 10.0
100.0	47.0	1	OTO1938M	100mm/47 OTO 1938	1944	ex-Italian SS	32	13.8	840	8 - 10	12.6

Medium guns

Caliber, mm	Bore Length, cal	No of bores	Type of mount	Guns used	Year	Ships used on	Max imal elevation angle, °	Shell mass, kg	Initial velocity, m/s	Rate of fire of one bore, rounds per min	Fire range / AA ceiling, km
101.6	40.5	1	CP Mk XXIII, XXIII*, XXIII**	4"/40 QF Mk XIX	1944	FF	60	15.9	396	15	8.9
101.6	44.4	1	CP Mk I	4"/45 BL Mk IX, IX*, IX**	1942	ex-British FS	30	14.1	800	10 - 12	12.7
101.6	45.0	1	HA Mk III, III*, III**, IV	4"/45 QF Mk V, V*, V**, V***, VC	1940	CVE, DD	80	14.1	728	10 - 15	12.7 / 9.4
101.6	45.0	2	Mk XIX	4"/45 QF Mk XVI, XVI*	1942	DE, FS	80	17.4	811	15 - 20	18.1 / 11.9
101.6	50.0	1	Mk 12	4"/50 Mk 9	1914	DD	20	15.0	884	8 - 9	14.6
105.0	45.0	1	Tbts LC/16	10.5cm Tbts L/45	1920	ex-German DD, MS	50	14.7	890	15	~14
105.0	45.0	1	Ubts LC/16	10.5cm Ubts L/45	1918	ex-German SS	50	14.7	890	15	~14
120.0	45.0	1	CP Mk XIV, XVI	4.7"/45 QF Mk IX, IX*, IX**, IX**A, IX**B	1943	DD	30	22.7	808	7 - 10	14.0
127.0	38.0	1	Mk 30 Mod. 80	5"/38 Mk 12	1945	CVE	27	28.7	792	12 - 15	13.8
130.0	40.0	1	M1919	130mm/40 M1919	1926	DD	36	34.9	725	4 - 5	18.9
130.0	40.0	1	M1924	130mm/40 M1924	1927	DD	35	34.9	725	5 - 6	18.7

Caliber, mm	Bore Length, cal	No of bores	Type of mount	Guns used	Year	Ships used on	Max elevation angle, °	Shell mass, kg	Initial velocity, m/s	Rate of fire of one bore, rounds per min	Fire range / AA ceiling, km
130.0	45.4	2	M1932	130mm/45 M1932	1937	CB, CV	75	32.1	800	10 - 12	20.9 / 12.0
130.0	45.4	4	M1932	130mm/45 M1932	1937	CB	75	32.1	800	10 - 12	20.9 / 12.0
130.0	45.4	2	M1935	130mm/45 M1935	1939	DD	35	32.1	800	10	~18.0
138.6	40.0	1	M1923	138.6mm/40 M1923	1929	DD	35	40.6	700	5 - 6	18.2
138.6	40.0	1	M1927	138.6mm/40 M1927	1930	CM, DD, SL	28	40.6	700	12 - 15	16.6
138.6	45.0	1	M1893	138.6mm/45 M1893	1897	CA, CL, SL, FS	25	36.5	725	4	15.0
138.6	50.0	1	M1929	138.6mm/50 M1929	1935	DD	30	40.6	800	12	20.0
138.6	50.0	2	M1934	138.6mm/50 M1934	1938	DD	30	40.6	800	6 - 7.5	20.0
138.6	55.0	1	M1910	138.6mm/55 M1910	1913	BB, FS	15, later 25	39.5	790	5 - 6	15.0, later 16.1
145.0	45.0	1	M1910	145mm/45 M1910	1915	FS	36	36.0	755	4 - 5	14.8
149.1	42.2	1	MPLC/17	15cm Tbts KL/45	1920	AMC, ex-German DD	30	45.3	680	4 - 5	14.5
149.1	42.4	1	MPLC/13	15cm SK L/45	1920	AMC, ex-German CL	19	45.3	835	5 - 7	13.5
149.1	42.4	1	MPLC/17	15cm Ubts+Tbts KL/45	1918	ex-German SS	30	45.3	680	4 - 5	14.5

Heavy guns

Caliber, mm	Bore Length, cal	No of bores	Type of mount	Guns used	Year	Ships used on	Max elevation angle, °	Shell mass, kg	Initial velocity, m/s	Rate of fire of one bore, rounds per min	Fire range / AA ceiling, km
152.4	55.1	3	M1930	152.4mm/55 M1930	1935	CL	45	54.2	870	7 - 8	26.5
152.4	55.1	3	M1936	152.4mm/55 M1936	1940	BB	75 later 85	54.2	870	7 - 8	26.5 / 15.0
155.0	50.0	1	M1920	155mm/50 M1920	1926	CV, CL	40	56.5	850	3 - 5	26.1
203.0	50.0	2	M1924	203mm/50 M1924	1928	CA	45	134	820	4 - 5	30.0
203.0	50.0	2	M1924	203mm/50 M1924	1932	SS	30	134	820	3	~25.0
203.0	55.7	2	M1931	203mm/55 M1931	1933	CA	45	134	840	4 - 5	31.0
305.0	44.6	2	M1906-10	305mm/45 M1906-10	1913	BB	23	432	783	1.5 - 2	26.3
330.0	52.0	4	M1931	330mm/50 M1931	1937	CB	35	560	870	1.5 - 3	41.7
340.0	45.8	2	M1912	340mm/45 M1912	1915	BB	12 later 23	575	780	2	14.5 later 26.6
380.0	45.4	4	M1935	380mm/45 M1935	1940	BB	35	884	830	1.5 - 2.2	41.7
381.0	45.3	4	M1935	380mm/45 M1935	1943	BB	35	879	800	1.5 - 2.2	41.7

FRANCE

Torpedoes

Caliber, mm	Type	Year	Ships used on	Full mass, kg	Length, m	Explosive charge	Explosive mass, kg	Fire range, km	Speed, kts
450	45cm M12D, Toulon	1914	surface ships	1012	5.75	TNT	145	8	28
500	G7	1918	ex-German ships and SS	1365	7.02	SW18	195	4 / 9.3	37 / 27
450	45cm M18, Toulon	1920	submarines	1020	5.88	TNT	145	3	34
550	55cm 19V, Toulon	1921	SS	1385	6.60	picric acid	238	2 / 4	43 / 35
550	55cm 19D, Toulon	1921	surface ships	1830	8.20	picric acid	238	6 / 14	35 / 25
550	55cm 23D, Toulon	1925	CA, CL	2068	8.28	TNT	310	6 / 14 / 20	43 / 35 / 29
550	55cm 23DT, Toulon	1925	DL, DD	2068	8.28	TNT	310	9 / 13	39 / 35
550	55cm 24V, Toulon	1926	SS	1490	6.60	TNT	310	4 / 8	45 / 35
550	55cm 24M, Toulon	1926	surface ships	1490	6.60	TNT	310	4 / 8	45 / 35
400	40cm 26V, Toulon/St-Tropez	1928	SS	674	5.14	TNT	144	2 / 3	44 / 35
400	40cm 26W, Toulon/St-Tropez	1928	MTB	674	5.14	TNT	144	2 / 3	44 / 35

Depth charges

Type	Year	Mass, kg	Type and mass of explosive, kg	Sinking speed, m/s	Maximal depth setting, m	type of piston
Guiraud 40 kg	1915		40		35	mechanical
Guiraud 70 kg	1915		70		35	mechanical
Mark 2	1917	191	TNT - 136	1.8	60	hydrostatic
Mark 3	1917	191	TNT - 136	1.8	90	hydrostatic
200 kg	1930s	260	200	3.0	100, later 120	hydrostatic
100 kg	1930s	130	100	2.2	100	hydrostatic
35 kg	1930s	52	35	2.2	100	hydrostatic
Mark VII	1940	191	TNT - 132	3.0	90 later 180	hydrostatic
Mark VII Heavy	1940	259	TNT - 130 minol from 1942 - 130	5.1	90	hydrostatic
Mark 6	1943	191	TNT - 136	2.4 later 3.7	90 later 180	hydrostatic
Mark 7	1943	338	TNT - 272	1.8 later 4	90 later 180	hydrostatic
Mark 8	1943	238	TNT - 122	3.5	150	magnetic
Mark 9	1943	154	torpex - 91	6.9	180 later 300	hydrostatic

DC racks

Type	Year	Number of DCs	Type of DCs
Mk 1 mod. 0	1918	8 or 13	Mk 2, 3
---	1930s	12	200 kg

DC throwers

Type	Year	Fire range, km	Fire depth, m	Explosive type and mass, kg	DC mass, kg	Number and caliber of bores, mm
Thornycroft 24cm ("K"-gun)	1917	0.06	90	TNT - 136; amatol from 1930s - 132	191	1 x 241
Mk 1 (Y-gun)	1917	0.027	90	TNT - 136	191	2 x 241
Mk 2	1918	0.027	90	TNT - 136	191	1 x 152
Mk 5 (Y-gun)	1918	0.027	90	TNT - 136	191	2 x 241
100/250 M1928	1930	0.25	100	100	130	1 x 116
Mark IV	1941	0.061 / 0.047	90	TNT - 132 / TNT - 130	191 / 259	1 x 241
Mark V	1944	0.071 / 0.057	90	TNT - 132 / TNT - 130	191 / 259	1 x 152
Mark 6 ("K"-gun)	1941	0.062 / 0.050	90	TNT - 132 / TNT - 130	191 / 259	1 x
Hedgehog	1943	0.18	180	torpex - 15.9	29.5	24 x 180

Mines

Type	Year	Type of laying	Type of fuse	Carried on	Targets	Lying depth, m	Full mass, kg	Explosive mass, kg
B1	1915	moored	contact	surface ships	surface ships		360	60
H1	1915	moored	contact	surface ships	surface ships		520	80
B2	1916	moored	contact	surface ships	surface ships		650	100
H3	1916	moored	contact	surface ships	surface ships		502	60
HS1	1918?	moored	contact	surface ships	surface ships		488	60
HS1M	1920	moored	contact	surface ships	surface ships		700	113
HS2	1920	moored	contact	surface ships	surface ships	40	1090	220
B3	1922	moored	contact	surface ships	surface ships	90	670	110
H4	1924	moored	contact	surface ships	surface ships	40	1135	220
H5	1928	moored	contact antenna	surface ships	surface ships, submarines	90	1160	220
HS4	1928	moored	contact	surface ships	surface ships	40	1150	220
H4AR	1930	moored	contact	surface ships	surface ships	40	1135	220
H5AR	1930	moored	contact antenna	surface ships	surface ships, submarines	90	1160	220
HS4AR	1930	moored	contact	surface ships	surface ships	40	1150	220
HS4P	1930	moored	contact	surface ships	surface ships	90	1150	220
HS4UM	1930	moored	contact	surface ships	surface ships	90	1150	220
H5UM1	1935	moored	contact antenna	surface ships	surface ships, submarines	180	1100	220
HS4V	1930s	moored	contact	surface ships	surface ships	90	1150	200
HS4UM1	1935	moored	contact	surface ships	surface ships	180	1150	220
B4	1936	moored	contact	surface ships	surface ships	90	530	80
H6	1930s	moored	contact	surface ships	surface ships	90		330
B4M	1940	moored	contact	surface ships	surface ships	90	530	80
B5B	1940	moored	contact antenna	surface ships	surface ships, submarines	90	1150	220
H5UM2	1940	moored	contact antenna	surface ships	surface ships, submarines	180	1100	220
HS4UM2	1940	moored	contact	surface ships	surface ships	180	1150	220
H7	1940	moored	contact antenna	surface ships	surface ships, submarines	75	665	4 x 100
HS5	1940	moored	contact	surface ships	surface ships	90	1150	220
HS6	1940	moored	contact	surface ships	surface ships	90	1150	200

IVAN GOGIN, ALEXANDER DASHYAN
FIGHTING SHIPS OF WORLD WAR TWO
VOLUME V
FRANCE
GATCHINA
2021